Well-Tempered Women

Well-Tempered Women

Nineteenth-Century Temperance Rhetoric

Carol Mattingly

Southern Illinois University Press
Carbondale and Edwardsville

04 03 02 01   4 3 2 1

Library of Congress Cataloging-in-Publication Data
Mattingly, Carol, 1945–
      Well-tempered women : nineteenth-century temperance rhetoric /
      Carol Mattingly.
          p.   cm.
      Includes bibliographical references and index.

      1. Woman's Christian Temperance Union—Language. 2.
Temperance—United States—History—19th century. 3. Women social
reformers—United States—History—19th century. 4. Women social
reformers—United States—Language. 5. Women orators—United
States—History—19th century. 6. Women orators—United States—
Language. 7. Temperance in literature. 8. Alcoholism in literature.
I. Title.
HV5229.M37 1998
363.4'1'097309034—dc21   98-16297
ISBN 0-8093-2209-9 (cloth : alk. paper)   CIP
ISBN 0-8093-2385-0 (pbk. : alk. paper)

For Lucy Freibert,

from whom I learned to appreciate nineteenth-century women. She is an inspiration and model for all women.

Contents

Part One. From Pedestal to Pen and Podium

Part Two. Controversy Surrounding the Cause

Part Three. Fictional Accounts of Feminine Concerns

Plates

Acknowledgments

I AM GRATEFUL for the generous assistance of the staff at the National Woman's Christian Temperance Union and Frances E. Willard Memorial Library in Evanston, Illinois, especially Alfred Epstein, curator of the Frances E. Willard Memorial Library, and Claudia Johnson Dobbs, hostess and guide at Rest Cottage. I gratefully acknowledge the Willard Library and the WCTU for their permission to reprint WCTU meeting minutes, pamphlets, letters, and other documents.

Lucy Freibert, perhaps the most inspiring teacher I've known, introduced me to nineteenth-century women and offered continued support throughout my graduate years and since. She will always represent the very best in academics and humanity for me.

Colleagues at Louisiana State University unselfishly provided both essential advice and continuing support. My special gratitude to Robin Roberts and Sharon Aronofsky Weltman, who read drafts of chapters more than once, providing intelligent suggestions and crucial reassurance. I wish to thank other colleagues at LSU: Sarah Liggett and Michelle Masse, who read and responded to portions of the text, and Emily Toth, who advised me in shaping the direction of this project. LSU supported me with a 1993 summer research grant and a 1996 spring semester research grant. I also benefited from a 1995 LSU Women's and Gender Studies Summer Institute. I am thankful as well for the staffs of the interlibrary borrowing office and microfilm reading room at LSU's Middleton Library and at the English department at LSU, as well as for the support of department chairs John Fischer and Jerry Kennedy.

Jerry Phillips's generosity in sharing his proficiency with biblical passages added immensely to my understanding of their meaning for nineteenth-century women. I am grateful as well to two readers at *Rhetoric Review*, Patricia Bizzell and Kathleen Welch, for their supportive and helpful comments on a portion of the text, and to the anonymous reader for Southern Illinois University Press. Acknowledgment is also made to *Rhetoric Review* for permission to reprint a revised version of "Woman-Tempered Rhetoric: Public Presentation and the WCTU" 14.1 (1995): 41–61.

Many individuals, knowing of my research interests, forwarded materials to me, especially John Kennedy and Linda Rogers. Jean Witherow and Natalie April, student assistants, helped with numerous details. Tracey Sobol, editor at Southern Illinois University Press, patiently guided me through the publishing process. And Alexandria Weinbrecht's careful copyediting has contributed to the quality of this book.

Finally, my daughters, Amy and Maggie, have talked with me and sent me materials about nineteenth-century women; their love and support sustains me in my work, as does that of my loving and reassuring siblings.

Chronology

1820s–1830s
Women join temperance societies led primarily by men, such as the Daughters of Temperance, an auxiliary to the Sons of Temperance, and the Order of Good Templars, which admitted women to membership and office.

1840s
Women begin organizing independent female organizations, both local and state, particularly in such states as New York, Pennsylvania, and Ohio.

1851
Maine passes a law prohibiting the manufacture or sale of alcohol, a law commonly referred to as "The Maine Law" by both advocates and foes of prohibition.

March 1852
The New York State Sons of Temperance meet but deny Daughters of Temperance member Susan B. Anthony permission to speak. The women withdraw, elect Mary C. Vaughan president of their group, and make plans to call a state women's temperance convention. (This date differs from that given in Stanton, Anthony, and Gage's *History of Woman Suffrage*. This date reflects coverage given by newspapers reporting the events.)

April 1852
Women form the New York Temperance Woman's Society in Rochester to counter actions taken at Sons of Temperance meeting. Elizabeth Cady Stanton becomes president.

January 1853
First New York State Woman's Temperance Convention. Susan B. Anthony presides for absent president Elizabeth C. Stanton.

Spring 1853
Susan B. Anthony, Amelia Bloomer, and Antoinette Brown travel New York State lecturing on temperance.

May 1853
The Brick Church meeting, called to plan the World's Temperance Convention of all major temperance organizations, excludes women delegates from participation.

June 1853
The New York State Woman's Temperance Society holds its second convention. Mary C. Vaughan is elected president. Stanton and Anthony leave the temperance organizations. (The *History of Woman Suffrage* quotes newspaper coverage of this convention under the header "First Annual Meeting of the Woman's State Temperance Society" [493] but later refers to it as the second [498]. Other accounts refer to this meeting as the Second Annual Convention.)

September 1853
The World's Temperance Convention meets in New York City. Since women have been excluded from participation, critics nickname the meeting the "Half-World's" or "Pseudo World's" convention.

In response, women call the Whole World's Temperance Convention, which also meets in New York City. The convention is called to counter the exclusionary practices taken by men in planning the World's Temperance Convention and is open to both sexes.

Autumn 1853
Lydia F. Fowler and Clarina Howard Nichols travel Wisconsin delivering temperance lectures.

Amelia Bloomer lectures on temperance throughout the Midwest, specifically Ohio, Indiana, Illinois, Michigan, and Wisconsin.

1861–1865
The nation is embroiled in the Civil War. Temperance women direct their efforts primarily at supporting the war effort.

1869
The National Woman's Suffrage Association breaks from the Equal Rights

Association (ERA) to protest the ERA's support for the Fifteenth Amendment to the Constitution.

1870
Ohio passes the Adair Law permitting wives and children of alcoholic men to bring suit against saloon keepers to recover damages.
The Fifteenth Amendment to the U.S. Constitution is ratified giving black men the right to vote.

1873–1874
Women join in the Woman's Crusade, the largest public demonstration by women in the nineteenth century. They march and pray in streets and saloons, protesting the sale of alcohol.

1874
The Woman's Christian Temperance Union (WCTU) is founded. Annie Wittenmyer becomes president.

1879
Frances E. Willard becomes president of the WCTU.
The National WCTU Convention adopts a suffrage resolution.

1889
The Iowa delegation, led by J. Ellen Foster, walks out of the National WCTU Convention and begins the Nonpartisan Woman's Christian Temperance Union.

1894
Ida B. Wells accuses Frances E. Willard and members of the WCTU of racism.

1898
Frances E. Willard dies at age fifty-nine.

1919
The Eighteenth Amendment to the U.S. Constitution is ratified, establishing national prohibition on liquor.
WCTU membership reaches its highest official number of 346, 638.

1920
The nineteenth amendment to the U.S. Constitution is ratified, extending suffrage to women.

Well-Tempered Women

Introduction: Silenced Voices

TEMPERANCE WOMEN MADE up the largest movement of women in the nineteenth century, and the largest group of women orators and rhetors as well. The quantity of material they produced alone justifies critical attention. However, their claim for critical study is by no means solely quantitative. Nineteenth-century temperance women, despite their lack of formal rhetorical training, exhibit an exceptional understanding of language use within the cultural context of their time in that they demonstrate remarkably effective rhetorical strategies in relation to their own purposes and the audiences they addressed.

Twentieth-century feminists often more comfortably identify with leaders of the suffrage associations, even though temperance women were enormously effective in creating change for nineteenth-century women. Such identification has been problematic. Lori D. Ginzberg, in recent efforts to contribute more broadly to our understanding of women's activism in the nineteenth century, has noted that "The historical focus on the radical demand for the vote as women's only significant political act . . . has had the effect of both foreshortening and distorting the history of women's participation in the political process" (29).

Perhaps because of my roots in a rural, poor community, I find it easy to understand and appreciate temperance women. I do not see them as conservative and complicit in their own oppression, charges often leveled against them. Instead, temperance women seem much like women I knew during childhood—strong, sensible women who recognized the real circumstances of their existence and strove, pragmatically, to improve life for themselves and for others.

Temperance women were remarkably effective for the very reasons they are often criticized. They presented arguments in comfortable, familiar language that made both women and men amenable to new ideas and evidence. Words are most effective when an audience admires its

1

speakers and finds the messages non-threatening. The great strength of temperance leaders was their ability to meld a progressive message with a rhetorical presentation and image comfortable to a large number of women and men. By the hundreds of thousands, women came to hear temperance women's ideas because they could identify with and admire these speakers. Men came to accept women temperance speakers and their positions because, through their rhetoric, these women provided a way for men to see change as imminent and non-aggressive. Temperance women connected theory to practice, and made the connection both important and comprehensible to the general populace through speeches, fiction, and even dress.

We are accustomed to binarisms, and nineteenth-century scholars have tended to label women's rhetoric in a dichotomous fashion—conservative/ liberal (or radical); consolidators/pioneers (Giele); arguments from expediency/from justice (Epstein); arguments from morality/from natural rights (Karlyn Campbell). However, with nineteenth-century women, and with temperance women in particular, binary labels do not fit so neatly. Temperance women represented broadly diverse attitudes. They wanted to change laws governing alcohol because they believed that the issues of temperance and woman's rights were one and the same. Many women explicitly noted their efforts to introduce the notion of woman's rights through the issue of temperance. For others, their intentions are less clear, since inadequate records prevent us from knowing their purposes. Women's temperance rhetoric is complex and varied and might, according to time, purpose, and author, fit any assortment of labels. Women who combined traditional rhetoric with an appeal for change mobilized hundreds of thousands of previously inactive women. Labels such as conservative and radical inadequately describe the complex speakers who successfully addressed a large community of people, united them, organized them, and moved them to action.

IN THE SPRING of 1994, I visited Evanston, Illinois, to see Rest Cottage (plate 1), where Frances E. Willard, president of the WCTU for most of its nineteenth-century history, had lived and to make use of the extensive materials on nineteenth-century temperance women in the Frances E. Willard Memorial Library. As I walked down Chicago Avenue in the direction of Rest Cottage, I found no signs of Willard's nineteenth-century neighborhood. Modern homes and tall apartment and office buildings lined the street. But then, seemingly out of nowhere, Rest Cottage appeared, a nineteenth-century treasure nestled amidst the numerous testimonies to modernity. The Woman's Christian Temperance Union (WCTU) had recently renovated the outside of the cottage; the inside, however, reminded me that the headquarters for the largest organization of women in the nineteenth century has been generally disregarded by the twentieth. Largely forgotten, Rest Cottage has not received the expenditure granted landmarks more acceptable to twentieth-century pride. Yet, while the inside of Rest Cottage needs restoring, the home remains a slice of time in the history of our country and of women. Both the WCTU headquarters and nearby Rest Cottage preserve valuable nineteenth-century history.

When I again visited Rest Cottage and the WCTU headquarters during the summer of 1994, I felt as if I had stepped back into the nineteenth century. I stayed nights in Rest Cottage, sleeping in Frances Willard's bed, surrounded by pictures and mementos from her life. There were no radios or televisions in the house, no working clocks, and I had forgotten to bring my watch. I did research in the Willard Library, a basement addition to the WCTU headquarters, surrounded by the papers and thoughts of nineteenth-century temperance women. I haunted Rest Cottage, imagining the women who lived there, examining Willard's extensive intact library, exploring the wealth of gifts given to Willard by admirers, as well as the other preserved relics of the greatest mass movement of women in the nineteenth century.

The last night I stayed at Rest Cottage, my daughter and I shared a meal with the Cottage's hostess and guide, Claudia Johnson Dobbs. We ate at Willard's dining-room table (plate 2), where Ms. Dobbs gave the Wesley blessing[1], as inscribed on the Blessing Tea Service; the service was probably a gift to Willard from John Wesley's descendants when she spoke in the Wesley Chapel in London. In the corner, a specially-lit cupboard illuminated the cupboard's glass door installed on Willard's fiftieth birthday, a gift from the WCTU portraying the rising sun to represent "a new day dawning for women." On the dining-room walls hung the prints given to Willard by Hannah Whitall Smith, a temperance and suffrage activist. After the meal, Ms. Dobbs gave us a tour of the home. Her wealth of knowledge, and her love for Willard and her home, gave life to this historical treasure.

Most of the house, which Willard's father Josiah built himself, remains as Willard left it, with the original furniture as well as the personal items of Frances, of her mother, Mary Willard, and of her long-time secretary, Anna Gordon, still intact. Four rooms of Rest Cottage have been made into a museum to hold the temperance memorabilia collected during Willard's tenure as president of the WCTU. Here visitors can view the huge bell made from melting one thousand opium pipes, Willard's gowns, and the Polyglot petition—a call for world prohibition written by Frances Willard and affixed with 7.5 million signatures from around the world, sewn into more than two thousand yards of white muslin.

The living room remains as Willard left it, containing the organ Willard bought with the first money she earned from teaching, as well as the collapsible desk she used when travelling. Here is the Willard family Bible, and an inlaid music box, a gift from Lady Henry Somerset that plays the favorite hymns of Frances Willard's mother. In the hallway rests Gladys, the beloved bicycle on which Willard learned to ride at age fifty-three, also a gift from Lady Henry.

Willard's upstairs study has a bay window, a gift from WCTU members to the woman they adored. The room contains the largest segment of Willard's personal library—her collection of works on rhetoric and contemporary writings on women's issues, such as her personal copy of the *History of Woman Suffrage* (signed by one of its authors, her friend Susan B. Anthony), as well as Willard's dictaphone and other accessories that helped with her voluminous writing.

The house is quiet, except during tours, but the National Woman's Christian Temperance Union headquarters, on the grounds behind Rest Cottage, bustles with activity. The union continues to admit only women as full members. Men may become honorary members, but may not hold office or act as voting delegates. The WCTU continues to sponsor three youth groups—the White Ribbon Recruits for children under six years of age, the Loyal Temperance Legion for those between six and twelve years, and the Youth Temperance Council for those between twelve and twenty years of age. All full and honorary members sign the total abstinence pledge and pay annual dues.

Rachel B. Kelly now serves as president of the forty-six state groups that contribute to the union's $360,000 budget. In addition to its many efforts toward educating the public, especially today's youth, about the dangers of alcohol, illegal drugs, tobacco, "and other threats to the health of the human body and the society in which we live" (*National WCTU* 7), the union maintains the Frances E. Willard Home as a museum.

The National WCTU continues to maintain its own publication house, Signal Press. The publishing service provides educational materials for teachers and for the public at large, including leaflets, booklets, books, posters, and videos. The WCTU also continues to publish the *Union Signal*, its bi-monthly magazine, the *Young Crusader*, a children's magazine, as well as various newsletters and directories.

Today's Woman's Christian Temperance Union has its roots in the last quarter of the nineteenth century and, to a degree, in the writings and speeches of women throughout the 1800s. Despite little formal rhetorical preparation, WCTU members actively worked to change their position in the second half of the nineteenth century. They were creating their own interpretations, images, and realities, educating and exploring ideas with one another, forming a large community of support—activities previously denied women.

In both fiction and platform speeches, temperance women were well aware of ethical appeal. They carefully constructed their ethos in an acceptable fashion, and attention to presentation was part of an overall strategy for gradually reconstructing and molding that ethos.

Evidence of women's difficulty in coming to public voice after centuries of silence surfaces over and over in temperance women's rhetoric. When Eliza J. Thompson recounts her leadership of women in their protest before saloons in 1873 and 1874, she describes her own fear, her inability to move or talk when chosen to be president of the group of women who would take to the streets in remarkably unfeminine demonstrations. When her minister asked that she come forward to take charge of the meeting, "her limbs refused to bear her." As do other women, she notes her greater ease at speaking in the company of women. Only after all men had left the room did she find both strength and voice:

> As the last man closed the door after him, strength before unknown came to me, and without any hesitation or consultation I walked forward to the minister's table, took the large Bible, and opening it, explained the incident of the morning; . . . I then called upon Mrs. McDowell to lead in prayer, and such a prayer! It seemed as though the angel had brought down "live coals" from off the altar and touched her lips—she who had never before heard her own voice in prayer! (Willard, *Woman and Temperance* 56–57)

Many women needed the support and comfort of other women to use their voices publicly, but they invariably expressed a joy at hearing those voices in a public arena for the first time.

Understanding the complicated fears and emotions women experienced when taking on a new role and when broaching accepted roles in speaking, Frances Willard instructed WCTU leaders to encourage other women's public voice as often as possible:

> When it comes to a vote after the parliamentary interval for remarks, mention that you are tired of your own voice and anxious to hear theirs, adding in your clearest tones, 'All in favor of that motion will please to say aye,' and let your final word be in the most decided sense a rising circumflex. You will be surprised to see the readiness with which you can thus call out the voices of the timid, partly out of good nature and partly because their musical perceptions lead them to put a climax to your incomplete inflection by their own. (*How to Organize* 7)

Willard's recognition of the difficulty for many women in uttering even one syllable in public presents a painful image of female voicelessness. In this context, especially, we should celebrate the successful process and the tremendous coming to voice represented in the voluminous speeches and public meetings held by temperance women by the end of the nineteenth century

TEMPERANCE WAS A major reform issue for most of the nineteenth century and represented the most important and far-reaching issue for women during that period. Yet, despite efforts in recent years to include women's voices in our understanding of our country's past, scholars have tended to ignore those of women associated with temperance. Karlyn Kohrs Campbell's valuable *Man Cannot Speak for Her* explicitly seeks to recover the rhetoric of women active in seeking greater rights, but Campbell overlooks the role played by temperance women. While she does devote one segment to Frances Willard, Campbell sees Willard's impact as transient (131) and independent of the feminist movement because she "generat[ed] discourse which was suited only to reinforce existing beliefs" (129). Campbell's subsequent edited volume, *Women Public Speakers in the United States, 1800–1925*, does include a number of women who were active both in temperance and in suffrage associations—Clara Barton, Antoinette Brown Blackwell, Clarina Howard Nichols, Anna Howard Shaw, Julia Ward Howe, and Frances E. Willard—but, with the exception of Willard, the selections emphasize their suffrage connections. However, the style often associated with temperance women is more fully appreciated in this anthology than in her first study, and the volume includes a more positive presentation of Willard.

In addition, while Gregory Clark and S. Michael Halloran's edited collection, *Oratorical Culture in Nineteenth-Century America*, explicitly seeks to reclaim nineteenth-century oratory and does include some women, there is no inclusion of temperance women. This omission is surprising. After all, the largest group of rhetorically active women in nineteenth-century America was comprised of temperance women. And leaders of the Woman's Christian Temperance Union systematically encouraged and instructed vast numbers of nineteenth-century women in rhetorical, organizational, and parliamentary techniques.

Contributing to the recovery of nineteenth-century African American women's voices, Shirley Wilson Logan's recent *With Pen and Voice* offers an anthology of African American women rhetors, including women important to the black woman's club movement. These women were also instrumental in the organization of the National Association of Colored Women at the end of the century. Chapter 4 discusses the connection between these important African American women and the WCTU.

Frances Willard has long fascinated scholars, and several recent works

focus explicitly on restoring Willard's voice. Amy Slagell's 1992 dissertation, "A Good Woman Speaking Well: The Oratory of Frances E. Willard,"
gathers and examines many of Willard's previously unavailable speeches.
And Carolyn DeSwarte Gifford's new publication, *"Writing Out My
Heart": The Journal of Frances E. Willard*, provides an edited compila-
tion of Willard's journals. Both works afford a more current appraisal of the
best-known woman orator of the century.

Even with recent interest in nineteenth-century women, and in Frances
Willard specifically, only Janet Giele, and in a more limited manner, Jack
Blocker, have examined the language of a large number of temperance
women. In her valuable study, Giele examines and compares the socio-
economic and educational backgrounds of temperance and suffrage leaders, finding little difference in their backgrounds. She also searches out
what these women had to say in the pages of the *Union Signal* and the
Woman's Journal, the official publications of the Woman's Christian Temperance Union and the National Woman's Suffrage Association, respec-
tively. Giele finds that the words used by suffrage women were more radical
than those of temperance women, but the language in the *Union Signal*
(beginning in 1883) is a limited sample of temperance rhetoric. The official journal presents temperance women in a light different from that of
their words at national and state conventions. Often, women who spoke
at conventions were more likely to be progressive than those who sought
the relatively safe space of the written word; and even progressive women
writing for the *Union Signal* would have been conscious that their audience included rank-and-file members who might require a more moder-
ate rhetoric. Temperance women nearly always presented non-traditional
ideas in a manner carefully crafted to appeal to a widely diverse audience. In doing so, they incorporated both traditional and progressive
ideas within their presentations, a strategy scholars often misinterpret as
conservative.

Past scholarship on the teaching of rhetoric has looked to educational institutions and academic texts for instruction in rhetorical skills.
But since women were most often excluded from and had little influence
on institutions of higher learning, those studies provide little information about the education of and communication among women. Because
the history of rhetoric has concentrated on the move from an oral to a
written tradition in male-dominated western history, women's voices have
been omitted. Women's movement toward attaining a public voice in the
nineteenth century took the reverse path, beginning largely in the more
acceptable (because less public) written form and moving toward oral,
public delivery. The temperance movement provides a unique look at
methods women used for teaching one another rhetorical skills in a manner "appropriate" to and successful for their gender.

Efforts at recovering nineteenth-century women writers have also largely neglected women writers of temperance fiction. Lucy Freibert and Barbara White's *Hidden Hands* includes an excerpt from Metta Fuller Victor's *The Senator's Son*, acknowledging the widespread availability and cultural importance of such fiction. Robert S. Levine also includes an examination of temperance fiction in mid-century America, including some by women, as a "central motif of the writings" in "Fiction and Reform," a segment of *The Columbia History of the American Novel.*

But as studies on nineteenth-century women writers flourished in the 1980s, little attention was given to writers of temperance fiction. Legacy, a new journal devoted specifically to nineteenth-century women authors, for example, began publication during that time but has not included women writers of temperance fiction. Most scholars of nineteenth-century women writers have ignored women's temperance fiction. The present volume shows, however, that women's temperance rhetoric, including fiction, is a rich and engaging field of study for feminist readers.

Women's temperance reform has often been incorrectly dismissed as a conservative representation of the nineteenth century's cult of true womanhood. In our secular age, scholars tend to disregard women associated with evangelical or religious causes not considered progressive by today's standards. However, because of the large participatory role women took within church organizations and reform causes, a vast number of women prepared for further involvement in public life through positions in such organizations. Numerous leaders credited their early activity within the church as providing initial interest and continuing preparation for their later public leadership roles. In addition, evangelical women created their own standards for Christianity, which they deliberately delineated from orthodox patriarchal religious organizations. Their own interpretation of Christian principles and their appeal to a "higher authority" justified their defiance of patriarchal authority and enabled them to demand greater rights for women. And, as chapter 3 shows, women temperance leaders provided the largest school for preparing women for public participation in the nineteenth century.

Temperance women and their rhetoric have also been neglected because our hierarchical, competitive society devalues a group it perceives as having "lost" when the Eighteenth Amendment was repealed. But these women brought about major political changes, including the passage of a constitutional amendment, a feat accomplished by few political movements. Temperance women were politically astute and effective; they were instrumental in achieving numerous local and state political gains in controlling the sale of alcohol, but they made gains in regard to other women's issues as well. They helped to raise the legal age of consent for girls in nearly every state, and they convinced the "average woman" of the need for woman's suffrage, leading to the passage of a second amendment to the Constitution still in effect today. It is not mere coincidence that the woman's suffrage amendment was added to the Constitution in 1920, one year after the passage of the prohibition amendment.

Well-Tempered Women adds to our knowledge about temperance women by examining new sources: temperance fiction, newspaper accounts of meetings and speeches, autobiographical and biographical accounts, and minutes of national and state temperance conventions. Each of these sources intentionally or unintentionally presents biased but informative perspectives.[2] Even so, *Well-Tempered Women* contributes new voices and new perspectives to our study of women and women's words in the nineteenth century.[3]

Because much of the material included in this book is not readily available, I often quote women's words at length. While I have tried to "see" from the perspective of the numerous women portrayed here and to present their story as much as possible in their own words, my own limitations and perspectives necessarily influence my work. Nonetheless, I believe the evidence supports my contention that the temperance movement, and especially the rhetorical sophistication of its leaders, was essential in women's growing awareness about and ultimate insistence upon a change in sexual inequalities in the nineteenth-century United States.

PART 1 OF *Well-Tempered Women* examines nineteenth-century temperance women's oral rhetoric. Chapter 1, "Woman's Rights in Woman's Wrongs: Temperance Women at Mid-Century," explores texts from early temperance speakers, both those who subsequently organized the woman's rights movement, such as Susan B. Anthony and Elizabeth Cady Stanton, and those who chose instead to remain active within the temperance organizations.

The majority of extant texts by women temperance speakers are from members of the Woman's Christian Temperance Union. Chapter 2, "Patriotic Reformers: 'Called by the Spirit of the Lord to Lead the Women of the World,'" examines the rhetoric of WCTU member Frances E. Willard, the primary leader of the WCTU during the final quarter of the nineteenth century, as well as other famous WCTU leaders, such as Mary Torrans Lathrap, often called the "Daniel Webster" of the temperance movement, and Eliza Stewart, referred to as "Wendell Phillips in Petticoats." Chapter 3, "Woman-Tempered Rhetoric: Public Presentation and the WCTU," examines the extensive network WCTU leaders created for teaching new members rhetorical skills.

Part 2 explores temperance women's rhetoric from perspectives outside those of mainstream, middle-class women. Chapter 4, "Dissension and Division: Racial Tension and the WCTU," focuses on racial conflict and alliances associated with the WCTU. Based largely on an essentialized image of women, the WCTU began to show signs of strain as an increasingly diverse membership threatened the unity and harmony of the organization. Chapter 5, "Red-Nosed Angels and the Corseted Crusade: Newspaper Accounts of Nineteenth-Century Temperance Reformers," analyzes press coverage of women temperance speakers. Newspaper reports focused on women speakers' physical appearance to an extreme, reflecting the great concern for dichotomous gender distinctions and the fear of any blending of gender roles.

Part 3 explores temperance fiction written by nineteenth-century women. Chapter 6, "'The Feelings of the Romantic and Fashionable': Women's Issues in Temperance Fiction," examines women's temperance fiction in its remarkably candid presentation of injustices toward women and its insistence upon greater equality. The temperance issue permitted women to broach otherwise clandestine topics openly, many of them remarkably similar to the concerns of today's feminists. Chapter 7, "'Wine Drinkers and Heartless Profligates': Water Drops from Popular Novelists," examines the abundant references to temperance in the writing of the most popular women novelists of the day, as well as in fiction labeled temperance and written by well-known literary women: Louisa May Alcott, Elizabeth F. Ellet, Grace Greenwood, Sarah Josepha Hale, Caroline Hentz, Caroline Kirkland, Elizabeth Stuart Phelps, Catharine Maria Sedgwick, Lydia Sigourney, Ann Stephens, and Harriet Beecher Stowe.

The conclusion, "Women of the Century," examines both the widespread success of the WCTU and the reasons for its diminishing strength. It also explores the parallels between women's groups at the end of both the nineteenth century and our own, as well as the importance to twentieth-century women of the most widely successful and popular woman's political movement: temperance.

Part One

***

From Pedestal to Pen and Podium

1

Woman's Rights in Woman's Wrongs:
Temperance Women at Mid-Century

> You who, clothed in the garb of womanhood, excuse your-
> selves from any participation in opposing the vice of drunk-
> enness, under the plea of sacrifice of female delicacy, or of
> departure from your proper sphere, look for a moment at the
> condition of the drunkard's wife and children, and the no-
> bler impulses of your nature will certainly prompt you to
> some effort to rescue and sustain female delicacy in the de-
> graded home of the drunkard.
>
> —"Address of the Woman's Temperance Convention"

BY THE MID-NINETEENTH century, many women recognized that the
temperance issue offered an ideal vehicle for speaking about women's
concerns. A serious problem in the nineteenth century, intemperance was
associated more with men than with women. W. J. Rorabaugh has convincingly shown the excessive use of alcohol, especially during the first
third of the nineteenth century, when "the typical American annually
drank more distilled liquor than at any other time in our history" (17).
Notions that alcohol promoted health had been a prevailing sentiment
in the United States. Americans also believed that drinking distilled spirits showed patriotism, because it supported home industries. In addition,
the well-established social custom of "treating," or buying drinks for
companions to display hospitality and friendship, also contributed to the
increased use of alcohol. But by the late 1830s, notions about the positive aspects of alcohol gave way to increasing fears of addiction and public disgust with inebriates.

13

Even though some women drank alcohol in large quantity, men drank far more. According to Rorabaugh, two-thirds of all imbibed distilled spirits were consumed by 50 percent of adult males, who comprised only one-eighth of the total population (11). As the century progressed, women drank even less proportionally because of cultural restrictions on such consumption. Therefore, intemperance came to be accepted as a problem characteristic of men rather than women.

Furthermore, men's intemperance uniquely served to highlight the many inequities and injustices within the legal system, especially with regard to married women. In the United States at mid-century, coverture, the traditional common law that united women's legal rights with that of their husbands, existed to varying degrees in every state. When women married, their personal property, and to differing extents their real property, their persons, their labor, and their children came under the ownership of their husbands. Therefore, all personal property and income—whether from rents, investments, or wages, and often from real property—were subject to a husband's disposal and could be confiscated by his creditors. While women's property might be misused or squandered by any husband, chances of loss became greater when husbands became alcohol abusers.

Laws regarding women's legal status varied greatly according to region. Southern states first instigated reforms beginning in the late 1830s, assuring a wife's ownership of, though not control of or income from, real property. Even in these states, wives might continue to own lands and slaves, but husbands were entitled to the control of both. The Panic of 1837 had encouraged such limited reform, partly out of sympathy for women left destitute when their husbands' creditors seized their property, and partly because men who married wealthy women wanted to protect their interests in their wives' property in case of financial disasters.[1]

Other states began making changes in their laws of coverture in the 1840s. Michigan allowed for a wife's separate estate beginning in 1844. By 1848, seven southern states and twelve northern states had passed legislation in varying degrees of generosity, restoring rights to married women. Most gave the wife ownership over her real, but not her personal property. Only one, Maine, permitted her the legal right to contract and manage her real property. In every state, children remained the legal property of the father, and only in Michigan and New York did women retain control over their own wages and income.

Women's inability to protect themselves or their children from abusive, irresponsible husbands who drank thus provided effective ammunition for speakers to point out women's precarious position with regards to the law. Official concern for needed reforms helped to focus public attention on problems with existing laws. Although a limited amount of legal reform improved conditions somewhat for some women, most were still vulnerable to the profligate behavior of husbands, and profligacy was more likely and less acceptable when husbands were intemperate. Women temperance speakers at mid-century sincerely believed that alcohol consumption should be controlled and that such control would improve conditions for women and their children. But they also wanted more far-reaching reforms and believed that addressing the issue of temperance effectively permitted them to reach otherwise inaccessible audiences in order to make their case for greater rights for women. Their presentation of women's rights by emphasizing wrongs women endured became an effective rhetorical means for temperance women throughout the century.

Resistance to increased rights for women was great and legal reform slow. Nineteenth-century wisdom, especially among those with the greatest power to legislate change, held that separating the material interests of a wife from her husband endangered the marital institution. As Nancy Cott has pointed out, marriage, often presumed to be a private matter, was instead very public and a primary means of control for those in authority ("Giving").[2] Because of the strong support for maintaining coverture, instigating change in the laws affecting marriage was far more effective when presented as protection for women and children victims of intemperate men.

Women who supported temperance reform actively supported a broad definition of woman's rights. Many believed that temperance, equal rights, and suffrage were equally important in advancing women's causes; however, they believed that the temperance issue would most effectively change attitudes about women's injustices and encourage women to become active on their own behalf. Some viewed women's temperance activity as an avenue for creating a changed consciousness as well as a move toward greater public participation on the part of women. Amelia Bloomer (plate 3) commented on the importance of women's temperance activity in changing attitudes among women. She referred to an 1852 woman's temperance society

> which became very effective and had much to do in breaking down the barriers and introducing women into temperance and other work. Some half-dozen women were employed by the society as agents on salaries of twenty-five dollars per month and their expenses . . . it was surprising how public sentiment changed and how the zeal of temperance women helped on the new movement of women. (Bloomer 85–86)

Many temperance women recognized the positive appeal of the issue, and their rhetoric reveals how skillfully these speakers argued for women's rights while overtly supporting the temperance cause. But it also reflects, I believe, the widespread, if repressed, unhappiness of many women with the failure of the legal system to protect them. While temperance women carefully named their addresses "temperance" lectures, sometimes modestly presenting benevolent pleas on behalf of suffering women and children rather than insisting upon their own rights, their promotion of equal rights is very thinly veiled. Framed in language that evoked concrete, familiar images of injustice, woman's rights issues could be safely heard and discussed by a broad spectrum of listeners through temperance rhetoric.

Temperance women were especially attuned to their audience, and, recognizing the need to meet women according to their level of awareness, they delivered speeches according to the consciousness of their listeners. For example, Clarina Howard Nichols (plate 4) and Lydia F. Fowler traveled the state of Wisconsin during the autumn of 1853 lecturing as agents of the Wisconsin Woman's State Temperance Society. Nichols acknowledged and tried to comply with the Society's concern that she "plead the cause of the poor and needy . . . without offending old-time ideas of woman's sphere" (Stanton, Anthony, and Gage 182). But, because of the prejudice toward women speakers, Nichols, as was often the case, was forced to defend women's right to speak at a number of stops. At one point, she was even excluded from speaking by men who deliberately spoke at length in order to usurp her lecture time.

Temperance speakers consciously chose a rhetorical strategy that served their purposes when they met such opposition. Nichols capitalized on her mistreatment to convince her audience of the need for greater rights for women, but she placed her argument within the context of abuses women suffered at the hands of intemperate men. She explained,

> Worse than unwise would it have been to allow an unjust prejudice against Woman's Rights, to turn the edge of my appeals for a law in the interest of temperance, when by showing the connection, as of cause and effect, between men's rights and women's wrongs, between women's *no*-rights and their helplessness and dependence, I could disarm that prejudice and win an intelligent support for both temperance and equal rights. . . . I assured my audiences, that I had not come to talk to them of "Woman's Rights," that indeed I did not find that women had any rights in the matter, but to "suffer and be still; to die and give no sign." But I had come to speak of *man's rights* and *woman's needs*. (183)

Nichols, understanding her audience and combining her purposes, effectively used wordplay on women's rights and wrongs to persuade her listeners of the validity of both her causes.

Speakers repeatedly recounted the effectiveness of temperance rhetoric in presenting audiences with the need for change in laws with regard to women. According to Nichols, her method worked well: "My audience had accepted woman's rights in her wrongs; and I—only woman's recording angel can tell the sensations of a disfranchised woman when her 'declaration of intentions' is endorsed by an Anti-Woman's Rights audience with fervent thanks to God!" (184). Nichols gained an ear for woman's rights among unsympathetic audiences by framing such rhetoric with complaints about intemperance. Her attitude is characteristic of the many women who believed in providing role models for women, in furthering women's acceptance as public speakers, and in enticing an audience to listen to women's grievances by using an indirect means of address. Within the context of temperance speeches, most audiences accepted the inclusion of what were considered woman's rights issues.

The Madison Argus's response to these addresses typifies many reactions to such speeches. Reporting that Nichols and Fowler had addressed a Madison, Wisconsin audience "upon the subject of the Maine Law,[3] and, *incidentally*, upon woman's wrongs and woman's rights" [emphasis mine], the newspaper editorialized,

> We have the usual prejudices of education, and the established usages of society, against the practice of women engaging in public lectures, or meddling in politics; but such prejudice has not blinded us to the fact, that in men's laws woman has not yet attained those rights and immunities which the laws of nature and necessity emperiously demand upon the fundamental principles of human equality; and we are free to confess that the intelligence, delicacy and grace exhibited by those lectures, more than half removed our scruples to female labor in such a sphere. No one could look upon their highly intelligent faces, without feeling that they were true women, acting from noble impulses, and outraging none of the instinctive delicacy of their sex. ("from the *Madison Argus*" 3)

The editor of the *Argus* recognized that the two women were breaching their accustomed roles and that they were including woman's rights issues in their delivery, but found the inclusion acceptable, placed as it was within the context of temperance. Thus, by carefully presenting their cause as an unselfish effort on behalf of suffering women and children, and by scrupulously maintaining the cultural expectations that defined their sphere (except for their uncharacteristic public speaking), these women "more than half convinced" powerful and influential newspaper editors to reconsider the legal position of their sex.

Wordplay on woman's rights and wrongs became a favorite means of address for temperance women. Amelia Bloomer even gave an address entitled "Woman's Rights and Woman's Wrongs." One account described that address as follows:

> She dwelt with much pathos upon the injustice of the laws of our country in regard to Woman, in the disposal of her property and her off-spring, and in *taxation* without *representation.* She said that it was only because the heart of man was so much better than the infamous laws which he had enacted, that Woman was not rendered the most abject *menial* upon earth. ("Woman's Rights" 3)

In spite of her emphasis on the need for greater rights for women, Bloomer dispelled negative notions about women speakers and the fear that women were becoming masculinized. She carefully attacked the law and not the man, even praising men's generosity, clearly wishing to persuade those whose power might help her cause. Her careful rhetorical stance even permitted her to speak of women's need for power; couching her desire for greater power for women as a selfless plea on behalf of abused women and children, she reached women who felt less free to insist on such powers.

> Who of our sisters are there, who do not weep tears of pity over the fate of this fair victim of the liquor seller's cruel business? . . . Who does not feel the wish for power to hurl down both the drunkard and the drunkard maker, and restore to their true position and happiness those who are subjected to cruelty? ("The Chivalry" 14)

Despite Bloomer's thinly cloaked appeals for greater rights and power for women, when she spoke in Detroit, the *Tribune* praised her "appearance and demeanor," calling it "modest and unassuming in the extreme" ("Mrs. Bloomer" 3). Thus her demeanor and conciliatory approach won receptive audiences that more confrontational woman's rights speakers could never hope to attract.

Throughout the country women spoke on temperance, almost always incorporating evidence that in another venue would have been opposed as arguments for woman's rights. Many insisted that women must have more rights in order to protect the helpless against the evils of alcohol. Others, while insisting on greater rights for women, assured audiences that they were not part of the woman's rights movement. They maintained a careful balance between encouraging listeners to question traditional assumptions and assuring them that they were not seeking disruptive changes.

Such was the case, especially on local or state levels, where speakers lived in the communities where they spoke and therefore understood their audiences. A good example is that of Mrs. R. Ostrander, president of the Wisconsin Woman's State Temperance Society, who assured members that they would not become a woman's rights convention. But her assurances masked only superficially her adamant efforts on the part of women. Ostrander's tactful but obvious oscillation between prodding women to claim greater rights and reassuring them about cultural codes exemplifies local temperance rhetoric. Her melding of traditional feminine expectations with persuasive appeals for change began with the opening of her address, as she modestly asked forbearance during her newfound position, while at the same time praising the new activity among women:

> I bring a warm heart to the cause which has convened us—and a willing one, too, to act in *any* position, and to perform *any* *duty* which shall subserve the interests of this cause; at the same time, I crave your forbearance and your charity for any imperfections during this meeting. The time *will come* when women will be at home, here, and everywhere, where humanity's call is heard. ("Mrs. Ostrander's Address" 2)

Ostrander deftly justified and emphasized women's right to act in any capacity in the name of temperance, but she carefully phrased that right as a duty, wording that made her suggestions more acceptable to many listeners. She also placed such duty in the context of the Old Testament "call to battle" by trumpet, adding further weight to the imperative of their action:

> The cause of *temperance* is one which, ever since its agitation in our country, has lain near my heart. I have watched its progress and rejoiced at its success. But, my friends, *heretofore*, we have watched afar off and rejoiced in silence. We did not dream that we had much to do but to weep and mourn in secret places over the misery Rum was creating, and pray to the Ruler of the Universe to stay the destroying flood. But a new era has arisen and a brighter day has dawned. The call now is, WOMAN! *be up and doing*! Let your voice be heard, as sure and certain as a trumpet's sound. We will not cease to *pray*, but we will unite our labors with our prayers. We will let *our faith be seen* by our *works*. (2)

Ostrander also celebrated women's new role. Later temperance women would more fully and directly incorporate praise for temperance women into their speeches, but early leaders already recognized the empowering force in rhetoric that celebrated women's work and glorified their activity. Ostrander carefully reassured those less confident of the propriety of women's new role: "Many there are whose hearts are true to the cause, but from timidity, or some other cause, stand aloof from this movement. But we will show them by our example—I trust we shall—that there is no danger—that we are not transcending our limits and getting "out of our sphere" (2).

Accordingly, Ostrander reassured women and men who feared the derogatory naming so often applied to reform women—that of becoming masculine or unsexed. But even as she reassured women, she scoffed at those who accused women taking public action of unbecoming behavior:

> Oh, I am sick of hearing this canting phrase—"*getting out of our sphere!*" Oh, that some giant intellect among our opposers would define our sphere—as *they understand it!*—so that we might, at least, see how far we may diverge from our *accustomed orbits* without danger of flying off to a returnless distance from the *great centres of attraction*—the "*lords of creation.*" (2)

At the same time that she challenged the rights of "the lords of creation" to define a woman's public role as improper, Ostrander once again strove to reassure the more timid in her audience:

> It is feared by some that this is to be a "Woman's Rights concern;" and hence the question has been repeatedly asked, "Is that subject to be agitated at your meeting?" My answer has been, No! The question to be discussed is the all-absorbing one of Temperance. (2)

While insisting that temperance alone was the issue of the convention, like other temperance leaders, Ostrander had ridiculed those who questioned a woman's right to public activity and praised women who had chosen to work outside the home. She further cloaked women's public activity in the sacred realm of tradition by drawing parallels between pioneering Wisconsin women and contemporary women, both justifying the activity of temperance women and implying a heroic courage: "Shall we stand still and see the combat thicken, and not lend *our aid*? Have we one drop of our revolutionary mothers' blood in our veins? Then let us respond to the call." Ostrander completed her address with a rousing call for courage and independence on the part of Wisconsin women. Once again, she associated opposition to women's public stance with negative connotations:

> Women of Wisconsin! Let not the fear of man—let not pride or opinion—let not the love of popularity, nor of ease, prevent your taking a stand, and performing your part in the

efforts that are being make [*sic*] to get a law prohibiting the sale of intoxicating drinks. Let the tears and groans and sighs, and poverty and crime, caused by intemperance, weigh heavier on your minds than all these considerations I have mentioned. Let your watchword be—"No rest, no ease, until Rum is banished from our land!" (2)

Ostrander's evocation of duty was a typical means of diffusing arguments against women's public involvement, since duty played prominently in those activities consigned to a woman's sphere. For example, in the late 1840s, Pennsylvania women were already holding their own temperance conventions and often cited such justification for their public activity. Following the pleas for formal participation from women, members emphasized that women "have solemn obligations resting upon us, and we should be unfaithful to the highest call of duty, false to the instincts of womanhood, and the pleading voices of love, if we should sit quietly down in careless ease while vice is thus spreading around us" ("To the Women" 1). These women took the charge of duty one step further, insisting that women would be failing in their true calling "if we did not exert ourselves to rescue those around us from the degrading vice of drunkenness" ("Address" 1). The Chester County, Pennsylvania women deftly manipulated charges against them and inverted strictures accorded to sphere in order to provide support for their undertakings. Such skilled acuity would mark rhetorical presentations of temperance women for generations to come.

Whenever permitted, temperance women lectured in churches, making it more difficult for their opponents to attack them. For example, when the *Milwaukee Morning News* criticized her for "taking the stump," Mrs. E. K. Fonda pointed out that the "stumps" where she had spoken were successively the Baptist Church, the Presbyterian Church, and the Methodist Church, and that she had been introduced by the pastor on each occasion ("The Morning" 3). Activity given religious sanction could hardly be condemned.

By mid-century, women temperance leaders were already committed to change for women, but they believed their cause could best be served by using a subtle, non-threatening, yet persuasive approach, and they consciously chose to work on women's behalf in that manner. However, a superficial examination of their rhetoric might belie their purpose, since they cautiously crafted their presentations to include words such as duty; they often claimed not to be speaking for the woman's rights cause; and they carefully presented their appeals as benevolent concerns for the weak.

Despite their efforts on behalf of change for women, today's scholars have shown little interest in temperance women because our record of women's efforts toward achieving greater equality has been dominated by those who believed in taking a more direct, aggressive approach. Since their ideas about the best way to proceed in effecting broader rights differed from that of temperance women, and because they often saw themselves in competition with temperance women, their perspective is worthwhile, but decidedly limited.

The accounts best known to today's scholars are the valuable and impressive collections amassed by Elizabeth Cady Stanton (plate 5) and Susan B. Anthony (plate 6). Because of our reliance on these and related sources, we often assume, as Anthony's biographer Ida Husted Harper tells us in *The Life and Work of Susan B. Anthony*, that Anthony and Stanton deserted temperance organizations because, Anthony suggested, "'they [temperance organizations] would not accept the principle of woman's rights'" (95). According to Harper, the New York State temperance organization that Anthony and Stanton had helped to found "passed into the hands of a body of conservative women, who believed they could accomplish by prayer what these two knew never could be done except through legislation with a constituency of women behind it" (95). As the examination of temperance women's rhetoric in this chapter demonstrates, this was simply not the case. Rather, temperance women chose a different, and arguably a more effective, rhetorical approach to delivering woman's rights messages.

In their *History of Woman Suffrage*, Stanton, Anthony, and Matilda Joslyn Gage provide an account similar to that of Harper's:

> Most of the liberal men and women now withdrew from all temperance organizations, leaving the movement in the hands of time-serving priests and politicians, who, being in the majority, effectually blocked the progress of the reform for the time—destroying, as they did, the enthusiasm of the women in trying to press it as a moral principle, and the hope of the men, who intended to carry it as a political measure. Henceforward women took no active part in temperance until the Ohio crusade revived into "The Woman's National Christian Temperance Union," of which Miss Frances E. Willard is president. As now, so in 1853, intelligent women saw that the most direct way to effect any reform was to have a voice in the laws and lawmakers. Hence they turned their attention to rolling up petitions for the civil and political rights of women, to hearings before legislatures and constitutional conventions, giving their most persistent efforts to the reform technically called "Woman's Rights." (512–13)

Because Stanton, Anthony, and Gage's work, along with that of Harper, has been our primary source for women's history of this period, scholars have mistakenly assumed that most women left the temperance cause and that those who remained were passive, timid women. Such negative accounts have produced distorted impressions about, and unfair dismissal of, the numerous women who spoke openly and widely for temperance reform.

Although Anthony and Stanton might well have regarded those women who remained active in the temperance cause as conservative because they refused to work exclusively for the woman's rights cause, their perspective that women, especially intelligent women, abandoned the temperance cause is inaccurate. Many women believed woman's rights and temperance to be inextricably intertwined. In addition, temperance women made a conscious, rhetorical decision to reach a broad-based audience by addressing the temperance cause. Many prominent temperance lecturers, including Amelia Bloomer, Clarina Howard Nichols, and Lydia F. Fowler were also among the most active and most effective speakers on behalf of equal rights for women in the country. They travelled widely, adjusting their message to a diverse population throughout the nation.

The tumultuous period Stanton, Anthony, and Gage cite as the culmination of women's active participation in temperance reform does mark a pivotal point for many women active in the movement. The turbulence began with the March 1852, New York meeting of all divisions of the Sons of Temperance from that state in Albany. The Daughters of Temperance were invited to send delegates,[4] but when Anthony, a delegate from the Rochester Daughters of Temperance, rose to speak, the presiding officer insisted that women were invited to listen only. Even more importantly, at a later "World's Temperance Convention," a group of men hissed and hooted to prevent Antoinette Brown (plate 7), an accepted delegate, from speaking. The minority, primarily ministers, drowned out Brown's efforts to be heard with such calls as "Shame on Woman," because of their disgust at women's attempt at public speech. Newspapers across the country carried the story, angering women and inciting them to active organization.

Anthony and Stanton did desert temperance organizations in 1853.[5] After Anthony was refused permission to speak, a small group of women called their own organizational meeting, choosing Mary C. Vaughan as president, Anthony as secretary, and Lydia Mott as chair of the business committee. The group subsequently called a state woman's temperance meeting at Rochester the following month, on April 20, 1852, at which Stanton was elected president, and Anthony, Bloomer, and Vaughan were chosen secretaries. At first, only women were permitted to speak and to hold office in the new organization, but when Antoinette Brown refused to participate because of unequal treatment for men, Stanton requested a change in this provision at the second year's meeting.

At that second year's convention, held June 1, 1853, Mary C. Vaughan was chosen president, and Stanton and Anthony abandoned the organization. Accounts regarding the reasons for their desertion differ. According to Ida Harper, some women opposed Stanton's re-election as president because of her radical views, and along with the majority of men who had been admitted, they defeated Stanton, electing Vaughan president instead. Anthony, elected vice president, declined to serve, Harper says, because "the vote showed they would not accept the principle of woman's rights and, as she believed thoroughly in standing for the equality of woman, she could not act as officer of such a society" (95). According to D. C. Bloomer's account of the gathering in his *Life and Writing of Amelia Bloomer*, Stanton was re-elected. But because the majority (including Amelia Bloomer) opposed Stanton's request that men be admitted on equal terms, "preferr[ing] that it should continue to be an exclusively feminine organization," Stanton declined to serve as president, and Anthony, chosen again to serve as secretary, declined as well (121). Bloomer's account, based on the perspective of Amelia Bloomer, is significant because Amelia Bloomer was, in many ways, the most influential person at the meeting. Although twentieth-century scholars are more familiar with Anthony and Stanton, Amelia Bloomer actually had attained far greater national and international name recognition because of her editorship of *The Lily* and the attention surrounding the "Bloomer" costume, the reform dress named for her (plate 8). At times, the *New-York Tribune* even referred to groups of women that included those better known today as "Mrs. Bloomer and assistants" ("Great Gathering" 5). If Bloomer opposed admitting males, she would have held great sway over many others present.

Personality might also have been at issue in the vote if Vaughan was elected over Stanton. Stanton's presidential address suggests her presumption of a knowledge and intellect superior to her audience, taking an "I told you so" attitude that might have offended other members.

> A little more than one year ago, in this same hall, we formed the first Woman's State Temperance Society. . . . We who had watched the jealousy with which man had ever eyed the slow aggressions of woman, warned you against the insidious proposition made by agents from that Society. We told you they would no doubt gladly receive the dollar, but that you would never be allowed to speak or vote in their meetings. Many of you thought us suspicious and unjust toward the temperance men of the Empire State. . . . our predictions have been fully realized in the treatment our delegates received at the annual meeting held at Syracuse last July, and at the re-

cent Brick Church meeting in New York. (Stanton, Anthony,
and Gage 493–94)

Although a brilliant philosopher and theoretician, Stanton did not always
display rhetorical acumen. Similar problems followed Stanton throughout
her life, most notably in the 1869 split of the Equal Rights Association
into the National Woman's Suffrage Association and the American
Woman's Suffrage Association, but also in numerous other disagreements
stemming from her refusal to compromise her own beliefs.

Accounts in the *History of Woman Suffrage* also suggest problems
associated with male membership:

> As it was decided at this second convention to admit gentle-
> men, a schism was the immediate result. . . . It was the policy
> of these worldly wise men to restrict the debate on temper-
> ance within such narrow limits as to disturb none of the ex-
> isting conditions of society. . . .
>
> Thus these politic gentlemen manipulated the association,
> eliminated the woman's right elements *per se*. . . . Those
> women who had no proper self-respect accepted the condi-
> tions; those who had . . . abandoned all temperance organi-
> zations, as the same proper pride that forbade them to accept
> the conditions of a proscribed call of men's conventions, also
> prevented their affiliation with women who would tolerate
> such insults to the sex. (498–99)

Stanton, Anthony, and Gage again depict a scenario in which a small
radical element (Stanton and Anthony, primarily) left temperance organizations to a conservative majority of women who permitted men to
control their proceedings, but there is little evidence to substantiate this
interpretation. Such women as Amelia Bloomer and Mary C. Vaughan
can hardly be termed conservative, because they actively and openly challenged a woman's traditional role. Others, such as Antoinette Brown and
Clarina Howard Nichols, also continued to work in both the woman's
rights and temperance organizations. Still others, such as Frances D.
Gage, Amanda Way, and Eliza Daniel Stewart, participated in equal rights
conventions, but devoted the majority of their time to temperance causes.
Way held a number of high offices in the Good Templars, while Stewart
belonged to and worked closely with a number of temperance organizations; both participated in the WCTU after its formation. Further, Stewart
was instrumental in the Woman's Crusade and in organizing the WCTU.

Amelia Bloomer had chosen not to join the Daughters of Temperance, of which Anthony was a member, because women were only accepted

into the auxiliary unit. Instead, she joined the Good Templars because they admitted both women and men as equal members. She published *The Lily*, a newspaper dedicated to temperance and woman's rights, and continued to belong to the Good Templars whenever there were organizations where she lived; she continued, as well, to participate actively in women's temperance organizations. When the Woman's Christian Temperance Union was formed in 1874, Bloomer became a member of that organization as well. The attitude of such progressive women who continued to labor for temperance might best be expressed by Bloomer's 1853 explanation:

> We cannot consent to have woman remain silent on the Temperance question till she obtain her right of suffrage. Great as is our faith in the speedy triumph of temperance principles were women allowed their right of franchise, and strong as is our hope that this right will be granted ere many years, we feel that the day is too far distant for her to rest all her hopes and labors on that issue. Let her work with her whole heart in this cause and, while she demands a law that entirely prohibits the traffic in strong drink, let her also obtain a voice in making all laws by which she is to be governed. (Bloomer 59–60)

Bloomer and other temperance women believed firmly in the cause of woman's rights, but they pragmatically recognized that support was easier to garner for the temperance cause. They made the tactical decision to work for both causes simultaneously, discerning their beneficial complementarity.

The use of temperance to call for the reform of laws affecting women is apparent in the attention these women give to the issue of divorce. At mid-century, divorce was a major point of concern for a multitude of people, provoking extensive discussion within the churches and among members of the press. Numerous changes had been made in divorce laws in the 1830s and 1840s. By the early 1850s, state laws were as diverse as those in South Carolina, which prohibited divorce for any reason, to those in Indiana, where lenient divorce laws and liberal residency requirements aroused fear among numerous social and religious leaders. Most states had adopted laws that permitted divorce for reasons of adultery, impotence, or abandonment, when the partner failed to return after a specified number of years. Some states had begun recognizing divorce for cruelty, but cruelty usually "presumed extreme physical abuse" (Halem 22).

Often divorces granted were a *mensa et thoro*, or partial divorces that permitted couples to live separately but refused rights to remarriage, rather than a *vincula*, or final divorces. Such divorces could be especially problematic for women with children, as they were thus prohibited the traditional means of support they might enlist in remarriage. As demands for more permissive divorce laws increased, and western states liberalized divorce laws and residency requirements, a growing fear that collapsing family units would endanger fundamental societal values, leading to the breakdown of the social order, spurred active debate regarding the proper direction for legal reform pertaining to divorce.

For example, Horace Greeley, temperance advocate and editor of the *New York Tribune*, published lengthy tirades against divorce on any grounds with the exception of adultery. Greeley's highly visible attacks were accompanied by those of other high-profile public and religious leaders, such as Yale president Timothy Dwight.[6] Thus, the topical nature of divorce afforded a popular issue for temperance women. Because few states permitted divorce for reasons of habitual drunkenness, temperance women could readily address this issue, calling for legal reform more favorable to women's needs by highlighting incidents specific to intemperance and evoking the image of suffering women and children. Both women who remained associated with temperance organizations and those, such as Stanton and Anthony, who departed, invoked portraits of women married to intemperate men in order to insist upon legal reform pertaining to divorce.

Even so, temperance women usually exhibited a greater consideration for audience than did women who chose to concentrate solely on the woman's rights issue. The content of Stanton's temperance speeches, for example, varies little from that of other temperance speakers, but her manner of presentation differs greatly. A look at Stanton's and Bloomer's arguments in favor of divorce for women married to drunkards illustrates the two women's disparate approaches. Stanton's appeal would have seemed harsh and unnecessarily accusatory to many listeners, with its third person imperatives and its ad hominem attacks on alcoholic men:

> Let no woman remain in the relation of wife with the confirmed drunkard. Let no drunkard be the father of her children. Let no woman form an alliance with any man who has been suspected even of the vice of intemperance; for the taste once acquired can never, never be eradicated. Be not misled by any pledges, resolves, promises, prayers, or tears. You can not rely on the word of a man who is, or has been, the victim of such an overpowering appetite. (Stanton, Anthony, and Gage 482)

Many temperance women, including Nichols, Gage, and Bloomer, spoke in favor of divorce and separation when women were married to alcoholics. Bloomer spoke in support of the divorce resolution at the first New York meeting in April, a speech more radical in some ways than Stanton's, especially since Bloomer insisted that women who refused to leave alcoholic husbands be forced to do so:

> We believe the teachings which have been given to the drunkard's wife, inculcating duty—the commendable examples of angelic wives which she has been exhorted to follow—have done much to continue and aggravate the vices and crimes of society growing out of intemperance. Drunkenness is ground for divorce, and every woman who is tied to a confirmed drunkard should sunder the ties: and if she do it not otherwise, the law should compel it, especially if she have children.

But, whereas Bloomer made a call similar to that of Stanton, she skillfully acknowledged the demand's radical connotations while incorporating rhetoric that would both encourage her listener to reconsider initial scorn for the proposal and diminish the shock of her suggestion:

> We are told that such sentiments are exceptional, abhorrent, that the moral sense of society is shocked and outraged by their promulgation. Can it be possible that the moral sense of a people is more shocked at the idea of a pure-minded, gentle woman sundering the tie which binds her to a loathsome mass of corruption, than it is to see her dragging out her days in misery tied to his besotted and filthy carcass? Are the morals of society less endangered by the drunkard's wife continuing to live in companionship with him, giving birth to a large family of children who inherit nothing but poverty and disgrace, and who will grow up criminal and vicious, filling our prisons and penitentiaries and corrupting and endangering the purity and peace of the community, than they would be should she separate from him and strive to win for herself and her children comfort and respectability? The statistics of our prisons, poorhouses, and lunatic asylums teach us a fearful lesson on this subject of morals!

Thus Bloomer capitalized on nineteenth-century images of pure, refined women by juxtaposing them with equally vivid portraits of degenerate drunkards. She also exploited her society's concern about the burgeoning class of destitute and dissolute people, especially children. She finished by again evoking the contrast between angelic women and drunken men, showing that hers was a common-sensical suggestion reinforced by traditional authority, noting that state lawmakers were considering such legislation seriously and would finally adopt it.

The idea of living with a drunkard is so abhorrent, so revolting to all the finer feelings of our nature, that a woman must fall very low before she can endure such companionship. Every pure-minded person must look with loathing and disgust upon such a union of virtue and vice; and he who would compel her to it, or dissuade the drunkard's wife from separating herself from such wretchedness and degradation, is doing much to perpetuate drunkenness and crime and is wanting in the noblest feelings of human nature. (Bloomer 87–89)

Bloomer was not the only skilled rhetorician among temperance women. Mary C. Vaughan, who, along with Susan B. Anthony, organized a separate meeting for women not permitted to speak at the Sons of Temperance meeting, and Lydia Folger Fowler addressed that secessionist group. In her speech, Vaughan said, "We have met to consider what we, as women, can do and may do, to forward the temperance reform. . . . [W]e are learning that our part in the drama of life is something beside inactive suffering and passive endurance" (Stanton, Anthony, and Gage 476). Unlike Stanton, who issued commands for women, Vaughan offered an invitation to women who might work toward reform, suggesting a community of women seeking a common goal. She placed herself as a learner among her listeners. She, like Bloomer, acknowledged that many would perceive their actions as radical, but she skillfully cast their opponents as intolerant: "We are aware that this proceeding of ours, this calling together of a body of women to deliberate publicly upon plans to carry out a specified reform, will rub rather harshly upon the mould of prejudice, which has gathered thick upon the common mind" (476).

Outlining women's grievances against liquor, she justified their involvement as "duty" and, in a lengthy, poignant appeal, effectively incorporated vivid adjectives and physical details to create concrete images for her audience. She concluded the list with the impassioned plea for helpless women and children that temperance women found so effective:

[She] has felt in her own person all the misery, degradation, and woe of the drunkard's wife; has shrunk from revilings and cowered beneath blows; has labored and toiled to have her poor earnings transferred to the rumseller's ill-gotten hoard; while her children, ragged, fireless, poor, starving, gathered shivering about her, and with hollow eyes, from which all smiles had fled, begged vainly for the bread she had not to bestow. Oh! the misery, the utter, hopeless misery of the drunkard's wife! (477)

Vaughan listed the characteristics of what she called "the masculine idea of womanhood," including one who is "gentle, mild, submissive" and "must necessarily enjoy and suffer in the extreme." But she refused to accept such a patriarchal notion, envisioning her own "true woman," one constructed by women themselves to take the place of "this false image of woman" (478). Vaughan did not call for divorce for wives of inebriates, but her speech and her position as president mark her as a strong advocate for women's release from suffering caused by alcoholic husbands.

Lydia F. Fowler also spoke at that meeting. Fowler was a practicing physician in New York City at the time—the second woman in the United States to attain a medical degree. In her address, she noted the sinister effect of intemperance on families and furnished anecdotal instances of the evils visited upon family members of the drunkard (Stanton, Anthony, and Gage 478). Her conversational narratives afforded a comfortable style for women more accustomed to parlor discussions; at the same time they provided tangible images and facts to support her call for change.

Numerous women were speaking publicly about temperance in the 1850s. Unfortunately, many newspaper accounts merely summarize or comment upon speeches. For example, the *New York Tribune*, in reporting on the April 20, 1852, New York Woman's Temperance Convention in Rochester at which Stanton was elected president, lists officers and simply mentions that Stanton, "upon taking the chair, read an address." The report then lists those from whom letters were read and explains that "Many speeches were made both by ladies and gentlemen—prominent among them which was an able address read by Mrs. Amelia Bloomer" ("Women's Temperance Convention" 5). Almost every early account of these addresses mentions their being "read," this apparently being the primary means of delivery for women. Women may have read their addresses because such mode of delivery was deemed more appropriate than looking at and speaking directly to an audience, and many temperance women carefully avoided offending listeners. Since these women modeled behavior for other women, however, and since such speakers as Stanton concerned themselves less with audience, a more likely interpretation seems to be that these women were simply inexperienced at public speaking and felt more comfortable reading addresses; none of them had access to the rhetorical training provided to men. The *Tribune* also reported that on the second day of the convention, "Mrs. Stanton and a lady from Genessee County, read long and interesting addresses," and explained that discussion of one resolution "called out Mrs. Bloomer in a long and eloquent address" ("Woman's Temperance Convention" 4).

In September of 1853, New York hosted the World's Temperance Convention; but since women had been excluded as full members from earlier meetings, including the May 12, 1853, Brick Church meeting that was held to plan the convention, many temperance women and men held a separate, simultaneous meeting that they called the "Whole World's Temperance Convention," labeling the men's convention as the "Half World's Convention" or the "Pseudo World's Temperance Convention." Women's addresses contained several standard characteristics, including an appeal for the sufferers of alcohol, a justification for women's public participation in the cause, and an insistence on the need for greater equality for women—clearly intended to appeal to women of diverse backgrounds.

A representative report comes from *The Pennsylvania Freeman*. As the newspaper suggests, it "condensed from the New York dailies and our own notes" the "report of its proceedings" ("Whole World's" 142); its record of speeches seems a fair account, comprehensive, but consistent with other newspaper descriptions. The *Freeman* printed parts of speeches by Antoinette L. Brown, Lucy Stone, and Clarina Howard Nichols.

According to the *Freeman*

> Rev. Miss Antoinette L. Brown [delivered] a clear and forcible speech.
>
> She said: The Whole World's Temperance Convention— room on its broad platform for everybody . . . —every man may come here and speak in his own tongue wherein he was born, about one of the most needed reforms ever launched on the ocean of events. Here is Woman invited to speak into the great ear-trumpet of the world, that all may hear. (142)

After establishing the equality in treatment at the Whole World's Temperance Convention, an obvious reproach to the men's convention without directly alluding to it, Brown evoked Pentecostal language to affirm the importance of her cause. Drawing from Acts 2, she suggested that each person could "speak in his own tongue," thereby signifying the beginning of a gospel power endorsed by God. She further drew upon symbolic Christian language regarding the church as the "ship" of Zion, invoking one of the most common symbols from the walls of the catacombs in presenting her suggested reforms as "launched on the ocean." She accordingly employed weighted Christian terms to provide a repertoire of meaning for her listeners and subsequent authority for her position. Having established the ordained righteousness of her cause, Brown brought her audience's attention to the harm alcohol does to the drunkard. But the largest part of her speech was an emotional appeal on behalf of suffering children. Brown, who refused to support Stanton and

Bloomer in their call for divorce, nonetheless did promote legal separation and very effectively presented the atrocities visited on innocent children by the evils of alcohol:

> Look at their degradation, when they are cursed with drunken parents. Look now in this dear little face. It would be fair enough, if there were only a soul life to flash over it. But it is an almost blank vacuity. You read there impressions of a gross nature, notwithstanding all that baby innocence. Yet you see a shadow over the face, reflecting the past and prophetic of the future. Poor child; with that worn little face smothered with dirt and filth. Fit emblem of your life is the little mole that lives under ground. There is sunshine in the sky, but you will never look upward. You may well bow your head, for your one talent is rolled up in the napkin of parental sin. God of justice, must there be every year thousands of such children born in our land? (142)

Brown carefully wove the image of destitution around children of drunkards, constructing the mole metaphor to emphasize their deprived lives, void of sunshine. While she could not support divorce, even under the hideous circumstances she presented, her doubts about bringing children into a world with no hope for a happy and fruitful life not only supported her arguments for legal separation but, intentionally or not, bolstered demands for more flexible divorce laws. She continued to assemble images of profoundly miserable children with dreadful prospects for their future lives:

> Here is another child, with baby smiles and baby tears crossing each other down its face, gushing up from its little heart struggling each for the mastery. If God would only take her to Heaven now, she would become one of the happiest of angel cherubs; but the fevered effect of the wine cup, delirium descends through her face, and the angels will weep over her own tears and will pluck out the smiles, while she is yet told that the wine cup will wipe out those tears better than the shame that caused them. They will lie down in an early grave; the earth will not be moistened by a single tear; no flowers will grow up over it; weeds and thistles will grow there, and the old sexton will throw them down with his spade as he passes on. We should grow weary in reading the destinies of children such as these—types of human depravity and human sin. They are the children of intemperance and so as surely as the cup of temptation is not taken from them, will they thus miserably perish. (142)

Brown's use of the word "cup" invoked Christ's agony at Gethsemane —"let this cup pass from me"—and further highlighted the danger of death, both physical and spiritual, to children born into families of alcoholics. She finished by turning her emotional appeal for children into a condemnation of lawmakers who sponsored and licensed the trade that so endangered children:

> Has the law nothing to answer for in all this? May good men be allowed to sign their names to sanction a traffic which produces results like these? Must they continue to sanctify intemperance and make the world buy their soul destroying drink, and then talk of a good moral character of themselves? Rumsellers good moral characters? The thief, the murderer, the libertine, can lay as good a claim to a good moral character as the patentees and patronizers of alcohol,—that genuine oil of licentiousness! They ought to be weighed in the balance together, to see which will be found wanting.

The *Freeman* report ended with "Miss B. concluded by urging the adoption of the Maine Law, and urging considerations of cheer and encouragement to all friends of the cause" (142). Brown thus juxtaposed suffering, helpless children with powerful and selfish lawmakers. Without explicitly supporting divorce, her analogies and rhetorical questions nonetheless added force to demands for changes in divorce laws. She further associated men with bad laws and the heartless abuse of power, and women and children with the evil consequences of their actions.

At the evening session, Lucy Stone (plate 9) addressed the assembly. Prior to her address, P. T. Barnum, of circus fame, had spoken: "sensible, shrewd, witty, pungent, full of sharp points and amusing illustrations, and though sometimes not peculiarly refined in expression, it kept the audience in excellent humor" (142). The lighthearted break prepared audiences to reconsider the devastating conditions of innocent children, but Stone built further on Brown's presentation by insisting that children not be born into such situations:

> Lucy Stone was then called by the President, to present the tragic side of the picture of intemperance, the comic features of which had been so amusingly given.
>
> Miss Stone was received with enthusiastic applause, and her speech was heard with an almost breathless silence broken only by applause. She presented a touching sketch of the sufferings and wrongs endured by women and children, resulting from intemperance, and the domestic ruin and woe it had caused. She desired that a public sentiment should be created, which would forbid marriage to the drunkard and would

dissolve the relation where either husband or wife was addicted to drunkenness, and defended her position with much
ability. She said:

> Let it constitute a crime on the part of any man or any
> woman, who shall assume the relation of a parent, who, by
> his or her habits of intemperance, would be likely to entail
> upon posterity this curse of domestic life. If it cannot be con-
> stituted by law, then let public opinion do that which law will
> not. Every child has a right to a healthful organization—has a
> right to come into the world with a fair heritage, that it may
> go back to its God without blemish, as pure as it was born.
> The husband and wife have or should have a right to a di-
> vorce from a drunken partner. (142)

Stone demanded rights for helpless children and for both men and
women victims of drunkards who might produce children subject to such
harsh conditions. She carefully placed her demand for rights within the
context of care and concern for the helpless, and, aware of the power of
custom, appealed for a change in attitudes. She anticipated criticism and
defended her position, insisting that her authority came from God.

> I know that texts and statutes will be quoted against us, and
> that usage too will be brought to bear against it, but truth is
> stronger than either of them. . . . If my position is true, I do
> not care who is against it or who is for it; for God's own life
> is in it—that life which never sleeps, but will one day come
> like leaven in the lump, will come without parchment, and
> will not come in characters that can be blotted out. (Loud
> applause.) I appeal to you, fathers and mothers; if you do not
> wish your sons and your daughters, when they go from your
> household, themselves and their daughters may be guarded
> against the miseries of intemperance. (142)

Stone's call for divorce was disconcerting for some members of the convention; Horace Greeley responded by dissenting from Stone's position
on divorce for drunkenness.

Stone again spoke the following evening, apparently under pressure
from members: "Lucy Stone being loudly called, came forward and spoke
for fifteen minutes in one of her happiest and most impressive efforts"
(142). In spite of the respected Greeley's demurring from Stone's position on divorce, she remained one of the most popular speakers at the
convention.

Clarina Howard Nichols, another favored speaker, also received special treatment at this meeting. According to the *Freeman*, "Mrs. N. was
received with applause, and spoke at length (the ten minutes rule being

suspended in her behalf) of the sufferings of woman by intemperance, and her duties, and of the responsibility of the church for the evil" ("Whole World's" 142). Nichols, in order to mollify those who might have contempt for women who spoke in public, justified her role by pointing out that women were the primary sufferers from alcohol; she painted men as the drinkers, women as the victims, a charge temperance women repeatedly invoked to deflect criticism. Nichols connected women's temperance activity with duty, and like other temperance women, she also assured audiences that she joined the temperance crusade only because men had failed to protect women.

> I cannot *present* to you woman's claim to the Maine Law more forcibly than by showing how it will restore the sweet harmonies of domestic life; it is because I believe this I take this position. And if I needed to make any apology for so doing, it is that woman is the greatest sufferer from intemperance. Woman, who is herself not addicted to this vice, suffers more than man; and it is to this point that I wish to direct your special attention. (142)

Having established woman as the victim, Nichols skillfully indicted the legal system, the presumed protector of the innocent and helpless, for its failure to protect women and children. She enumerated incidents, including but not limited to intemperance, whereby the law allowed the good of women and children to be sacrificed, very effectively establishing both the need for a change in the legal system and the necessity for women to take public action.

> The laws of this country have bound her hand and foot, and given her up to the protection of her husband. They have committed her soul and body to the protection of the husband, and when he fails from imbecility, misjudgment, misfortune, or intemperance, she suffers. The mother cannot hold in her own hand the bread she earns to feed her babes and children; even the clothes she wears can be taken by her husband to satisfy his inordinate appetites. If intemperance did not invade our homes and tear them from over our heads; if it did not take from us our clothing, our bread, the means for our own self development, and for the training of our children in respectability and usefulness; if it did not take our babes from our bosoms, I would not stand here. (Loud Applause) (142)

Thus, Nichols effectively incorporated graphic images of clothing and food, even children, being torn from the bosom of women made helpless to provide for their suffering children by the law of the land. She also used repetition—"if it did not"—to drive home the impression that she reticently took the public stage out of necessity. But she also justified divorce for women more broadly than for reasons of intemperance to include imbecility, misfortune, and misjudgment. Having brought her audience to the point of accepting her demands, Nichols chose to complete her address with a statement of understanding and an offer of assistance, ending with an anecdote she knew her mostly female audience would enjoy:

> It seems to me that the great cause of humanity is very much in the position of a little child that a friend of mine lately met. She was traveling in a stage coach, when she saw a man with an infant a few months old in his arms; my friend was exceedingly interested in the babe, and wondered that the father should be carrying an infant so long a journey. She naturally fancied that the child's mother was dead, and her big heart yearned toward the little desolate one. She asked the man where the babe's mother was? He replied that she "would not come along with it, and when husband and wife disagree they must separate." "What," she eagerly inquired, "and *you* take the little babe?" To which he answered that he did, for he had "both the right and the power." "But," my friend inquired, "when the little one is hungry, can you feed it?" "Oh! yes," he replied, "I can feed it, I have a pocket full of cakes." (Laughter and cheers.) And so man has gone through the world in every department of life; in the legislative, and in all the out-of-door avocations, and he has thus carried with him a "pocket full of cakes" until humanity has become dyspeptic. (Loud applause.) And what we now ask is that it may be restored to the mother of humanity, to drink the milk of human kindness which God has stored so bountifully in the breast of women. (142)

As was often typical with women's temperance speeches, Nichols began her speech with an appeal for relieving the suffering of women and children victims, and she concluded with a call to "Christians of every name to engage in this work." Thus, her accusations and claims regarding the injustices toward women were sandwiched between and connected with the cause of temperance. And like many speakers, she narrated humorous but touching anecdotes that further highlighted women's strengths and supported her demand for equality. Women speakers thus subverted the ridicule and humor that was often addressed toward them by redirecting the joke.

So many women wished to lecture that speakers strictly adhered to an allotted amount of time; such cooperation and sharing underscored a theme of unity and sisterhood typical of women's temperance organizations throughout the nineteenth century. But, although a large number of women spoke, newspapers reported in detail only the addresses of the best-known women, simply summarizing or mentioning speeches of others. For example, the *Freeman* noted that

> Mrs. Vaughan, the President of the Women's New York City Temperance Society, spoke of the operations and success of that organization, concluding with an appeal for the Maine Law, urging women until they are permitted to vote to *electioneer* for it. (142)

The newspaper account put the attendance for the first evening session at 2,500 to 4,000 persons and for the second evening at over 3,000. Although the newspapers did not print all the women's speeches in full, they actually gave more space to women's addresses than to men's presentations at similar conventions. Very popular male speakers, such as Horace Mann or Gerrit Smith, might find welcome print for their entire addresses, but generally men's speeches were summarized, if the content was given at all. Because of the novelty and controversy surrounding their public roles, women aroused more interest in their activities; women's addresses, therefore, received greater coverage.

Women reformers differed, understandably, on some of the finer points of women's advancement, yet their appeals for women were remarkably similar. Some could not accept the notion of divorce, for example, but felt comfortable promoting legal separation. Others were uncomfortable even with the notion of marital separation. Women reformers' beliefs about how best to further women's cause—through a direct and assertive approach or by means of an indirect, non-threatening one—was more likely to determine the paths they chose, although such decisions sometimes reflected the circumstances of their own lived experiences. Some, fearful of fathers or husbands, undoubtedly were forced to refrain from overt participation. For instance, Eliza Daniel Stewart, in her report of the Ohio Woman's Crusade, noted that a Crusade woman "turned to a miserable inebriate" during one of their marches saying, "'Your wife ought to be with us.' A fierce light came into his eyes as he answered, '*I'd kill her if she was!*'" As Stewart noted, the woman "could not, dared not, lend a helping hand, for fear of that imbruted husband" (172). Such was surely true for many women, but such incidents offered ready material for leaders who encouraged other women to come to the aid of those unable to speak for themselves.

Others, fearful of injuring loved ones, chose modified courses. For example, Antoinette Brown requested that Caroline M. Severance accompany her as a delegate to the World's Temperance Convention to test the convention's sincerity in promising to include women. Severance, a prominent speaker for both temperance and woman's rights in her own state of Ohio, nonetheless demurred at taking a highly visible or controversial role in New York. Severance agreed to accompany Brown, but asked that she be allowed to "go in quietly" because "I have in this city venerated grandparents, whose feelings I greatly regard, and would not willingly or unnecessarily wound"; Severance felt that she should "take no active part in what will seem to them an antagonistic position for woman, and uncalled for on my part" (Stanton, Anthony, and Gage 153).

Paulina Wright Davis reported similar complications among a committee of seven organized to plan a national woman's rights convention: "[T]he work soon devolved upon one person [Davis]. Illness hindered one, duty to a brother another, duty to the slave a third, professional engagements a fourth, the fear of bringing the gray hairs of a father to the grave prevented another from serving" (Stanton, Anthony, and Gage 216).

Stanton also finally gave up the "Bloomer" costume because of the wishes of her brothers and father. According to Ida Harper, the women who wore Bloomers were constantly harassed, "Their husbands and children refused to be seen with them in public, and they were wholly ostracized by other women" (114). Harper says, "Mrs. Bloomer wore the costume eight years, but very few held out one-fourth of that time" (114). "Mrs. Stanton was the first to capitulate" (115). Stanton apparently discontinued wearing the Bloomer after "two or three years," because "the pressure brought to bear upon her by her father and other friends was so great, that she finally yielded to their wishes and returned to long skirts" (Bloomer 70).

Because of such pressures, women temperance speakers secured audiences for their addresses and recruited women for their cause by avoiding agonistic presentations. They effectively presented their case for greater rights for women—for changes in the law of coverture giving women legal rights to their personal and real property, to their own income and wages, and to their children. They also convincingly argued the need for more flexible divorce laws. By emphasizing such needs in relation to intemperance, and insisting upon women's duties toward and concern for those in need, women forcefully and permissibly encouraged and participated in public debate over issues of great concern to them.

The complex rhetoric of temperance women can help us to understand more fully the complicated choices women made. Only superficial examinations allow for the dismissal of women's temperance rhetoric as conservative and unimportant. The women who worked so arduously for temperance reform at mid-nineteenth century made complicated and sophisticated rhetorical decisions that represent a complex weaving of women's philosophies and historical circumstances. The product was often a beautiful, varied, and sophisticated rhetoric.

2

Patriotic Reformers: "Called by the Spirit of the Lord to Lead the Women of the World"

We are here to-day as the representatives of a great and growing society—a society so large and so far reaching in its influence that its name is a household word wherever the English language is spoken.

—Annie Wittenmyer, 1878 Presidential Address to WCTU

BY THE FINAL quarter of the nineteenth century, women had firmly established temperance as a woman's issue. Beginning in the 1820s, women had comprised a substantial portion of membership in temperance organizations,[1] and since at least the 1830s, they had published fiction presenting temperance as an overwhelming concern for women. From the 1840s, women had organized in independent, exclusively female organizations to fight for temperance, publishing their proceedings and resolutions in state and local newspapers. By the early 1850s, numerous women had begun to speak publicly in support of temperance, some confronting retail dealers and occasionally destroying their wares.

Often men's fiction and speeches helped to solidify this perception of women as the principal movers and beneficiaries of the temperance movement, and laws passed in some states furthered the notion that women were the primary sufferers of intemperance. For example, in 1870, Ohio passed the Adair Law, which permitted wives and children of alcoholic men to bring suit against saloon keepers to recover damages.

By the time women established the Woman's Christian Temperance Union (WCTU) in 1874, they felt little further need to defend their participation in the temperance cause. In earlier years, they had most often portrayed women as victims in an effort to justify their public action on behalf of themselves and their sisters. However, late in the century their rhetoric rarely pointed to female vulnerability, emphasizing instead women's courage, intelligence, accomplishments, and their capacity as role models and heroines. Addresses were often part of formal occasions—the annual meetings of the national or state Woman's Christian Temperance Union—or other stately gatherings, such as the meetings of the National and International Councils of Women or holiday celebrations, such as the Fourth of July. Such speeches, then, tended to be ceremonial in nature. Occasions demanded dignity, and proceedings were decorous and often ritualistic, incorporating devotional exercises, familiar hymns, and prescribed tributes. Speeches were typically formal, inspirational, eulogistic, and celebratory in nature; however, members of the WCTU made the occasion and rhetoric their own. Instead of eulogizing traditional male heroes and leaders, they made use of such occasions to craft their own history and heroines—a history of women's accomplishments with heroes and role models who were female.

While rhetoric on these occasions celebrated women, WCTU women also deftly made use of women's prescribed role both to establish their authority and to challenge traditional limits for women, thereby refashioning an image of women that better satisfied their own needs and wishes. Their motto, "For God, and Home, and Native Land," demonstrates representative ways in which they employed established cultural expectations to serve their own purposes. Simply juxtaposing native land (defining women as patriotic warriors and suggesting their rights as citizens) with God and home (customary areas of influence for women) broadened traditional notions of woman's place. The motto also provided multipurpose themes, and while the traditional resonance of the motto's segments alleviated fears and reassured the skeptical, the same theses paradoxically permitted women the authority to remake their image and to demand greater equality.

The WCTU was itself a celebration of women, dedicated to improving the image of and conditions for women. Only women could be voting members. The union built, or tried to build, monuments to women. The Woman's Temple (plate 10), intended to house the national WCTU, was also expected to provide revenue for the organization and to produce income for investors; but only women were allowed to invest. The Woman's Temperance Publication House, in which only women could own stock, employed women exclusively. Women served as business managers, editors, and publishers; even the typesetters were women. All such employments by women were atypical in the nineteenth century, and the union celebrated its position as the vanguard for women's new roles. The union's newspaper, The *Union Signal*, was likewise edited by and produced by women. The organization even founded a National Temperance Hospital, whose board of managers was made up of women, and the WCTU was instrumental in founding and funding such aids to women as child care centers and homes for "fallen women."

This celebration of women marked the rhetoric at WCTU meetings as well. Ceremonial speeches traditionally venerated outstanding figures or heroes, but customarily women had been absent from speeches that commemorated bravery and exalted accomplishments. Members of the WCTU generated their own tradition of exemplary women, taking every opportunity to establish contemporary women's common heritage with historic heroes. They confirmed women's virtue and worthiness by defining an admirable legacy, by situating noble actions, and by offering testimonial evidence.

Sometimes temperance women drew from the Bible, from history, and from mythology to chronicle women's fame and strength. In her 1883 president's address, for example, Frances Willard eulogized such paragons from all three sources: "Let not the lessons of history be disregarded. Of old the world had its Semiramis and Dido, its Zenobia and Boadicca, nay, better still, its Miriam and Deborah. Later on Russia had her Catharine, and England her Elizabeth" (*Minutes of National Tenth* 53).[2] When using historical models, Willard thus chose to present women famed for their ability as rulers, some also as noted warriors; they were hardly reticent women confined to the home. In addition to citing admirable historic and mythological women, Willard praised well-known contemporary women. Speaking before educational groups, she commended popular writers, such as Elizabeth Barrett Browning, Julia Ward Howe, Harriet Beecher Stowe, Dinah Mulock ("Woman's Work" 162). Before the National Council of Women, she extolled women who excelled in academic and professional pursuits—women who had scored highest of all entrants on exams at Harvard, at the Paris law school, and in Latin and English at Calcutta University ("Women and Organization" 32–33). But preeminent among heroines selected to form a history of noble women were women chosen from their own ranks; speakers drew analogies between powerful and admirable women of history and members of the union: "But in my thoughts I always liken the Woman's Christian Temperance Union to Joan of Arc, whom God raised up from France, and who in spite of their muscle and their military prowess beat the English and crowned her King!" (Willard, "Woman's Work" 162).

Leaders of the Woman's Crusade provided especially worthy heroic examples. While almost forgotten now, the Woman's Crusade became the label for the numerous active protests by temperance women between December 1873 and November 1874. These protests represent the largest public demonstration by women in the nineteenth century; a minimum of 57,000 to 143,000 women participated in at least 911 Crusades throughout the United States.[3] Crusaders' participation differed according to location, but most often women protested the sale of liquor by marching and praying, inside or in front of saloons.

Such public participation required great courage. Women were ridiculed, both in the streets and in the press, and they often braved physical harm as well.[4] In her history of the Crusades, Eliza Stewart (plate 11) attests to the physical exhaustion women experienced (365), to their being jostled and spit upon (379), to their being doused with dirty water and beer in the cold of winter (150), and even to how one woman, a seventy-year-old president of the Temperance League of Bucyrus, Ohio, was dragged through the streets, her arm lacerated to the bone (351). Jack Blocker documents newspaper reports of further violence toward women: some were drenched with paint; accosted with water from force pumps and hoses; pelted with rotten eggs, stones, old boots, and even bricks; threatened by mobs so large and violent that police protection was inadequate; and forced by husbands to leave the streets. One spouse even publicly horsewhipped his wife for her participation ("*Give*" 76–77). Press backlash against temperance women's public activity was extensive, but women united to fight intemperance publicly; they learned that their activity could draw considerable attention to their complaints. At every national meeting of the WCTU, speakers capitalized on these crusaders' courage and strength to build a canon of valiant heroines.

In creating a history in which courageous women played the major roles, Crusade leaders often related their stories to union members, offering testimonial support to the lore of the Crusade. Members ritualized homage to their brave Crusade pioneers. They honored the special capacity and power of their leaders with the title "mother," e.g., Mother Stewart (Eliza Daniel Stewart) and Mother Thompson (Eliza J. Thompson), to signify their importance as founders of the Crusade, cleverly associating "the most glorified role of the nineteenth-century woman" (Ryan 162) with the typically heroic term of founder. In this way, they served as counterparts to the founding "fathers" of patriarchal history, and members provided these special leaders with distinctive seating and extraordinary recognition.[5]

The Crusade leaders themselves contributed to the historic mosaic, not just by relating their own stories and those of other brave women, but also by publicly and graciously acknowledging and extolling other leaders. After being recognized and offered a seat of honor at a national meeting, Eliza Thompson

> expressed a wish that Mrs. George Carpenter, of Washington Court House, join them; saying, that while she was the first lady who prayed in a saloon, she thought the ladies of Washington Court House, who were led by Mrs. Carpenter, were

entitled to the first honors of this Convention, as the saloons were first closed at that place, as the result of the effort of Christian women. (*Minutes of National Sixth* 19)

From their first meeting, women had honored Crusade leaders. Annie Wittenmyer (plate 12), who was to become the WCTU's first president, evoked the memory of the Crusade to establish the courage of temperance women: "The Crusade has shown that the women . . . can face the cannon and the mob" (17). In praising Crusade women, Wittenmyer and other leaders often drew upon women's knowledge of and comfort with biblical texts for traditional battleground language of bravery. Members regularly used such militant rhetoric, identifying women as warriors, their cause as a war, and their arena as a battleground.[6]

Brave leaders who had led the Crusade were singled out and honored at the conventions, often with gifts of the women's own work and with glowing tributes to their courage. At the 1878 convention in Baltimore, Frances Willard presented a quilt made by temperance women to Eliza Thompson and delivered a lengthy tribute to her, drawing upon women's traditional arts to weave a new image. In her accolade, Willard dismissed traditional, patriarchal annals and referred explicitly to temperance women's valuable new chronicle: "History! What attraction has its ancient record for you who are steadily making America a history more inspiring than any that her archives have yet furnished" (*Minutes of WCTU Annual* 49). WCTU leaders were creating and extolling their own history, a history of courageous and admirable women.

Willard ensconced Crusade leaders as veritable heroines: "Pioneers in this great reform . . . we point you to the veteran's post, the post of honor" (50). Later, lest any doubt the importance of that post of honor for Thompson, or for her followers, Willard placed them in company with traditional national heroes: "[Y]our Crusade quilt shall take rank with the Declaration of Independence, and the names of John Hancock and the immortal fifty-six who signed below him, shall not be more fragrant in the memory of grateful hearts than those of yourself and your associates" (51–52). Members told and retold the early stories of the Crusade. Narratives about Crusade heroines became a typical part of annual addresses, both state and national, with numerous references to the "heroic" Crusade or the "heroic day of womanhood" (Lathrap, *Poems* 286).

Leaders often extended the praise universally to WCTU members. Wittenmyer, justifiably proud of having helped to create this historic organization, liked to remind union members of their singular, historical importance as "representatives of the largest and most influential society of women that has ever been organized in the history of the world" (*Minutes of National Sixth* 7).

Individual members received such recognition as well, as speakers repeatedly recognized women worthy of praise and admiration. In her address of welcome at the fourth annual meeting in Indianapolis, for example, Sarah P. Morrison helped to establish a "roll of honor" for women by hailing individual leaders:

> From the Excelling City, and a faithful watcher for the Temperance cause in all states, we greet the honored President of the Union [Wittenmyer]. From wherever they work, and for whatever is still left undone, irresistible Mrs. Livermore and invincible Miss Willard. From crusade-conquered Brooklyn, Mary C. Johnson, charmer of hearts in the Old World and New. And, successful from travels abroad, and for labors at home, our dear heart, Mrs. Malloy. Greetings to Foster and Foster, though lawyers, at peace with themselves and the world, and to that firm of Robinson & Co., where a mighty spirit animates a little woman-preacher and bread-winner. Greetings to Jehovah-trusting Mother Stewart, and to one who has proved a mother to a nation, our lady at Washington. But who can mention all the favored names of this fast-increasing and living Roll of Honor? Are they not all written in the Lamb's Book of Life? "Inasmuch as ye have done it unto one of these, my brethren, ye have done it unto me." (8)

Here Morrison deftly identified and praised worthy leaders, situating them as worthy disciples recognized by Christ; she paralleled members on the WCTU's "Roll of Honor" with those given eternal salvation—those written in the Lamb's Book of Life (Phil. 4.3). She also, significantly, acknowledged these women's nontraditional roles as lawyers, preachers, and bread-winners.

At the national meetings, members publicly and formally recognized one another as often as possible. They often voted special thanks to individual members, applauding and consecrating their special and valuable contributions: "That this Convention hereby expresses its hearty thanks to Mrs. Mary T. Burt for the remarkably efficient and faithful services as publisher during the last year, and its earnest hopes that she may be abundantly prospered in her future work for the cause she has so ably served" (*Minutes of Fourth* 177).

They recognized women by calling role for vice-presidents (there was one from each state), for committees, and by reporting, in detail, activity of members from each state for the various departments. They even formally recognized young women pages, careful to honor women of all ages.[7]

In keeping with the ceremonial nature of national meetings, members emphasized unity as a primary theme, and the limited role permitted nineteenth-century women facilitated rhetorical stress on solidarity. Traditionally, women had been identified in relation to others in their lives, and nearly all early addresses began, "Women, Sisters, Mothers," most women in attendance fitting comfortably under all three titles. Thus, these women once again made positive use of cultural restrictions to create a sense of community, repeatedly using terms applicable only to women and inclusive of all women. From its inception, the WCTU defined itself as "exclusively a convention of ladies, and that no man be admitted as delegate under any pretext whatever" (*Minutes of First* 15) and resolved that "all good temperance women without regard to sect or nationality are cordially invited to unite with us in our great battle against the wrong and for the right" (29). While insisting on their privilege of excluding men, their use of the term "ladies" dispelled fears of "strong-minded" and "unsexed" women, thus disarming opponents.

The presidents were especially concerned to bring women together. In address after address, they emphasized "comradeship among women" and evoked biblical commands for unity, often opening their presentations with such themes. At her annual address at St. Louis, for example, Willard began,

> [W]e must stand by each other in this struggle. Side by side, shoulder to shoulder, we must move forward, with no break in the ranks, no aspersions, no careless, harsh or cruel judgments, but the tenderest and most persistent endeavor to keep the unity of the spirit, if not of method, and, above all, the bond of peace. Let the criticizing world see plainly that concord has the right of way in the Woman's Christian Temperance Union. (*Minutes of National Eleventh* 405)

Willard's calls for "no break in the ranks," for a "unity of spirit," and for the "bond of peace" drew directly from Paul's statement of unity, providing Christian authority for her appeal.[8] She also diligently avoided exclusive language in an effort to make the WCTU comfortable for all women. "No sectarianism in religion, no sectionalism in politics, no sex in citizenship" became a familiar phrase in almost every presidential address she delivered. She emphasized acceptance and understanding between "North and South, Protestant and Catholic, of white and black, of men and women equally" (*Glimpses* 451).

Others echoed this call to unity. In greeting members, speakers conscientiously employed inclusive terminology. In her 1874 welcoming address, Mrs. Dr. L. D. McCabe of Ohio carefully hailed women of all regions: "Sisters of the Atlantic," "Sisters of the Pacific," of the "South" and so on. She told members, "We rejoice that we are thus united, and for life in this blessed temperance reform" (*Minutes of First* 10). At the 1885 convention, Willard even asked members to take the following pledge: "I promise by God's grace, to say nothing discouraging about the work and nothing disparaging about the workers" (*Minutes of National Twelfth* 91). Willard explained that

> Under this rule we may frankly avow our difference of opinion from other men and women in the great army, but always without questioning *their motives*. Thus only, as I believe, can we "minister grace in them that hear us." Can we not rise to this level of a practical, everyday Christian charity and maintain it throughout the year to come? (*Minutes of National Twelfth* 91)

Temperance women drew upon and modified traditional rhetorical strategies in other ways in order to serve their purposes. They made positive use of cultural restraints both to authorize their public stance and to construct their own image. The use they made of themes in their motto clearly represents such efforts. In the three major theses of the WCTU motto, God, home, and native land, WCTU women invoked the language deemed appropriate for women within their society, but they fashioned that language to the service of their own interests. In evoking the first segment of their motto, "For God," they referred to their special commission from God to provide authority for their undertakings, but they also used that association to establish women's rights and importance. Annie Wittenmyer, the WCTU's first president, described members' importance as absolutely vital to social and moral progress:

> We have been called by the spirit of the Lord to lead the women of the world in a great and difficult reform movement, and thousands in our own and other lands are looking to us with hope and expectation. The drink system is the common enemy of women the world over, and the plans we inaugurate will be eagerly sought after by the women of all civilized nations, and as the success of all moral reforms depends largely upon women, the world will halt, or move in its onward march towards millennial glory, as *we* halt or march. (*Minutes of Fourth* 141)

Wittenmyer likened the temperance reform movement to the Protestant reformation, establishing WCTU members' special charge in its leadership. Taking the Reformation's elimination of authority one step further, members repeatedly confirmed their own unique relationship with God, affirming that they required no male, ministerial intermediaries.[9] Instead, they established their own divine appointment as leaders the world over.

Such references to direct appointment from Christ were numerous.

Mrs. S. D. La Fetra told members, "It was the voice of Christ that called together the white-haired and white-souled women of that first crusade, and it is the *Christ in the Union, the Christ in the temperance,* and the *Christ* in the *woman* that has been, in all this movement, the secret of its success and power" (*Minutes of National Sixth* 13). Others echoed this call, such as Mary T. Burt, "It is Christ and His gospel from which have come our high commission" (139); Sarah P. Morrison, "All called of God in the noble crusade" (7); and Clara L. Roach, "The women of the West, baptized with the Holy Spirit, entered upon this crusade" (19).

The women accordingly relied in part on their special relationship with God to establish authority. In noting women's intense interest in Christianity in the nineteenth century, Ann Douglas has noted the partnership between ministers and women to maintain some semblance of power through religious alliances. But WCTU members exhibited little concern for a partnership with ministers. They recognized the power of established religion, acknowledging and deferring to it when necessary and when it served their purposes. Ministers, for example, had charge of facilities women needed for holding meetings and conventions, and they could influence public opinion. But even seemingly positive comments show thinly veiled disdain for established clergy in most references by WCTU women. For example, in an annual address as President of the Michigan WCTU, Mary Torrans Lathrap (plates 13, 14) told members,

> be sure to seek and hold the most friendly relations with the churches. . . . the hardest thing, sometimes, is to be patient with the poor, belated people, who open sleepy eyes, and utter opinions about the temperance reform, which, like crawfish, back up to us out of the middle ages of darkness. But still be patient. If pastors are not ready with help, remember that brain-work is costly, and they have the care of all the churches. (*Poems* 305)[10]

But these women also sometimes criticized ministers openly and seldom praised them, firmly committing themselves to establishing a Christianity that more closely adhered to their own interpretation—one not of "fashionable church-membership . . . kept like canned fruit, bottled up at a fixed price of pew rental or other contribution," but one based on a Christian way of life. Temperance women were proud that they lectured without fee and that they ministered to all classes: "God be thanked that the womanhood of Christendom begins to go out into the highway and hedge, shaking into the laps of the people the rich, ripe fruit of the gospel tree without money and without price!" (*Minutes of National Sixteenth* 98).

Women capitalized on their confidence and newfound roles to demand equal status and responsibility, especially insisting upon women's right to powerful positions of leadership in religious authority. These women no longer needed approval from men. In fact, they often premised their mandates on the failure of the established church to perform responsibly. For example, Dakota President Mrs. H. M. Barker told her membership, "[W]e are astonished to see a minister or two and a few church members marching in line with the worst elements of every community, and we notice the weapons they use are the same as the brewers and gamblers carry" (Barker 25).

Lathrap, herself an ordained minister, often indicted the clergy of established churches for their inadequacy in meeting Christian expectations as defined by women. She highlighted their failure in many instances to provide church facilities for women's temperance meetings, for refusing to license women to preach, and for supporting for political office men aligned with liquor interests. Lathrap further castigated these "Christian men" for their refusal to work with those most in need. "Has the church . . . become so dainty it can only build tabernacles on the mountain, but refuses to go to those possessed with devils below?" she asked. In thus referring to the transfiguration of Jesus, Lathrap placed herself and other members in the company of Christ, who led his disciples back to the people when they wished to build structures of glory on the mountain. She effectively reversed notions of women and men to show that while women willingly and bravely worked among the downtrodden, "dainty" Christian men avoided or feared such work (*Poems* 355). And she criticized the church explicitly for its treatment of women: "Church and State unite in one thing if in no other; viz., in defining a position for women and so far as possible keeping them in it" (399).

In 1888, Willard even delivered an ultimatum to ministers. Noting, as did many speakers, that women made up the great majority of church membership, Willard addressed the debate between those who would "stay in the church and help reform it" and those who proposed a "Church Union," organized by the WCTU for "those who are unwilling longer to leave inoperative the protests of their souls against a government of the church by its minority." Willard asked members for a four-year reprieve before taking action, as she would "fain give her [the church] a little time in which to deal justly by the great household of her loving, loyal, and devoted daughters" (*Glimpses* 463–65).[11]

But many references suggest that women believed they were already creating their own church. For example, as early as 1874, Mrs. Runyon of Ohio told members, "God seemed by a wondrous touch to lift a nation of noble women up, and tonight they are assembled to gather strength, for the continuance of their work" (*Minutes of First* 16). Runyon confirmed that the union already afforded the necessary ingredients for a church—assembly of the faithful and work in the name of Christ.

Even though not formally departing established religion, WCTU women refused merely to accept an established Christianity; they constructed their own, differentiating explicitly between organized patriarchal religion and a God-centered Christianity. They saw themselves as divine agents. When they drew religious warrants for their work, they most commonly likened women of the WCTU to Christ's apostles and their new commission to a Pentecostal visitation. Matilda Carse told members,

> [W]hen we speak about this Gospel temperance movement of the women—born from the Pentecost of the Crusade— . . . we speak about the germ of a new church in which, as Christ declared, there shall be neither male nor female, and in which the signing of the pledge shall be a prerequisite of membership. (*Minutes of Fourth* 136)

Carse's "new church" would recognize women's equality with men and actively work to abolish the abuses of alcohol. She explicitly defined the *women's* temperance movement as that which was Pentecostal. Like other temperance women, Carse drew upon St. Paul's charge that "There is no longer Jew or Greek, there is no longer slave or free, there is no longer male and female, for all of you are one in Christ Jesus" (Gal. 3.28) to negate ministers' claims that Paul demanded women keep silent in the churches.

Language drawing upon Scriptural references held deep and comforting meaning for nineteenth-century women, who were well-versed in biblical words, delivering a connotation not readily accessible to many twentieth-century readers. For example, Mattie McClellan Brown claimed, "The women of this nation have been set apart as the apostles of the temperance people" (*Minutes of First* 23). When Brown noted that women had been "set apart," her listeners would have instantly recognized her words as acknowledging members' sanctity, understanding that the Greek word for sanctify meant to set apart. And Wittenmyer's reference to the union's beginnings "Coming up out of the crusade with the breath of a Divine inspiration upon it" (*Minutes of National Sixth* 11) would have, likewise, evoked Genesis for members, suggesting that Christ was breathing a "Divine inspiration" into them.

So comfortable were women with such language and meaning that they often sent greetings to one another at their conventions by suggesting a reading from the Bible, realizing that their sisters would understand the message. For example, in 1881, the American Woman's Suffrage Association sent such a telegram to the convening WCTU convention in Washington: "'Greeting.' Read Proverbs 31st, 25th to 31st" (*Minutes of WCTU Eighth* 17). Similarly, on the death of one of their members, participants at the national WCTU convention dispatched the following telegram:

> To the family and friends of Mrs. S.J.C. Downs, Newark, N.J.:
> The National Woman's Christian Temperance Union in Convention assembled expresses its tenderest sympathy in your great loss which we deeply mourn as ours also. Read 2d Timothy, 4th Chapter, 7th and 8th verses. (*Minutes of WCTU Eighteenth* 15)

Since most women were much better versed in Scripture than men, such conversation also gave them a common language with comfortable and familiar interpretations exclusive primarily to women.

Women valued theology and derived much comfort from their religious affiliations; they appreciated the positive role religion had played in their lives and marveled at the power they felt in their new leadership roles. Lathrap acknowledged that "It was here I first learned the art of public speech in the prayer and class meetings of this church" (*Poems* 374), and in her "Report of Lyceum Bureau" at the third annual meeting in Newark, Mrs. S. A. McClees cited the union's evangelical approach as helping women come to voice:

> After two years of prayer and effort in home missionary labors, on behalf of the inebriate classes, the Christian temperance women developed a latent power as speakers, under circumstances and conditions which a few years previous would to themselves have appeared simply appalling, if not absurd. Women who had but lately found no wider sphere than the domestic or social circle for their *special pleadings* in favor of all things good and true . . . suddenly found themselves facing vast audiences, standing in sacred places, altars and pulpits, side by side with fathers and brethren of the ministry, to give the same solemn admonitions to which they had lent reverential ears since childhood days. (*Minutes of Third* 107)

McClees thus highlighted a previously unthinkable reversal, the transition from women as silent listeners to women as voiced participants and leaders before large numbers of people. She credited women's tradition in and comfort with missionary training for their rapid progress.

Mary Rider Haslup, president of Maryland WCTU, expressed a similar belief: "Many of us remember how God's Holy Spirit came upon the women of the Crusade, and weak, timid ones suddenly found themselves preaching and teaching Temperance and righteousness" (17). In noting that women became filled with the voice of the Holy Spirit, Haslup evoked the Pentecostal experience of Acts 2, suggesting that although listeners might think them curious, even inappropriate, temperance women could be secure in the knowledge that they were speaking from the strength of the Holy Spirit.

Women leaders sometimes used their special relationship with God to establish authority with other union members. When some members expressed concern for the WCTU's official call for the ballot, evangelist Hannah Whitall Smith, evoking Ephesians and employing traditional military rhetoric, cited God's special calling to establish influence for that position:

> Dear friends, the commission has come to some of us in a heavenly vision, that God is calling and preparing the Christian women of this country to wield a weapon in our warfare against the liquor traffic, which will be as regards all human instrumentalities by far the most effective weapon God has yet given us, and we dare not be disobedient to this vision. . . . Let me beg you, my dear sisters, not to turn away from the revelation. Do not let any prejudice hinder you. . . . when the vision comes, be obedient to it.

Smith further criticized the established male clergy and implied that women would be more Christian in their leadership than the present ministry: "Heretogore [sic], I grieve to say, the church has been last of all in reforms. I long to see Christians prepared to take the front ranks in this reform which is surely coming" (*Minutes of WCTU Annual* 32).

The second part of the WCTU's motto evinced woman's place in the home, but also provided authority for these women. As accepted guardians of the home, they easily invoked their special right to leave the home in order to defend it and their loved ones. The Illinois WCTU, for example, had passed a resolution in 1875 declaring that "since woman is the greatest sufferer from the rum curse, she ought to have power to close the dram-shop door over against her home" (*Glimpses* 446). Such claims were not new. In fact, women's right to active public roles at mid-century had been based largely on such warrants. But WCTU women not only justified their public roles by references to their homely duties, they also reshaped the image of the woman, often as one whose household duties were complemented by an equal responsibility to public employment and service.

For example, in 1884, Willard celebrated women's role in education by noting that "two-thirds of all our teachers are women to-day" ("Woman's Work" 162); she further explained that the change in women's home life had permitted rising numbers of women to seek employment. Placing responsibility for the change on men, Willard told the National Educational Association, "[Y]ou, our brothers, invaded our realm" (162). She noted the many glorious changes that men had wrought, such as building railroads, and then explained the "wonderful havoc" men had created in the home:

> [T]hey took the wash-tub and carried that out of the house and built great laundries, and they set little nibbling fingers at work on the weaving and spinning, and did it by steel fingers, and it did not tire the women's fingers any more, and they are going at such a rate that I predict that they will soon have the cook-stove out of the house. (163)

Willard credited men's ingenuity with women's having time to participate in public activities: "[B]ecause you have accomplished so much already is the reason that women's hands are free to take up this splendid work of teaching, and these grand endeavors of philanthropy" (163).

Lathrap also enumerated major changes in the last half of the century that had changed conditions for both women and men. Labor-saving machinery, she explained, had emancipated women as well as men, providing them with more time. Educational opportunities, and subsequent financial independence, had empowered women. These components, "time and a trained brain" and the "hundreds of avenues now open" offered a situation in which "the woman of to-day, without depending on husband, or brother, or son, has more money than the woman of days gone by" ("President's" 30), thus providing women with more numerous options.

Women temperance speakers repeatedly referred to the "new woman" they believed they were helping to construct. While the "new woman" outlined by temperance women is far less radical than the one most often recognized at the end of the nineteenth and beginning of the twentieth century, she might certainly be seen as a precursor of the later formulation. Unlike later New Women, temperance women venerated women's connection with motherhood and the home, and they cherished their religious associations; at the same time, they argued for dress reform, for women's right to earn their own living and to be independent of men, and to women's right to equality generally. As Carroll Smith-Rosenberg suggests, they were able to "defy proprieties, pioneer new roles, and still insist upon a rightful place within the genteel world" (245). Many of them lived the life of the independent, single woman. While not openly insurrectionist, their behavior exhibited much of the outspoken and independent attitude that the early twentieth-century New Woman would refine and flaunt.

Even in the early 1850s, as noted in chapter 1, temperance women had rejected the "masculine idea of womanhood"—the "submissive woman"

(Stanton, Anthony, and Gage 477–78). And from the very beginning of the WCTU, speakers purposefully highlighted the union's new, unique woman, differentiating her from earlier generations. In addressing women at the first annual meeting, for example, Mrs. Dr. P. S. Donelson

> said that the scene presented to her view was a wonderful one, and one which would have been impossible five hundred, or even one hundred years ago. The impossibility would not only have been a legal and moral nature, but also an intellectual one. In those days woman was often no more than a slave to man. (*Minutes of First* 5)

At the 1881 convention in Washington, D.C., Lathrap even posited the need to redefine women's roles as the organization's reason for holding conventions: "If you should ask us *why* we came, we face, in the answer, two problems—the problem of *womanhood* in America; and the problem of civilization in America—as the reasons why we are here" (*Minutes of WCTU Eighth* 29). In elaborating on the problem of womanhood, Lathrap defined women of her century as radically different from previous centuries: "The women of this century are no more like the women of the last century than is the noonday like the morning. God has given to us such wealth of talent, such weight of responsibility, such a wide place in which to stand we must necessarily do what the women of the last century could not do" (29).

By repeatedly enumerating the ways women of the late nineteenth century differed from women of previous generations, temperance women were prescribing their own model for women. Willard often included this theme in her annual addresses: "The W.C.T.U. is doing no work more important than that of reconstructing the ideal of womanhood. . . . Woman is becoming what God meant her to be and Christ's gospel necessitates her being the companion and counsellor, not the incumbrance and toy, of man" (*Minutes of National Fourteenth* 90).

Willard enjoyed reflecting on the differences the union had made for women. Celebrating the tenth anniversary of the Woman's Crusade, she stressed the difference those ten years had made to women: "Then custom's pinched lips declared 'thus far and no farther,' and we rebelled but yet obeyed; now nothing can restrain our ardent footsteps, save the loving 'thus far and no farther' of God" (*Minutes of National Sixteenth* 48). And for the women of the WCTU, God rarely said "no farther" to their public involvement.

Temperance women's new image of woman was also promoted in their exercise of the third theme of their motto, and it was in this theme that they most stringently demanded greater rights by evoking their own loyalty to country. They often did this by placing themselves alongside

traditional patriotic heroes of the republic. In her 1886 presidential address, Willard established union members as loyal disciples of the nation
by commemorating their relationship to earlier patriotic women:

> We are but the third generation from our Revolutionary Fore-
> mothers. If each of you could clasp with your mother and she
> with hers, these links would bridge the distance that sepa-
> rates us from Abigail Adams, the Mother of the Revolution;
> Martha Washington, its most stately lady; and Molly Pitcher,
> its most notable heroine. Like ourselves, those women bowed
> before the Cross and were devoted to the flag. (*Minutes of
> National Thirteenth* 142)

Such rhetoric confirmed the worthy lineage of every American woman,
including all union members, radical marchers, and their humble mothers—all notable, heroic, and participants in the creation of a great nation.

Lathrap was perhaps most effective rhetorically in establishing
women's patriotic rights. She referred to the Crusade in her address before the National Council of Women in 1891, a speech in which she proposed to relate the union's record, a "history at once unique and
impressive" ("National WCTU" 141). Lathrap immediately situated the
Crusade in relation to the Civil War: "A decade after the close of the
Civil War the Woman's Crusade startled the nation, compelled attention, and defied ridicule" (143). She explained the need for the Crusade's
'war' as a result of the government's attempt to pay for its own war by
licensing liquor for revenue. In her address, Lathrap contributed to the
notion of heroic foremothers, taking the opportunity to acknowledge
the impact of Crusade leaders and recognizing and extolling the accomplishments of other union members. First, she praised the courage of
women to persevere against great opposition, employing strong, repeti-
tious verb phrases to accentuate the vehement and scurrilous nature of
their enemies:

> Cursed at the bar of the legalized saloon; hissed on the floor of
> the Beer Brewers' Congress; scorned by conventions of politi-
> cal parties; misrepresented by the all-powerful press; denied
> its prayer in halls of legislation; sneered at in palaces of fash-
> ion, where the wine-glass tempts to destroy; criticized by con-
> servative pulpits; and unwelcome often even in the Christian
> church, it has been left to this organization of ballotless women
> to arouse all classes of opposers and find for themselves the
> hate of hate. (141)

Lathrap's rhetoric deftly combined agonistic, masculine language of war with softening, feminine attributes. Her strong verbs, all including harsh "s" sounds, are followed in each case by at least one prepositional phrase, and often two, providing a soothing rhythm between harsh actions. In addition, the alliterative nature of most of the phrases further offset the strident, repetitive verbs.

Lathrap continued by carefully crafting an image of WCTU women as patriotic "warriors" in the service of their country—not victims, but victors, "a force in the Nation's life"—by showing the respect and admiration they had won. She once again made use of repetitive verb phrases, but this time she chose benevolent, favorable ones to extol women's accomplishments and to highlight the valuable praise they had earned. Here, as she turned to the positive force of women's work, Lathrap further softened the language by increasing the number of rhythmic phrases following each verb.[12]

Again applying militant language, Lathrap defined the women's "battle-ground" as one "between right and wrong," but she differentiated the women's healing war from the earlier divisive one by noting the unifying strength of the WCTU; at the same time, she established the union's worthiness by attesting to its primacy in unifying a recently divided country, a feat men had been incapable of: "This was the first organization sufficiently national in spirit to cross the swordline between North and South, bearing the lilies of peace to homes and hearts on both sides of the line, until the past was beguiled of its sting in the high endeavor of a common cause" (147).

But Lathrap primarily confirmed the wartime contributions of her women warriors, highlighting their sacrifices and substantiating validity for their demands:

> With the going of the men to the battle field and to death, the farm, the shop, and the store, as well as the home, were left to the hands of the women; . . . when the cost of the nation's struggle came to be counted, it was found that its women had freely laid on the altar such costly gifts that all past relations were changed. (144)

She cited the Civil War's impact as a major force in changing women. Such acknowledgment honored the strength and fortitude often cited by women who believed their role during the war to be equally as important and difficult as that of men, though its significance was rarely conceded. She seized the opportunity to demonstrate that demands made upon women went beyond the conventional, and that their role during the war was equally courageous and patriotic:

> [A]s they marched away there stood behind them another

army, without any music, without any ambition, without any
promotion. And they took care of the children, and ran the
churches, and paid the preachers, and stayed by the stuff,
and scraped lint and rolled bandages, and then, in God's midnight, went down on their faces and prayed for power to say,
"Thy will be done," when the worst news came, and when it
did come wrapped themselves in crape and went on scrap-
ing lint and rolling bandages for those who were no [*sic*]
dead. (144)

Lathrap further evoked women's patriotic rights by highlighting their
kinship with other public-spirited models. She pointed to women's predicament, much like that of Revolutionary heroes, as taxpayers without
representation: "Thinkers, tax-payers, and unwilling partners in the cost
of evil legislation, the women of the country could not stand idly by when
another danger was being grown by law and not rebuke it" (144). Thus,
Lathrap carefully led listeners through the narrative of patriotic women's
bravery and loyalty, confirming the enormous cost of their contributions, and evoking parallels that would justify their demands for greater
equality. By establishing women's patriotic heritage and their generous
contributions given without fanfare, Lathrap demanded women's right
to reap advantages from educational and financial gains based on merit.

Others often seized opportunities to analogize women with traditional military heroes. Before the Decoration Day (Memorial Day) crowd
in Indianapolis honoring the Blue and Gray, Willard praised members of
both sides in the recent Civil War conflict, including Lee and Sherman as
well as soldiers from specific states. Again emphasizing the unity between
North and South, Willard sandwiched between her examples of military
heroes two of the best-known women temperance leaders—Northerner
Mary T. Lathrap of Michigan and Southerner Sallie F. Chapin of South
Carolina—praising these women from the two regions and placing them
in the company of these established heroes.

On another occasion, Willard paraphrased Lincoln's Gettysburg Address to praise this organization of women that was "in nowise guided,
moulded or controlled by men" ("Address" 474), noting that the society
was "'of the women, by the women,' but for humanity" (475). In addition to evoking similarities between the WCTU and the national government, Willard's words drew a parallel between the nation's "new birth
of freedom" established by the Civil War and the nation's chance for a
new freedom from the evils of alcohol, accompanied by women's chance
for a new freedom from oppression.

WCTU women consistently built on traditional rhetoric and ritual,
modifying it for comfort and for public consumption. In carefully creat-

ing their own history, members chose to use glorious and immediate antecedents. During the 1870s, formative years for the WCTU, Crusade leaders told their own histories—narrating their battlefield experiences as part of the U.S. Sanitary Commission during the Civil War, relating, episode by episode, women's victories during the Crusade, and citing achievements of union members. In establishing worthiness, they also regularly gave testimonials citing the bravery of Crusaders and WCTU members. They compared members to already famous women and paralleled women's activity with that of traditional patriotic heroes.

They employed other traditional means of establishing virtue as well. Speakers' illustrious family heritages were often cited, including prestigious marital relations. The WCTU had many professional members whose titles acknowledged their credentials, and such accomplishments were always recognized—Dr. Mary Burnett Weeks, Dr. Bessie V. Cushman, Rev. Anna Howard Shaw. But members also publicly recognized prestigious associations with regards to family and marriage, hence, such forms of address as Mrs. Dr. P. S. Donelson and Mrs. Governor Wallace. Such affirmations of familial lineage and relationships that established prestige and economic power contributed to their credibility.

WCTU members maintained an atmosphere of decorous proceedings, at once professional, businesslike, and feminine in nature. They sought the protection of traditional cultural expectations for women at the same time that they insisted on changing them. They appealed to concepts of religion, home, and patriotism—in many ways acceptable venues for women's energies—but insisted on changes within each of those arenas. They saw themselves as leading the vanguard in a new era for women, and they took great pride, and exhibited much skill, in establishing and celebrating that new era.

National leaders made use of the ceremonial nature of their annual meetings to inspire and motivate members, as well as to establish their authority and credibility with the press and public at large. Their glorification and celebration of women—historic and contemporary—instilled pride in members and inspired their continuing work and leadership among local unions upon their return home. Such eulogizing was important, as well, for giving members a voice, an obvious strategy of WCTU leaders. In creating worthy heroes and role models for women, leaders hoped to further women's commitment and promote their self-esteem. As I will show in the next chapter, involving women and bringing them to voice marked one of their greatest achievements.

3

Woman-Tempered Rhetoric:
Public Presentation and the WCTU

[W]omen are growing too wise and strong to use either tears
or tirade as weapons of defense.

—Mary Torrans Lathrap, 1888 Presidential Address to
Michigan State WCTU

IN 1873, AFTER MORE than a decade of teaching young women, Frances
E. Willard recognized the difficulties for women within educational institutions designed by and for men: "[T]o give ladies an 'equal chance'
with gentlemen, means something more than to control a college wholly
by men, arrange its surroundings solely for men, give the instruction entirely by men, and then, forsooth! open the doors *alike* to both sexes!"
("A New Departure" 158).

Willard, the first woman president of a woman's college and the first
Dean of Women at Northwestern University, chose to leave institution-
alized education because she became frustrated with what she perceived
as demeaning treatment of her ideas and unjustified challenges to her
authority. She and other leaders of the Woman's Christian Temperance
Union (WCTU) proceeded to create their own network for teaching
women outside the recognized establishments for education that they
found to be uncongenial to women. Their creation became the largest
and most effective organization for teaching women rhetorical skills in
the nineteenth century.

Organizations such as the WCTU were essential to women's learning to take on public personas because the nineteenth century offered
limited formal education in rhetoric for women. At coeducational institutions, for example, women might be admitted to classes but still be

58

refused permission to participate in rhetoric and elocution classes. At the first coeducational state institution, Oberlin, separate courses for men and women focused students' attention on the body and gestures for men and on voice and text for women—performance for men, listening for women. Women might choose to attend the men's rhetoric classes, but they were not permitted to speak; at graduation, male classmates delivered orations while women's compositions were read for them by the professor of rhetoric. By 1858, women received permission to read their own compositions, but were not allowed to address their audience. As late as 1870, one Oberlin graduate shocked her graduation audience when she looked directly at her audience to deliver her composition instead of demurely reading it, eyes lowered. Not until the late 1870s and 1880s were women students permitted to address mixed audiences, and even those audiences were comprised of members and guests of women's literary societies. (Lawrence 64–66, 78–81)[1]

Even attending rhetoric classes must have been only marginally helpful for women. Miriam Brody has convincingly outlined the traditional rhetorical curricula that assumed a masculine rhetor and denigrated the feminine. Brody traces gendered metaphors that equated good rhetoric with the masculine and poor rhetoric with the feminine or effete. She begins with the classical model of statesman-warrior-hero that evolved through history, continually constructing a rhetoric that took the masculine as the ideal. By the late nineteenth century, for example, Brody notes prominent Harvard lecturer Edward Channing's call for a "'masculine, earnest and impressive'" rhetoric and his disparagement of "'treacherous allurements'"(113). In addition, school texts, Brody explains, merged "heroic ideals of the older, manly warrior-civic statesman and the manly entrepreneur" (116), leaving little room for the feminine.

Such modes of rhetoric would have been especially problematic for women because of the late-nineteenth century's pronounced cultural dichotomy between male and female roles, and its subsequent strictures on woman's persona. In addition, many women were particularly shy about public presentations, since such highly visible activity was not part of their expected role. Yet, despite different expectations for women, most institutions of higher learning continued to approach rhetoric from a combative, "masculine" model, and textbooks presumed a male speaker, failing to address women's particular needs.

Even if institutions of higher learning were in some measure helpful for women, most women could not attend. Yet women were increasingly called upon to make public presentations in some form. Many late-nineteenth-century women, instead of seeking rhetorical skills at institutions of higher learning, sought and received such instruction within the reform movements—women teaching women. The largest of these organizations and the most effective in teaching women rhetorical skills was the WCTU, especially successful because new members learned public presentation from skillful teachers who understood women's particular needs; in addition, the WCTU provided an explicit audience and committed purpose, not one defined by classroom strictures or institutional priorities.

Leaders of the WCTU created a widespread network for teaching women rhetorical skills. As Willard points out in *A New Profession for Women*, a pamphlet encouraging young women to become a part of the WCTU, "Nearly all these workers [union members] have learned to speak acceptably in public without manuscript or notes." Willard also notes the need in the Temperance Literature and Press Departments for women with a "skillful pen." WCTU leaders made every effort to encourage and to make space for women's rhetorical involvement.

From its inception, the WCTU encouraged women to become active participants in public life. At its very first meeting at Cleveland in 1874, members passed a resolution declaring that the union would be "exclusively a convention of ladies, and that no man be admitted as a delegate under any pretext whatever" (*Minutes of First* 15). When other women's groups were prodded into admitting male members, the WCTU stood firm. Willard explained the reasoning as follows:

> These organized movements are, as we think, God's great recruiting station for the new war in which He is enrolling, drilling and disciplining. If men were at the front in these societies, as they would necessarily be if there at all, women would not develop so rapidly, or become so self-respecting and individual in character: they need to learn how to use the weapons with which the future is certain to equip them. . . . We work alone in order to become experts so that we can hold our own when we go into societies with men. That is the short of it. (*Minutes of Nineteenth* 140)

Perhaps women also felt more comfortable learning their new skills exclusively in the company of women. Willard later remembered, "Very few could make a speech at that early period—we gave speechlets instead, off-hand talks of from five to fifteen minutes" (*Glimpses* 349). Nonetheless, the WCTU created a tremendous network for providing leadership opportunities for women: scores of offices and departments on the national level, and thousands on state, district, county, and local levels, that would require workers to become publicly active writers and speakers. At its fifteenth annual convention in Detroit in 1888, for example, Willard announced that the National WCTU had forty departments (*Glimpses* 458). Each national department was headed by a superintendent with an associate in each state and local union (*Glimpses* 370). At the same meeting, Willard announced that Ohio had five hundred local unions.

Many members were already receptive to encouragement toward and instruction in public speaking. Evangelical women, who comprised the majority membership in the WCTU, would have grown up hearing homilies and lectures at church services and other community functions. Many of them likely participated in such functions to some degree themselves. For example, in her introduction to *"Writing Out My Heart": The Journal of Frances E. Willard*, Carolyn DeSwarte Gifford notes the many participatory exercises young Methodist women in the second half of the nineteenth century might have experienced: openly reporting on personal religious progress, leading class meetings, and participating in oral examinations and debates (19). This active involvement made them receptive to being fostered by WCTU leaders.

Such encouragement was constant. At the second annual meeting of the WCTU, Auretta Hoyt, Chair of the Committee on Lecture Bureau, urged women not to bring in "foreign speakers" but to "step to the front themselves" (*Minutes of Second* 65). Other leaders repeatedly advised members to speak and to encourage others to do so as well. In her many instructional manuals, Willard suggested that leaders elicit voices of women members as often as possible. As noted in the introduction, she charged leaders explicitly to "call out the voices of the timid." Willard understood the significance of voice for women who had known only silence, and her purpose was always to have women speak:

> Do not go through the dumb show of 'the lifted hand,' nor imbecility of 'manifest it by the usual sign' (when there are several signs), but call out that most inspiring response, the human voice divine. Remember too, that thus you educate women out of the silence which has stifled their beautiful gifts so long. (*How to Organize* 7; *Woman and Temperance* 618)[2]

Willard recognized also that women in the WCTU represented various stages of openness to and experience in speaking. She and other leaders tried to provide for all women, whatever their previous backgrounds. At the same time, leaders were sensitive to the practicalities of the organization's financial needs and, given nineteenth-century audiences' receptivity to the oral, could correlate their joint purposes of promoting women to speak and assisting in the organization's economic stability. Caroline B. Buell (plates 15, 16), corresponding secretary for the national WCTU, in *The Helping Hand; or the A-B-C of Organizing a WCTU*, quotes Bessie V. Cushman to union members:

> Much is truly said of the value of the written word, but were

it possible literally to "sow the land knee deep with temperance literature," there would be no less need of speakers. It is
a mistake to "put all the money into tracts," as some advise.
Good speakers bring more money into the treasury than they
draw out, taking the entire year into the account. The leaflet
cannot substitute, and should not supplant, the lecture. The
Bible—chief gem of the world's literature—does not make
preaching unnecessary. (23)

Historian Elizabeth Putnam Gordon notes the nineteenth century's
receptivity to oral presentation: "In this era, before the advent of the auto-
mobile, phonograph and moving picture, temperance mass meetings
everywhere were popular, and large audiences assembled to hear the
women speakers" (47). To assure women's participation, the WCTU not
only encouraged women to make public presentations, it provided members with many opportunities for doing so. Besides numerous local and
state meetings and conventions, each year members addressed national
convention delegates and guests, as well as congregations in the host city.
Newspaper accounts of annual conventions attested that "nearly every
pulpit in the city will be occupied by the temperance women to-day"
("Close" 8), where women served as guest speakers on the Sundays following the conventions. In 1885, for example, when the annual convention was held in Philadelphia, "forty churches were opened to speakers
on the Sabbath" (Willard, *Glimpses* 410), and often several women spoke
in one church.

Speakers addressed a broad range of audiences, from prison inmates
and "fallen women" to congregations of well-to-do churches; from re-
mote "North Woods lumbermen" (Willard, *Glimpses* 419) to international groups and organizations. In addition, the WCTU held national
camp meetings "conducted wholly and addressed largely by women"
(Elizabeth Gordon 18) and owned buildings at the popular chautauquas
around the country, a means of encouraging WCTU women to participate in the gatherings.[3] In her promotional pamphlet, *The WCTU at
Chautauquas*, for example, Lillian Mitchner suggests, "The value of the
Chautauqua Assembly to the average individual cannot be over esti-
mated. It offers an easy opportunity to hear the best talent that can be
obtained in the lecture field . . . and to avail oneself of the benefits to be
derived from attendance upon the various classes in physical culture,
elocution, Sunday school work, etc." Mitchner continues with instructions for establishing a WCTU department in a chautauqua, encouraging members to organize such departments, suggesting hints for creating
programs, and providing a sample WCTU program.

By 1885, the national organization had established a department
for "Training Schools" (later changed to "School of Methods" and sub-

sequently to "Schools of Methods and Parliamentary Usage"), hoping for a year-round training school in addition to summer camps and chautauquas. By 1886, four national camps existed. The curriculum at the shortest, a four-day institute at Mt. Lake Park, Maryland, included one morning devoted to "Parliamentary usages" and another "taken up by ten-minute talks on the 'Best Methods of Influencing Public Opinion,' the subjects being on the 'Press' the 'Platform' and 'Literature'" (*Minutes of National Thirteenth* 188). Sessions frequently addressed the work of particular departments. Anna Smeed Benjamin, National Superintendent, explained the need for such schools:

> When a woman is thoroughly versed in the work of a department and is able to present it so clearly and concisely and comprehensively as to make every hearer not only an interested listener but a forever-after-determined, enthusiastic doer (so far as opportunity permits) she is the leader for which we long. (*Minutes of Twenty-First* 304)

State unions also formed state, district, county, and local schools, which could be numerous. For example, in 1896, Mary A. Hadley, state superintendent for Indiana, reported as follows: "Forty-three schools were held immediately following the semi-annual spring conventions of one and one-half days, each including two evenings. Total enrollment, 1,296; average attendance, 30; visitors at day meeting, 611; evenings, 5,260; parliamentary drills, 26; Schools at Summer Assemblies, 3" (*Report of National Twenty-Third* 227). Camps differed according to state. One "California School was a practical drill in extempore speaking" at which "women without the slightest preparation made brief, bright speeches" (230).

WCTU leaders were uniquely equipped to teach rhetorical skills. Among the best educated women in the country, many of them had been university teachers, often of rhetoric, or were active in professions that allowed them to hone rhetorical strategies. For example, the two women most active in calling the Cleveland convention at which the national WCTU was organized were Jennie Fowler Willing and Emily Huntington Miller. Willing was a professor of English language and literature at Illinois Wesleyan University; she had served in many public capacities and had even been nominated to the post of Illinois Superintendent of Public Instruction, although she declined because of so many other commitments. Miller graduated from Oberlin College, published a wealth of writing, and became president of the Woman's College of Northwestern University. Other influential early leaders included J. Ellen Foster, a practicing Iowa attorney, Mary Torrans Lathrap, a licensed preacher, and Mary Allen West, twice superintendent of schools in Knox County, Illinois. The two WCTU presidents during its first quarter century, Annie Wittenmyer and Frances E. Willard, had years of experience as active, effective speakers, and Willard was an experienced teacher of rhetoric as well.[4]

WCTU leaders also taught public speaking and writing to women in their travels across the country, both by modelling and by careful one-to-one instruction. For example, both Wittenmyer and Willard travelled extensively while serving as officers of the organization, addressing audiences daily and helping to organize local WCTU organizations. Other officers also travelled widely to encourage women's participation. In addition, leaders created their own texts for women, many of them published by the WCTU's own publication house, and made them available as conveniently and inexpensively as possible. For example, according to the 1901 *Catalogue of the Woman's Temperance Publishing Association*, state and local unions might obtain "national" leaflets, including Willard's *How to Conduct a Public Meeting*, $.75 per one hundred. "Department" leaflets cost even less: one thousand for $1.50 (*Our Leaflets*). To further facilitate sales, Julia Colman, Superintendent of the Department of Literature, categorized leaflets, pamphlets, and books so that interested parties would know which publications complemented one another, which most appropriately served for distribution at various types of meetings, and which would appeal to specific groups, such as lawyers, ministers, doctors, and teachers.

Not only did the WCTU supply a wealth of inexpensive instructional materials for members, its wide distribution also provided members a ready means of publication with large circulation. By 1890, the WCTU's publication house was printing 125 million pages annually (McKeever 365). Many works were reprinted so often that no publication date was listed in order to facilitate reprinting. The 1901 catalogue lists ninety-eight different women authors for publications and one hundred seventy-six total contributions by women, even though the catalogue lists no author for many pieces.

In addition to writing for the WCTU's publication house, women published with the various tract societies, with Sunday school publication houses, and with the National Temperance Publication Association. Significantly, the majority of temperance authors were women. At the 1875 WCTU convention, Willard quoted John Newton Stearns, who was the publishing agent and editor for the National Temperance Publication Association for thirty years: "[He] referred to the dearth of temperance literature prior to the present work of the women. He stated that now women were writing three-fourths of the temperance tracts and books" (*Minutes of Second* 49).

Many of those publications have been lost. Efforts to blanket the country with an inexpensive plethora of materials may be partly to blame. Publications, even handbooks of hundreds of pages, lacked sturdy covers and bindings. In addition, twentieth-century appraisals of the temperance movement have devalued such materials. Even at the WCTU headquarters in Evanston, Illinois, only an incomplete collection remains. Extant materials, however, do provide some measure of understanding how leaders instructed members in public presentation.

What they show is that their counseling considers needs specific to women in the nineteenth century. WCTU leaders were sensitive to the particular strictures for women speakers, realizing they must carefully establish the authority to speak. Theoretically, as noted in the previous chapter, they combined a modified version of the classical "good" speaker with patriotic and biblical allusions in order to establish credibility and create authority for their public roles. On a practical level, they offered step-by-step outlines and instructions for beginning speakers. Recognizing the prejudices peculiar to women speakers, they carefully addressed ethical appeal above all other concerns. Willard repeatedly counseled women, "Womanliness first—afterward what you will," understanding speakers' primary need to dismantle resistance to women's messages by presenting a reassuring feminine persona. This strategy worked well for temperance women. Since gender representations in the nineteenth century were so closely connected to dress and appearance, temperance women comforted the skittish and disarmed the critical, because all outward appearances defined them as first and foremost "womanly."

Thus, leaders were acutely aware of women's need to present both a moral and feminine character. Whereas male speakers, in order to be effective, presented strong, masculine personas, women found it necessary to reassure audiences that their public stance did not masculinize them. And while men might be heard and taken into account even with a somewhat tarnished character, the same was not true for women. Buell emphasized that "one general rule should always be observed. For *leaders women of consecration should be chosen*: women *who can and do command the respect of the community* for their devoted and religious lives and whose *influence is without doubt on the side of Christianity and pure living*" (5; Willard, *Do Everything* 187).

Mary Allen West, editor-in-chief of the *Union Signal*, the WCTU's official newspaper, also implored Union members to consider ethical appeal: "Choose a lady who has true Christian courtesy and the power to express herself in a clear, bright, pleasant manner. It is through her your Union is known to other Unions and the State and District Officers" (*Leaflet*). Leaders modeled a dignified, but not elaborate, dress for members. Correspondence between Anna Gordon, Willard's private secretary, and Willard's mother attests to the concern of all three that Willard appear appropriately dignified. Their letters discuss the amounts and styles of lace for Willard's dress, for example, representing their wishes that Willard look adequately fashionable and feminine, but in no way showy.

Willard campaigned for more "reasonable" dress for women, but those efforts were combined with a pragmatic belief that members must present an acceptable appearance. Willard even had appropriate dresses and skirts designed specifically for WCTU members (plates 17, 18). As another means of presenting a proper ethos in dress, leaders continually encouraged members to wear their Union badge, a white ribbon that symbolized membership in the WCTU, but which also stood for purity and peace.

Sensitive to the limited background and timidity of novice members, many of whom were unaware of even the fundamental decorum of public meetings, leaders presented basic, specific explanations for proper procedure at gatherings, most likely providing the necessary assurance for some women to make their first efforts at public speech. For instance, Buell's suggestions include the following:

> Always *rise* and address the Chair, and wait to be recognized before beginning to speak. The Chair should then give the name of the lady. (40)

> Use the voice to be heard. (40)

> In announcing the congregational hymn . . . ask the audience to rise and join in the singing. (32)

> Do not vote by the uplifted hand. (40)

In addition, Willard, always attuned to the particular needs and problems women might face, often gave very specific outlines to help speakers and WCTU organizers. In *How to Conduct a Public Meeting*, Willard suggests that those presiding over a public meeting not use the "'cut and dried' method, where the President reads every word she says, and if her sight blurred, or her spectacles are mislaid, finds herself all out at sea" (2; *Woman and Temperance* 624). Instead, Willard encourages members to use common sense and "[p]lan matters thoroughly beforehand. Rehearse if necessary; you do this for a wedding, and we shall never wed the WCTU to the people's heart until we conduct our meetings without hitch or flaw" (3; *Woman and Temperance* 624).

By making the connection between uncomfortable public address and the more familiar events in women's lives, Willard deftly weakens the fearful and unfamiliar aspect of speaking in public. She then gives some specific details, encouraging women to avoid terms associated with the masculine:

> Teach without seeming to do so. Carefully skip all such "hard words" as "Take notice," "I call your attention," "Do you understand?" and on no account include a sentence with that irritating grammatical non-descript "See?" Put yourself in the

attitude of a learner along with the rest; thus your style will be suggestive and winsome rather than authoritative and disagreeable. (*How to Organize* 5; *Woman and Temperance* 616)

Willard then provides a seven-point general outline for speeches that includes a history of the organization, reasons women should join the organization, and even answers for likely questions, suggesting, as she often did, that women use a conversational or narrative form of delivery: "I have often given these in anecdotal form, telling just what women, old and young, grave and gay, had said to me about the convictions resulting from their own observation and experience which had led them into temperance work" (*How to Organize* 6; *Woman and Temperance* 617).

Union leaders recognized the need for a receptive audience and stressed a rhetoric that heeded appearance as well as speech. They attended to personal image, careful of their own attire and exhibiting their white ribbon badges, but they ensured that meeting halls promoted a specific image as well. For example, Buell suggests, "Make the place in which your meeting is to be held as attractive as possible. It helps the lecturer to speak, it helps the audience to hear, and it plainly says to both, 'These women have put work into this meeting, and it is worth our while to do our part if they consider it of so much importance'" (28). Even more emphatically, E. G. Greene insisted, "*Remember* to bring the flowers and mottoes, make the place cheery, giving forth a welcome—*we expect you, look!*" (48).

Willard also stressed visual rhetoric, imploring women to decorate with flowers and banners of their own work and design, as well as with national flags and state escutcheons so as to add a conducive atmosphere based on patriotic authority. State WCTU shields represented the pride of the state of origin; a shield from Colorado, for example, was made "of solid minerals, gleaming with gold, silver, and copper" (Lathrap, *Poems* 320). In addition, Willard reminded members of the positive influence of music, especially religious music: "[D]on't forget that a hymn with the gospel ring in the united voices that sing it; a solo from some sweet woman's heart and voice, or from that of some good and true man, a chorus lifting the audience to concert pitch, will utterly transform your audience as to its receptivity" (*How to Conduct* 3).

The attention to a comprehensive rhetorical presentation served more than one purpose. The "womanly" atmosphere and patriotic and religious tones made reserved women comfortable without offending more liberal women. In addition, such an atmosphere deflected criticism from outside the organization. Although the press sometimes openly criticized WCTU speakers, the atmosphere created by the women generally disarmed harsh critics.

Such rhetoric also served to establish the rights of WCTU members to become public persons. Their motto, "For God, and Home and Native Land," represents the warrants they used to draw authority for their public stance. Women made use of biblical allusions throughout their speeches, included the word "Christian" in their organization's name, and began every meeting with religious hymns and prayers. They further insisted upon their right to work for temperance and to demand the vote so that they might protect their homes. Their celebration of women's traditional skills—embroidered and quilted samplers of the national motto and other temperance memorabilia displayed throughout their meeting halls—reinforced this warrant. At almost every convention, the women presented needlework they had created themselves. For example, at the 1883 annual convention, Anna Gordon (plates 19, 20) presented the Union with a banner she had embroidered herself, and the organization often honored select members by presenting them with quilts or other handmade articles created by local or state unions. Finally, members evoked patriotism by displaying national flags and state shields at each meeting, even making special displays of patriotic acts. At the 1878 annual convention, for instance, they borrowed and displayed the national flag from Fort McHenry. Their public work became a duty: to God, for home, and in the service of country.

Leaders also presented instructional models for women, often taking a chatty or narrative approach. In her famous *Do Everything: A Handbook for the World's White Ribboners*, Willard uses a story format to exemplify a model approach for forming local and state unions, as well as for public speaking. In Chapter 6, "My Visit to Cheerible; or, How to Conduct a Public Meeting, and How to Carry on a Local Union," Willard narrates her visit in first person, but the obvious purpose is the presentation of a model for members, from the arrival of the speaker through the conducting of a temperance meeting. In suggesting a model for speaking, Willard writes, "I then talked a while, putting what I said into the narrative form. I wonder if it would be a good plan to reproduce, as well as I am able, that talk right here?" (82). Willard then presents what she calls an "outline" of her presentation to complete her "model Local Union" (82–86), but the very detailed outline might actually be used by novice speakers as presented.[5]

Sometimes leaders offered specific directions for demonstrations to accompany speeches. Julia Colman, superintendent of the Department of Literature for the WCTU from 1875–90, wrote over five hundred books, tracts, and pamphlets, and also travelled the country lecturing and demonstrating how speakers might use a testing device she had created (Willard and Livermore 1: 195–96). Like many WCTU leaders, Colman deliberately identified the temperance movement with the broad public interest in science, further establishing her authority and credibility.

Colman's *The Temperance Handbook for Speakers and Workers* offers ten "outline temperance lectures" with detailed instructions for providing complete scientific presentations. Included is a list of the necessary supplies for each experiment, directions for executing the experiment, and a list of "further items and information for filling out this lecture"—an itemization of temperance pamphlets and publications to provide even greater background for the speaker and for circulation among guests at presentations.

In her preface, Colman describes her effort "to make some of these scientific laws plain to the comprehension of the average mind." Part 1 provides detailed background for speakers, while Part 2 offers "Ten Scientific Lectures, with Full Directions for Their Illustration with Simple Chemical Experiments" (84).

Colman calls them "outline" lectures, and a speaker might readily expand upon or adapt given material to her own personality and need. But, as with Willard's outlines, a novice member could readily follow most of the proposed lectures and demonstrations verbatim. For example, the first lecture is called "Our Mysterious Enemy Unveiled," which leads listeners step-by-step through the history of alcoholic beverages to an experiment for determining whether or not a drink or food contains alcohol. Since alcohol was often used both to promote the storage life of provisions and to enhance the flavor of bland or poorly kept foods, spirits often comprised a considerable portion of a food. Colman then lists necessary supplies: "A testing apparatus with rubber tube and a condenser of some sort, (perhaps a bottle on ice,) a slop bowl, two plates, and one small, shallow pan, a bottle of alcohol, matches, gunpowder, hard cider or homemade wine, porter, port wine, gin, matches and candles" (93).

The supplies are adequate for conducting any of six experiments for determining the presence or absence of alcohol in a beverage or food. Colman does not provide an exact procedure for all of the experiments, but rather for at least one or two experiments per lecture, she guides the reader carefully through an appropriate procedure.[6]

Although the WCTU leadership approached its goal of widespread public participation by women within a decade, it planned as well for future needs by deliberately preparing for its own replacement. As part of her effort to prepare future generations, Willard heads a section in *Woman and Temperance* with the question, "Who Will Take Our Places?" and she addresses *A New Profession for Women* "To Young Women who are Ready for Work." This concern for preparing girls and young women who would take the place of current leaders of the organization prompted a great deal of work and numerous publications. A multitude of pamphlets and books targeted young people. In addition, Gordon worked with children in her travels throughout the country and at every national convention, helping them to speak and sing as part of the convention program. She published numerous books and pamphlets providing instructions and presentations for young speakers. Her *Recitations*, for example, a collection of speeches for young people, joined similar works by others such as Julia A. Ames and Louise Penny, who wrote or edited works designed for children's recitations; all included extensive parts for girls.

Leaders organized a WCTU children's organization, The Bands of Hope (later the Loyal Temperance Legion), and a youth group, the Youth Temperance Council. They also created an organization specifically for young women, The Young Woman's Christian Temperance Union. After 1882, one evening at each annual convention was "assigned to the young ladies. . . . They are to be our successors," explained Willard, "and their training must begin." She outlined her hopes for this new generation of leaders: "We have had to forge our own weapons and to learn the manual of arms upon the battle-field. Happily this will not be so with them, for they will enter with the hard-worn heritage of our experience. . . . Gentle girlhood will march onward to our places if we but give the signal" (*Minutes of National Ninth* 60).

The concern for preparing young women for public roles prompted Jennie F. Willing, one of the founders of the WCTU, to devote a full chapter in her *The Potential Woman* to the issue of public address for young women. Although she titled the chapter "Talking" and includes references to and suggestions for conversation, Willing actually justifies and presents instructions for formal public speaking. First, she places the current situation into context:

> The gift of speech has been bestowed alike upon men and women; but women have not been permitted the scope of theme, nor the practice that men have reserved for themselves. Women, like all who have not had a fair field, have fallen into diplomacy, carrying by favor points that they are not permitted to win by direct argument. They understand that nothing pleases an egotist more than to have one listen well to his talk. So they say, "Yes," and "No," and keep up a gentle jingle of the small bells of assent and applause, hoping to gain by pleasing what they are not allowed honorably to claim; their hearts, meanwhile, hungering for the mental food of excellent ennobling speech. (111–12)

Then Willing offers authority for young women's right to speech, drawing upon numerous biblical passages to support their prerogative for speaking (118–19). She also offers more contemporary role models to justify a woman's right and ability to speak—Susannah Wesley, Catherine Booth,[7] and Quaker women—finally suggesting that young women take the advice of "good, wise old Sojourner Truth: 'What's de use o' makin' such a fuss about yer rights? Why dun ye jes' go 'long an' take em?'" (124)

Willing encourages young women to develop their intellects, urging them to become active readers: "use pencil and commonplace book, so as to enrich your own thought with that which was planted for that very purpose" (117), and to avoid pathetic appeal—"emotional appeals to the sensibilities"—because "people cannot live and grow robust on custards and whipped cream" (126). She then warns against faults in what she refers to as the "mechanical part" of speaking—offenses that would be particularly problematic for women speakers: "mannerisms, loudness, coarseness of voice or words, the giggling habit . . . the simpering and affected, the slangy, the haughty, the ostentatious; your own common-sense protests against all these faults" (116).

Whatever the age, and regardless of previous experience, the WCTU provided extensive rhetorical training for women. Active participation in the WCTU suggests that women were more interested in pursuing, and more diligent in providing for, rhetorical education for women than previous studies of the nineteenth century suggest. The WCTU's "school" offered both encouragement and effective instruction, crafting a means for overcoming prejudicial and institutional obstacles for women speakers. Women taught women with a sensitivity to the rhetorical circumstances peculiar to women, as well as with an understanding of women's fears, displaying a remarkable rhetorical sophistication.

In spite of the fact that more women in the nineteenth century sought public voice through the temperance cause than in any other, and that leaders, especially Frances Willard, were among the most beloved and respected women of the century, late-twentieth-century scholars have virtually ignored their contribution to nineteenth-century rhetoric. Such treatment stems, I think, partly from contemporary scholars' discomfort with temperance women's religious/evangelical associations, despite the fact that many temperance leaders attributed their earliest rhetorical training to empowering church related activities. A closely related cause rests in our natural inclination to value the ideas and motives of those most like us; in doing so, feminist scholars, whom we would expect to appreciate this major movement of women, have recovered and esteemed leaders of the suffrage movement instead—women such as Elizabeth Cady Stanton and Susan B. Anthony. And due to our admiration of such women as Stanton and Anthony, we have also accepted their explanations and interpretations in the accounts they have left behind—their personal papers and especially their *History of Woman Suffrage*. Such accounts provide a valuable but limited perspective about other leaders whom they often saw as competitors, women who chose a remarkably different rhetorical strategy for achieving improved conditions for women.

While the temperance movement is often seen as a failed movement, temperance women, through their rhetorical acumen, created effective change for women, both politically and personally. They were successful in changing local and state laws pertaining to women in every state, laws raising the age of consent for girls, for example, and for improving property and legal rights for women. And they were instrumental in gaining the passage of two amendments to the federal Constitution: the Eighteenth, or Prohibition Amendment, and the Nineteenth, Woman Suffrage Amendment. The WCTU, more than any other group, successfully encouraged late-nineteenth-century women to become publicly active and provided the necessary instruction for them to do so. The organization provides a model of rhetorical precision by a group outside mainstream educational and political institutions.

Pl. 1. Rest Cottage, home of Frances E. Willard

Pl. 2. Dining room, Rest Cottage

Pl. 3. Amelia Bloomer

Pl. 4. Clarina Howard Nichols

Pl. 5. Elizabeth Cady Stanton

Pl. 6. Susan B. Anthony

Pl. 7. Reverend Antoinette Brown (Blackwell)

Pl. 8. Amelia Bloomer
in Bloomer dress. From
the archives of the
Seneca Falls Historical
Society.

Pl. 9. Lucy Stone

Pl. 10. The
Temple. Courtesy
Frances E. Willard
Memorial Library
and the National
Woman's Christian
Temperance Union,
Evanston, Ill.

Pl. 11. Eliza Daniel Stewart (Mother Stewart), a leader of the Woman's Crusade

Pl. 12. Annie Wittenmyer, first president of the WCTU

Pl. 13. Mary Torrans Lathrap, participant in Woman's Crusade and president of the Michigan WCTU

Pl. 14. Mary Torrans Lathrap. Sketch from *St. Louis Post Dispatch*, 24 Oct. 1884.

Pl. 15. Caroline Brown Buell, corresponding secretary of the WCTU

Pl. 16. Caroline Brown Buell. Sketch from *St. Louis Post Dispatch*, 24 Oct. 1884.

Pl. 17. The Willard Dress. Courtesy Frances E. Willard Memorial Library and the National Woman's Christian Temperance Union, Evanston, Ill.

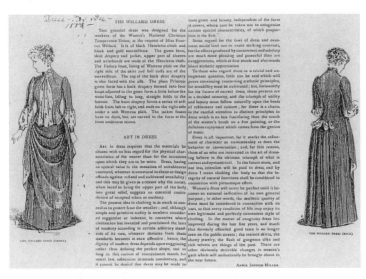

Pl. 18. The Willard Dress, with text. Courtesy Frances E. Willard Memorial Library and the National Woman's Christian Temperance Union, Evanston, Ill.

Pl. 19. Anna A. Gordon, private
secretary to Frances E. Willard
and third president of the WCTU

Pl. 20. Anna A. Gordon. Sketch
from *Baltimore Morning Herald*,
19 Oct. 1895.

Pl. 21. Frances Ellen Watkins Harper, National Superintendent, WCTU Work among Colored People. Reprinted by permission of Moorland-Spingarn Research Center, Howard University.

Pl. 22. Frances Ellen Watkins Harper. Sketch from *Baltimore Morning Herald*, 20 Oct. 1895.

Pl. 23. Scene at the opening session of the WCTU in Music Hall. From *Baltimore Morning Herald*, 19 Oct. 1895.

Pl. 24. National WCTU in session. From *Baltimore American*, 19 Oct. 1895.

Pl. 25. A chautauqua salute at the WCTU Convention. From *St. Louis Star*, 15 Nov. 1896.

Pl. 26. Frances E. Willard, second president of the WCTU

Pl. 27. Frances E. Willard. Sketch from *St. Louis Post-Dispatch*, 24 Oct. 1884.

Pl. 28. Emily Pitt Stevens

Pl. 29. Emily Pitt Stevens.
Sketch from *St. Louis Post-Dispatch*, 24 Oct. 1884.

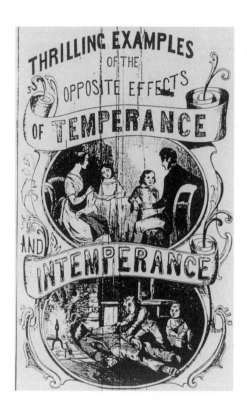

Pl. 30. Cover of *The Fountain and the Bottle*. Edited by a Son of Temperance.

Pl. 31. From "Amy" by Caroline H. Butler

Pl. 32. Legree and his drivers. From *Uncle Tom's Cabin* by Harriet Beecher Stowe.

Pl. 33. Mr. Lindsay insists that Ellen drink wine. From *The Wide, Wide World* by Susan Warner.

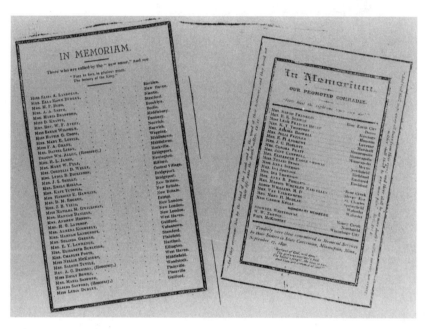

Pl. 34.
Memorial pages from Connecticut and Minnesota state minutes, 1890

Part Two

Controversy Surrounding the Cause

4

Dissension and Division:
Racial Tension and the WCTU

She is simply endeavoring to do what is impossible—please
the anti-lynch people and not displease the south.

—"Frances, A Temporizer," The *Cleveland Gazette*

IN MANY WAYS, the women of the WCTU reflected the times and culture of which they were a part. Divisions apparent within the nation
often surfaced among members. For example, Frances Willard made numerous overtures to Catholics despite the fact that the WCTU membership was almost completely comprised of Christian evangelists. She often
met with opposition from members who represented a typical fear of
"papists." Debates over whether and how to include immigrant popula-
tions also surfaced. In both cases, rhetoric differed according to where
members lived. For example, in Minnesota, although there were many
efforts to solicit membership among immigrants, members often spoke
negatively of Germans because of their control over the growing brewing
industry in that area; in Boston, members' disdain was directed primarily at Irish Catholics. Attitudes toward African Americans also reflected
the regional and cultural background of members, but racial relations
within the union, unlike other divisions, became a subject for national
and international debate.

Frances Willard's biographers and others who have written accounts
of the WCTU have ignored or glossed over many differences within the
WCTU, including racial tensions aired publicly by the most vocal African American woman activist in the 1890s, Ida B. Wells. One biographer,
Mary Earhart, does mention the Willard/Wells conflict; but Earhart does
not seem to understand the seriousness of the charges made by Wells, and

she wonders that "criticism persisted" even after the 1894 presidential address Willard had hoped would put the matter to rest. Ruth Bordin, in
Woman and Temperance: the Quest for Power and Liberty, also addresses
the issue briefly, attributing the major criticism to "A British antilynch-
ing society," probably because Wells's charges were first published in
Fraternity, the official newspaper of a British anti-lynching organization; but Bordin fails to mention Ida. B. Wells at all. Her efforts concentrate, instead, on providing evidence of black participation within the
WCTU and on showing that "Black women appreciated the WCTU's
limited acceptance" (84). Black women did often value their connection
with the WCTU, but primarily for the agency it afforded them in fulfill-
ing their own purposes.

Similarly, biographers of Ida B. Wells have relied almost solely on
Wells's view of the WCTU in addressing any connection between black
women and that organization. They have thus ignored the participation
of other highly influential black women in the WCTU and the value those
women placed on their membership, as well as the sometimes committed support of white WCTU members.

Although there was unquestionably racism within the WCTU, there
was also acceptance, and many African American women found the organization beneficial for their own purposes. This chapter examines the
Wells-Willard controversy but also goes beyond the controversy between
these two powerful rhetors to explore other issues of race within the organization and to discern attitudes among members of both races.

In 1893, during her second anti-lynching campaign in England, Ida
B. Wells accused Willard and the WCTU of complicity in the lynching of
blacks. Wells told her English audiences of the failure of American religious and moral leaders to speak out in opposition to lynching. According to Wells, the press continually asked her about specific prominent
leaders, such as Dwight Moody and Frances Willard, and she charged
those leaders with a continued refusal to speak out against lynching. Wells
was particularly critical of Willard, suggesting that Willard had not only
failed to take a stand against lynching, but had seemed to condone it. She
based her premise on a portion of an 1890 interview in which Willard
praised Southerners and suggested that Northerners had unfairly judged
the South. Willard had told a New York newspaper reporter,

> I pity the southerners, and I believe the great mass of them are
> as conscientious and kindly-intentioned toward the colored
> man as an equal number of white church-members of the
> North. . . . The problem on their hands is immeasurable. The
> colored race multiplies like the locusts of Egypt. The grog-shop
> is its center of power. The safety of women, of childhood, of the

home is menaced in a thousand localities at this moment, so that the men dare not go beyond the sight of their own roof-tree. (Thompson 56)

While Willard did not mention lynching *per se*, the disparaging image equating African Americans with the multiplying locusts that plagued Egypt, and the suggested connection between blacks and saloons, were enough to have incited Wells's anger and shock today's reader. But even more problematic, Willard's juxtaposing the safety of women and children with the Southerners' "problem" supported exactly the kinds of racist myths and suppositions Wells was devoting her life to eradicating. As equally adept as Willard in rhetorical acumen, Wells made use of Willard's statement to draw international attention to her cause.

Wells created a maelstrom within the press with her accusations and continued to command attention by extending the confrontation. After her return to the United States, she persisted in her criticism of Willard and the WCTU in her public addresses; she also requested permission to address the national WCTU convention. Her request was denied, WCTU leader Anna S. Benjamin later told the *Baltimore Sun*, "on account of the rather too fervid language of her oratory" ("The Union" 8). The following year, Wells did attend the 1894 national convention as a fraternal candidate, having, according to Benjamin, "with the shrewdness of a politician . . . induced a society of some kind to send her" (8). Benjamin continues:

> The union, in courtesy, was thus compelled to receive the woman with other delegates and she seized the opportunity to soundly score the union as being indifferent in the welfare of the negro. Her violent attack was replied to at the time and assurance was made that the negro was the recipient of Christian Sympathy of the union. She refused to be convinced and she has since spoken against the WCTU. (8)

At the convention, WCTU leaders had minimized Wells's effect, not only by limiting her time for speaking, but also by positioning her address after that of two members of her own race who praised Willard and the WCTU. Rev. Wm. Boyd, former minister of the African Methodist Episcopal Church, had been introduced and spoke briefly (*Minutes of Twenty-First* 36). Then, Lucy Thurman, "representing the colored people, presented a bunch of yellow and white chrysanthemums tied with yellow and white ribbons" to Frances Willard (39), "chosen, Mrs Thurman said, because Miss Willard is queen of women, the chrysanthemum is queen of the autumn and that particular variety queen of all ("WCTU" 1). Shortly after, Wells was introduced and permitted to speak briefly. The 1894 *Minutes of the Twenty-First Convention* make only brief mention of Wells's appearance at the convention: "Miss Wells, fraternal delegate from the African M.E. Mite Society, was here introduced" (39), providing no details about the content of her speech. In addition, I have been able to find no mention of Wells's presentation in then contemporary newspaper reports.

At the same convention, Willard attempted to defend herself in her presidential address by explaining that "Much misapprehension has arisen in the last year concerning the attitude of our unions toward the colored people, and an official explanation is in order" (129). After referring to her own background as the daughter of abolitionist parents and her longtime loyalty to and support of blacks, Willard elaborated on the "State rights" policy of the WCTU, by which the details of organization were left to the states.

> It is needless to say that in the Northern and Western States colored women join the same local unions as white women, and that they have always been among our national superintendents. The President of a colored State WCTU is a full voting member of our Executive Committee, just the same as the President of the white WCTU who comes from the same State. (129)

In truth, although occasionally both races formed one union even in the South, many black unions chose to be separate, not only in the South, but in the North and West as well.[1] And apparently the equal treatment Willard suggests, while the letter of the law, often failed in practice, especially in the South. However, while separate unions in the South provided one issue for Wells's accusations, the more volatile issue was that of lynching.

Willard's defense became even more precarious as she tried to justify other segments of her earlier remarks. She commented on less controversial issues, such as educational qualifications for the ballot and corrupt political practices, sandwiching the more sensitive rape issue briefly between those matters and her indictment of white men. Still, Willard's efforts appeared awkward as she tried to appease her critics without really acknowledging any mistake on her part:

> Some years ago on my return from the South I was interviewed by a representative of the New York *Voice*, and stated that as one result of my observations and inquiries I believed that it would be better if not only in the South but throughout the nation we had an educational rather than a color or sex limit put upon the ballot. To this opinion, without intending the slightest discrimination against any race, I still adhere. I also said that in the South the colored vote was often marshalled

against the temperance people by base political leaders for their own purposes, and still hold to that statement. Furthermore, I said that the nameless outrages perpetrated upon white women and little girls were a cause of constant anxiety, and this I still believe to be true; but I wish I had said then, as I do now, that the immoralities of white men in their relations with colored women are the source of intolerable race prejudice and hatred, and that there is not a more withering curse upon the manhood of any nation than that which the eternal laws of nature visited upon those men and those homes in which the helpless bondwoman was made the victim of her master's base desire. (130)[2]

Willard's efforts at silencing her critics was ineffective for a number of reasons. Frances E. W. Harper (plates 21, 22) and other black women leaders had also expressed concern about universal suffrage that included the illiterate, although they most often suggested that an answer lay in educating them, and black women leaders had long expressed concern about the enormous alcohol problem within the black community. The associated abuse of alcohol and politics among both races was well-known; election day was a dangerous day to be on the streets in many places because of the free flow of alcohol, given that polls were often located in saloons and politicians purchased alcohol freely for potential voters. But in her comments, Willard again pointed specifically to black voters as the primary problem, and Willard's first two reaffirmations reveal her white, middle-class assumptions.

But Willard's reassertion that outrages were perpetrated against women and children—the implication being that black men posed a danger to innocent white women and children—must have infuriated many black leaders. The fact that Willard included a reprimand to white men—situated primarily in the past and associated with the evils of slavery—could hardly assuage anger at this kind of accusation. After all, white men were not likely to be lynched.

Later in her address, Willard explained that "It is inconceivable that the WCTU will ever condone lynching, no matter what the provocation" (133), placing her on record as opposing lynching; but the inclusion of the phrase "no matter what the provocation" suggests her stubborn adherence to the notion that black men were raping white women and children. Willard then offered a resolution stating the union's opposition to lynching, but her near repetition of earlier inflammatory rhetoric undercut the formal condemnation of lynching, and the southern delegation blocked formal passage of her suggested resolution.

The confrontation between Wells and Willard continued for several years. Willard had made personal reference to Wells in her 1894 annual address. When Wells suggested that, in situations in which rape was given as the reason for lynching, often "the relationship between the victim lynched and the alleged victim of his assault was voluntary, clandestine and illicit" ("Miss Wells" 1), Willard seized upon Wells's statement to charge that Wells, by her statements "concerning white women having taken the initiative in nameless acts between the races . . . has put an imputation upon half the white race in this country" (*Minutes of Twenty-First* 131).

However, Willard's 1894 defense explains Wells's charge that Willard promoted the lynching of black men. Wells had long insisted that whites used the notion that black men raped white women as a myth to excuse lynching. She had provided statistics to show that the majority of reasons given for lynchings were actually for reasons other than rape. In suggesting that "nameless outrages" were "perpetrated upon white women and little girls," Willard had, Wells believed, supported the lynching of black men, because the rhetoric of Willard's statement, even if not explicitly justifying lynching, did in fact support the assumptions on which lynching was based.

Wells continued her criticism of Willard. Immediately following her appearance before the 1894 national WCTU convention, Wells presented a lecture before the Tawawa Literary Circle, which the *Cleveland Gazette* had labeled "a perfect success" and "one of the most thrilling talks against, and exposes of, lynching the people of to-day can possibly listen to." The newspaper then printed Wells's specific references to Willard:

> "I pointed out to Miss Willard," said Miss Wells, "her error. We did not expect this from one who has stood so long for humanity. We have to give the facts. *In giving them no imputation is cast upon the white women of America, and it is unjust and untruthful for any one to so assert.* I wish it were possible not to make such allusions, but the Negro race is becoming as to its honor as the white race." ("Miss Wells" 1)

Wells was both an eloquent orator and sophisticated rhetorician. She had carefully chosen the time and place to criticize Willard for her racist comments. Willard had made her pejorative comments in 1890 to the reporter of a New York temperance newspaper. Not until late in 1893, while she was in England where the press more willingly examined accusations about lynching, did Wells choose to include Willard in the controversy. In the U.S., as evident in her Tawawa address, Wells carefully avoided *ad hominem* attacks, crediting Willard by noting that such rhetoric was unexpected from someone with Willard's history of work for humanity; she continued that "she had the greatest respect for Miss Willard personally, and heartily indorsed her great temperance work, but she thought some of her positions on the lynch question untenable" (1). Wells left more direct attacks to others. Both Rev. R. C. Ransom, who shared the Tawawa platform with Wells, and the editor of the *Gazette* leveled stronger criticism at Willard personally.

At the Tawawa address, Rev. Ransom criticized "a scheme of a few misguided Afro-Americans who were foolish enough to want to present Miss Willard a bouquet in the name of the Afro-American ladies of Cleveland, that, too, in the face of her adverse comment upon Miss Wells and the race's cause in her (Miss Willard's) annual WCTU address" ("Miss Wells" 1).

The *Gazette*, a black owned newspaper, reported the audience's recognition that such an act "would have been not only a back-handed 'blow in the face' for Miss Wells and the race movement she leads, but a rank insult to every Afro-American lady in the city." The newspaper then went further in criticizing directly those black women members of the WCTU who did publicly support Willard, noting the

> peculiar conduct and actions of the two "colored" delegates (from Michigan)—Madams Preston and Thurman. Strange to say these women sided with Miss Willard as against Miss Wells and the race, and therefore in no sense were they representatives of our people. . . . Afro-Americans should remember (them) as woman [*sic*] who forsook Miss Wells, their race and its greatest cause at present to cling to a woman (*white*), Miss Willard, portions of whose annual address is an insult to the race. (1)

The outrage expressed at those black women who honored Frances Willard is intensified by the specific use of the term "Afro-American" for black women generally, but of "colored" in reference to those felt to be complicit with denigration of the race.

In an accompanying editorial, "Frances, A Temporizer," the *Gazette* criticized Willard because she

> waited a long time and then "beat all about the bush" before going in on the lynch question. When she did go in (not far either), Miss Willard could not refrain from doing two things which neither add to her prestige nor accomplish what she desired. They were her covert attack upon Miss Ida B. Wells and the cause she represents at present, and the casting of a little "sop" to the south when she said in substance that she didn't believe there were white women in the south who encouraged Afro-Americans there to make certain advances to them.

The newspaper became even more explicit about Willard's not taking a stronger stand against lynching:

The fact is, Frances E. Willard is a *temporizer* as far as our people's interests are concerned. Her views on lynching and the color line in temperance work do not, as she thinks, need further explanation, but they do need and badly, too, revision and change. They stamp her plainly as a *temporizer*, pure and simple. (2)

Willard continued her efforts to rescue her image. After 1894, she recognized and praised Lucy Thurman's work as the national Superintendent of Work among Colored People each year in her presidential addresses. She announced that she had sent resolutions against lynching each year to every state in the union, explaining that they had generally been adopted and "in no instance so far as I can learn have they ever been voted down" (*Report of National Twenty-Second*, 90). She also called for such resolutions from the national WCTU in both 1894 and 1895. When the executive committee proposed doubling Willard's salary to $2000, Willard asked that the additional thousand be apportioned instead to WCTU works, with $200 of the amount to be an additional appropriation to the Department of Work among Colored People (61).

Members also tried to improve perceptions of the union and of their leader. Although the southern delegates had opposed Willard's 1894 anti-lynching resolution, the 1895 convention passed the resolution without dissent, sending a copy to the *New Era*, "the organ of the colored women's association" (20). The resolution barely cloaks members' anger at what they obviously believed to be unjust accusations:

> *Resolved*, That white ribbon women who wear the badge of peace, ought never to have been placed in the position of having to defend themselves from the charge that they favored the lynching of any human being, anywhere, under any circumstances; and we keenly feel the false position in which we have been placed, and repudiate any imputation inconsistent with the law of Christ, which, as everybody knows, is totally at variance with the torture or killing of any human being without opportunity to have his case fairly presented and to be tried by a jury. We do not multiply epithets on this subject, because it is not necessary. We leave that to those who have misrepresented our position; but we have never hesitated, and do not now, to place ourselves squarely on record in regard to lynching and other lawless proceedings in our own or any other country, now and always, and we believe that when women have a share in making laws such atrocities will disappear from the face of the earth. (12)

But, immediately prior to this resolution, the union had passed a resolution declaring the organization's intent to build public sentiment against and to work for laws to prevent "the awful outrages" committed against women and little girls. Although the union had always stood for the protection of women and had worked diligently to raise the age of consent in state laws, and although the defining modifier "white" was eliminated and no mention was made of special concern for the South or of black men, the placement of such language before the lynching resolution appears to be an attempt to mollify southern white women.

Despite assertions that they should never have to defend themselves on such charges, the union included such resolutions for a number of years after the 1894 convention. After that year, financial support for Lucy Thurman's work increased, both in the amount allocated her department and in individual donations. In 1895, she reported that "last year I could not report one penny that had been given to the work," but in the current year $175 had been "placed in my hand" (*Report of National Twenty-Second* 208).

Emilie M. Townes attributes the roots of Willard's uncharacteristic racial rhetoric to the 1890 Atlanta convention, where Willard was influenced by wealthy and influential white southerners. It does appear that her inflammatory remarks began upon her return from that convention. Townes also suggests that Willard was unable to understand Wells's criticism: "The issue was not one of temperance or illiteracy but the effects of radical racism and disenfranchisement. Blacks died due to the charge of rape that was actually a subterfuge for white southern and northern hegemony" (165). Willard did seem unable or unwilling to understand the deep implications of her suggestions and how they might support the lynching mentality. And she was unquestionably infatuated with the attention of southern whites, choosing, either consciously or unconsciously, to court their favor.

After 1885, Willard was obviously aware of the growing dissension within the union, and she struggled to combat divisiveness. However, she failed to completely squelch prejudicial rhetoric toward blacks and other minority groups, which was surprising in light of her earlier record of support for and praise of minorities, and she eventually began to contribute to such rhetoric herself. Her efforts at uniting northern and southern white women seem to have superseded her concerns for unity between black and white members.

Wells was not alone in leveling racist charges against Willard. Perhaps the most notable opposition came from Frederick Douglass, a long-time friend and mentor of Wells and an acquaintance of Willard. Douglass criticized Willard, along with other high-profile religious and political leaders, for naming African Americans a "problem." But while Douglass also charged Willard specifically with implying that black men posed a danger to white women and children, he stopped short of making the explicit charge linking Willard with lynching.

Douglass later, in February of 1895, signed a letter to the British press in defense of Willard. The statement began

> It has come to our knowledge that wrong impressions con-
> cerning the attitude of Miss Willard toward the colored people
> in America have been made in certain quarters, and as an act
> of justice we desire to put on record that no such criticisms
> would be for a moment received in her own country by those
> who have any adequate knowledge of Miss Willard's charac-
> ter and career. (Earhart 361)

The letter continued with an explanation of why WCTU state organizations managed their own "internal affairs," acknowledged the work
of the WCTU as a "society . . . of wide range and womanly benefi-
cence," and ended in noting the good Willard had achieved in her work
as a reformer:

> In view of these facts we feel that for any person or persons
> to give currency to statements harmful to Miss Willard as a
> reformer is most misleading and unjust. Through her influ-
> ence many of the State Unions have adopted resolutions
> against lynching, and the National Union has put itself on
> record in the same way, while the Annual Addresses of the
> President have plainly indicated her disapproval of such law-
> less and barbarous proceedings. (361)

Douglass's was the first signature appended to the document, but the note was also signed by other very prominent personages: authors Julia Ward Howe, Edna Cheney, and Elizabeth Stuart Phelps Ward, abolitionist William Lloyd Garrison, and five others.

Willard's problems with the South and with the treatment of African American members had begun much earlier than the 1893–94 con-
flict with Wells. The organization had special departments for any group members deemed in need of unique attention. To that end, two departments, the Department of Southern Work and the Department of Work Among Colored People, existed throughout most of the 1880s.

In 1889, however, white union members from the South balked at being represented by a separate department. By that time, apparent dissatisfaction was surfacing among some black members as well, and Willard's efforts to placate southern white members increased anger among blacks members.

At the sixteenth national meeting in Chicago, southern members presented the Executive Committee with the following proposal signed by forty-three members from thirteen southern states:

> Dear Sisters: —The Southern delegates, whose names are subjoined, after careful deliberation, address to you the appeal that the Department of Southern Work be abolished for the following reasons:
>
> 1. The South is in no sense a missionary field; each State supports its own work and pays money into the national Treasury: and, so far as we know, none of our States have ever received aid to the amount of one dollar from outside, except in the gratuitous labors of Miss Willard and Mrs. Buell.
>
> 2. It is painful to be reported as a missionary field, as are the colored and Foreign work.
>
> 3. The Southern States occupy positions identical with States of other sections, and prefer to come into National Conventions under identical conditions.
>
> 4. The Southern Unions believe it is contrary to our platform, "No Sectionalism," to make special provision for Southern work. (*Minutes of National Sixteenth* 56)

The WCTU had courted southern women and had merited high praise for its ability to join North and South after the divisive war that had so ruptured the nation. Willard often called for acceptance and understanding "between North and South, Protestant and Catholic, of white and black, of men and women equally" ("Decoration Day Speech" 450). And she had been praised profusely for her efforts toward unification. A typical example is that of Col. Bain of Kentucky: "Miss Willard in the South, and Mrs. Chapin [Superintendent of Southern Work] in the North, have done more to bring together the divided sections, than all the politicians who have ever gone to Washington" (*Minutes of National Ninth* lv).

But the word "equally" in Willard's invitation began increasingly to show a disparity, and the Southerners most courted were southern white women. Signs of discontent began to surface well before 1889, but the southern delegation's admonition that its own classification with "colored and Foreign Work" caused pain among its members implies a prejudicial superiority that must have increased the rupture.

Frances E. W. Harper also made a formal statement at that convention. Harper had been an officer of the Philadelphia and of the Pennsylvania State WCTU since 1875, and Frances Willard introduced her formally to the national convention in Newark in 1876. By 1883, Harper was listed as national Superintendent of Work among Colored People, and by the 1889 meeting, she had an associate, Sarah J. Early. Both Harper

and Early gave routine reports at the 1889 convention, but Harper also
offered the following recommendations:

> 1. That the Superintendent of this department be sustained in
> the work by the local unions.
>
> 2. That the Superintendent of this department be informed by
> State Corresponding Secretary or otherwise of the appoint-
> ment of State Superintendents.
>
> 3. That in dealing with colored women that Christian courtesy
> be shown which is due from one woman to another. (*Minutes
> of National Sixteenth* 26)

Harper had made her recommendations prior to the proposal offered by
the southern delegation; they suggest Harper's already growing frustration with members and officers who refused to work closely with her or
other black leaders. The first two items imply poor cooperation on the
part of state and local officers with their national superintendent; the
third suggests unequal treatment of black members, despite the union's
claim of equality.

Harper, a strong feminist and advocate of temperance reform, had
hoped that the WCTU could provide leadership that would promote both
the cause of women and of her people. In an 1888 essay entitled "The
Woman's Christian Temperance Union and the Colored Woman," Harper
provides a history of the Woman's Crusade for her black audience and
explains her involvement with the union:

> For years I knew very little of its proceedings, and was not
> sure that colored comradeship was very desirable, but hav-
> ing attended a local Union in Philadelphia, I was asked to
> join and acceded to the request, and was made city and after-
> wards State Superintendent of work among colored people.
> Since then, for several years, I have held the position of Na-
> tional Superintendent of work among the colored people of
> the North. When I became national Superintendent there were
> no colored women on the Executive Committee or Board of
> Superintendents. Now there are two colored women on the
> Executive Committee and two on the Board of Superinten-
> dents. (Boyd 205)

Although Harper seems to want to be optimistic about the possibilities
for African Americans within the WCTU, she candidly admits to the
mixed results she herself has experienced:

> Some of the members of the different Unions have met the

question in a liberal and Christian manner; others have not
seemed to have so fully outgrown the old shards and shells of
the past as to make the distinction between Christian affiliation and social equality, but still the leaven of more liberal
sentiments has been at work in the Union and produced some
hopeful results. (205)

The issue of mixed or separate unions itself seems not to have been problematic for Harper. She tells of her "pleasantest remembrances of my
connection with the Woman's Christian Temperance Union" in the state
of Missouri. There, state president Clara Hoffman "declared that the
color line was eliminated." Although black members were given the
option of joining the same union as their white counterparts, "There
was self-reliance and ability enough among them to form a Union of
their own." Members named the union the Harper Union, after the national superintendent. In this case, black members did have the option
of joining an existing white union or forming their own. Black women
in the South were seldom given that choice.

Harper relates other instances where unions "have been opened to
colored women," but complains of prejudicial treatment in the South:

> Southern white women, it may be, fail to make in their minds
> the discrimination between social equality and Christian af-
> filiation. Social equality, if I rightly understand the term, is
> the outgrowth of social affinities and social conditions, and
> may be based on talent, ability, or wealth, on either or all of
> these conditions. Christian affiliation is the union of Chris-
> tians to do Christly work, and to help build up the kingdom
> of Christ amid the sin and misery of the world, under the spiri-
> tual leadership of the Lord Jesus Christ. (Boyd 206)

Harper, while supporting and retaining hope for possibilities within the
WCTU, did not hesitate to take the union to task for its failure to live up
to promises of equality, and especially for refusing to offer the Christian
fellowship that members professed was at the very heart of their organization—a fellowship they repeatedly claimed to extend to all groups.

The most problematic segment of Harper's essay for Frances Willard
and for the WCTU addresses the notion of equal membership for African Americans. As national superintendent, Harper had received a request for information from a black union in Atlanta, asking "if black
sheep must climb up some other way" and requesting information about
proper procedure if that were the case. In her essay, Harper related
Willard's opinion "That the National could not make laws for a State. If
the colored women of Georgia will meet and form a Woman's Christian

Temperance Union for the State, it is my opinion that their officers and delegates will have the same representation in the National" (Boyd 206). Thus, Willard maintained support for the states' rights policy of the organization, but offered an "equal but separate" strategy by which African American unions were recognized; in fact, African American state unions in the South were usually referred to as number 2, as in Georgia State Union #2. State presidents served on the national executive committee, and, at times, other state officers served on various national committees.

Harper could accept separate unions on the state and local level, recognizing that black members might choose to create their own unions and that separation was not always a result of discrimination. But she expected Christian fellowship at all levels and equal authority for black members on the national level.

The request of the southern delegation that the Department of Southern Work be abolished was problematic in another sense. In claiming that each southern state "supports its own work and pays money into the national Treasury," the delegates were simply echoing claims Harper had made for her constituency earlier. In her departmental report to the 1887 convention in Nashville, Harper made clear that, although she had given more than one hundred addresses during the year,

> I have neither asked, that I remember, nor received pecuniary aid at any time from the national Union since I have been Superintendent of this Department, except that at one time I received some circulars for my work from headquarters which were not charged to me, and at present my department is paying its own expenses. (*Minutes of National Fourteenth* ccxiv)

Implications of racial tension are discernible in other rhetoric at the 1887 convention. Harper had asked for clarification on several matters. She asked that the parameters of her work be defined. Here, she again stated that her department paid its own way. In addition, Harper asked that she be allowed to "aid in securing items for the letter to be prepared for the colored people" (57). A successful author of both poetry and prose, she apparently felt that her expertise, both in writing and in knowledge about her own people, was not fully appreciated.

At times, the official rhetoric of the convention also seemed to equivocate on such important matters. In response to a communication from a local black union's request for representation at the national convention, the executive committee recommended "that the General Officers be requested to give particular attention to the work among colored people, and address to them at the earliest possible moment a letter explanatory of plans and our relation one to another" (23). Such phrasing defers any real answer to the legitimate request of the local union. In a

move that might have further frustrated black members, the union passed
the following resolution with regards to the Department of Work among
Colored People several days later:

> Whereas, the colored vote is an important factor in the future
> success of Prohibition and we are impressed with the impor-
> tance of educating the colored women; therefore,
> Resolved, That we give our hearty approval and sincere
> sympathy to the department of work among this people, and
> that we recommend the States to push the work of organiza-
> tion among them, and as a National WCTU we will co-oper-
> ate to the extent of our power. (45)

Such supportive rhetoric, without material practice, would have further
disheartened Harper and her constituency.

Harper must have noticed other discouraging signs in attitudes regarding race. At early conventions, Harper was presented to the convention formally and with praise. After the mid-eighties, however, Sallie
Chapin and other southern white women were most often singled out
for special recognition. Harper must have noted the change in tone as
southern whites became an increasingly important focus of the convention. Her growing realization that the WCTU would not provide the
equal access she envisioned for members of her race must have been
painful. In her 1888 essay for the *A. M. E. Church Review*, Harper wrote,

> Believing, as I do, in human solidarity, I hold that the Woman's
> Christian Temperance Union has in its hands one of the grand-
> est opportunities that God ever pressed into the hands of the
> womanhood of any country. Its conflict is not the contest of
> a social club, but a moral warfare for an imperiled civiliza-
> tion. Whether or not the members of the farther South will
> subordinate the spirit of caste to the spirit of Christ, time will
> show. (Boyd 206)

The official minutes of the 1889 national convention contain no
reference to discussion about eliminating the Department of Work among
Colored People, or of Harper's or Early's refusal to continue as superintendents, but in a copy of the minutes for that year at the WCTU headquarters, its owner, Cornelia B. Forbes, President of the Connecticut
WCTU, has marked through the names of both women. In this and in
other yearly minutes, Forbes had drawn through the names of women
who no longer held offices and had written in names for replacements;
or she had simply crossed through some names, suggesting they no longer
held official positions. On page 9 of the 1889 minutes, she has crossed

out the names of both Harper and Early, suggesting that some action was taken, either pertaining to the status of the department or to the two women's positions. Since both Early and Harper continued with the union in official capacities, it is likely that they were protesting the separate departmental status for African Americans.

In 1890, the Department of Work among Colored People was officially dropped and the field incorporated into the Department of Organization. Fourteen women were named national organizers, including Sallie F. Chapin and three designated specifically for "work among the colored people": Harper, Early, and Mary Marriage Allen (*Minutes of WCTU Eighteenth* 315).

Harper continued her association with the union as both organizer and lecturer throughout the century, but the position proved an uncomfortable one at times, especially at the height of the Wells-Willard controversy. In 1894 when Wells spoke at the national WCTU convention, Harper's report as organizer both encouraged and chided white members. Harper noted that African American women, also interested in organized efforts on behalf of women, more likely joined the King's Daughters, Christian Endeavor, and other organizations. "And yet," proclaimed Harper, "if the work of temperance was vigorously and patiently pushed among them by women in whose friendship they could trust" their numbers within the WCTU might increase. She also implicitly referred to the Wells-Willard conflict:

> Were it true that the worst things said against the negro are sad, and frightful verities; that from his presence such dangers lurk around peaceful and happy homes, as make it unsafe for fathers and husbands to go far beyond their roof tree, then I hold that the deeper the degradation of the people the louder is their call for redemption. ("Mrs. Harper's")

By acknowledging charges against black men without acceding to their verity, Harper used the hypothetical to insist that white women work with greater compassion and acceptance toward the African American race. Refusing to side with either Wells or Willard by explicitly and deliberately diminishing the significance of their quarrel, she called instead for understanding and directed effort on behalf of her race. She presented as a proper example the work of whites among freed African Americans on South Carolina's Sea Island of St. Helena, where whites "act as friends, advisers and teachers" and where only one murder in thirty years had been committed. She insisted that "Between every branch of the human race in the Western Hemisphere there is a community of interests, and our interests all lie in one direction, and we cannot violate the one without disserving the other" ("Mrs. Harper's"). She concluded by asking that work among African Americans be carried on "not as a matter of charity but as a means of self-defense for the country." Thus, Harper chose not to join the controversy but to mediate toward improved relations between the races.

If Harper found prepared presentations rhetorically difficult during this dispute, how much more problematic were occasions when she was questioned directly about her perspective on the great controversy? In 1895, a reporter recounted her reply to explicit questions about Ida Wells's lectures on southern lynchings, noting that "Mrs. Harper replied slowly and apparently measuring the effect of her words." Harper responded,

> I do not approve of Miss Wells' vehemence in dealing with the subject. She is a little too sweeping in her charges. I think that she is unable to discuss the matter salmly [sic], because some of her friends were shot down in the Nashville affair and her mind has been set unduly against the whites. I look at the lynchings as the eruptions of a disease lingering in the body politic, caused by the war. The old-time prejudice still remains, but I believe that it is growing less and less day by day. I do not believe lynchings of negroes who assault girls are brought about alone by the color of the criminals for I have noticed that some white men when accused of similar offenses have had the summary punishment meted out to them. No, I believe that the white man is coming to treat the opposite race more as brothers.
>
> That the better class of whites in the South do not uphold the indiscriminate hanging of negroes was evidenced by the action of the Governor of Georgia a year or two ago in offering $200 for the apprehension and conviction of parties guilty of such a crime. I am only sorry that meetings of the colored people were not held and the reward increased by their subscriptions. ("About")

Harper had been a friend of Wells; she had even titled her novel *Iola Leroy* after Wells (Wells used the pseudonym "Iola" for much of her early writing). Thus, Harper carefully chose her words, distancing from Wells's attacks while offering a sympathetic understanding of Wells's position. She also acknowledged the lingering prejudice and discrimination toward blacks. As she often did, however, she held open her hope for cooperation between the races, recognizing an effort toward achieving justice among "better" whites, a move that might also encourage other whites to seek that classification. Typical of her rhetoric throughout her career, she recognized problems in racial relations, but chose to advance a notion of hope as she mediated among diverse and contradictory positions.

In 1893, the Department of Work among Colored People was rein-
stated at the request of Lucy Thurman of Jackson, Michigan, who also
requested that "its superintendent shall be a colored woman." The motion carried "after considerable discussion," but specifics as to that discussion are not included in convention minutes (*Minutes of National
Twentieth* 37–38). Thurman was chosen national superintendent of the
department, and eventually, by the end of the century, two associates had
joined her: Margaret Murray Washington of Alabama and Frances Joseph of Louisiana.

Washington's accession to national superintendency within the union
reflects divergent approaches among black activists as well. Margaret
Murray Washington was the third wife of Booker T. Washington, whom
Wells consistently criticized for promoting prejudice against higher education for African Americans as well as for encouraging a reduced curriculum for African Americans in elementary and secondary education.
She claimed that he aided the white South "to establish and maintain
throughout the country a color line in politics, in civil rights and in education" (Thompson 259). The disagreement between black leaders, such
as Wells and Washington (or more publicly debated, that between Washington and W. E. B. Du Bois), reflects differing philosophical underpin-
nings with regards to the best course for advancing rights and improved
conditions for blacks. In fact, this disagreement has continued through
the twentieth century for black leaders, most notably in the leadership
styles of Martin Luther King and Malcolm X. The disagreements between black leaders resemble those between temperance women and
suffrage leaders, making it understandable why these women chose to
affiliate with the organizations they did. Like temperance women, Washington chose a more pragmatic, less confrontational position than that
of Wells. Like Stanton, Wells had little patience for the gradualism Washington supported, insisting instead upon immediate equal treatment and
equal rights for her people.

Despite the controversy within the WCTU and the criticism Wells
and some other black leaders leveled at the union, black membership in
the organization continued to grow, and many of the leading black women
in the country retained their association with the union, usually becoming officers. The reasons for this must have been complex, but some moti-
vations seem likely.

For one, personal contact among white and black leaders must have
been an important factor in the attitudes of black women leaders. While
Harper did not hesitate to take WCTU members to task, and did so on a
number of occasions, her personal relationship with many of the women
seems to have been rewarding. Harper once wrote, "One of the pleasantest
remembrances of my connection with the Woman's Christian Temper-

ance Union was the kind and hospitable reception I met in the Missouri State Convention, who declared that the color-line was eliminated" (Boyd 205). Harper noted other reports from state superintendents of instances in which white members had "invited the colored sisters to join them" (Boyd 206). And Harper knew many white women leaders, as she was sometimes their guest as she travelled the country in her official capacity as superintendent. Her acceptance and kind treatment among some leaders must have helped to sustain her.

Further, black women were accepted into many of the local WCTU unions in the North, and white women helped to organize separate black unions when that was the choice of black members. In the South, separate unions provided a means of networking and of gaining the respectability black women found imperative at the end of a century that questioned their integrity and morality.

WCTU membership afforded other benefits to African American women. In the South, the separation of unions provided a substantial number of leadership roles for black women. By the end of the century, Alabama, Arkansas, Georgia, Louisiana, North Carolina, Tennessee, and Texas all had black women state presidents and officers who assumed responsibility for their unions;[3] the state presidents were also national vice-presidents and members of the Executive Committee. Some also served on other national committees as well. Lucy Thurman acknowledged the value of such leadership opportunities for black union members, noting that she "always favored the organization of unions among the colored women for it will be to them just what it has been to our white sisters, the greatest training school for the development of women" (*Report of National Twenty-Second* 208).

Association with the widely respected WCTU afforded an avenue for many black women to move around the country as lecturers and organizers, and as representatives of their unions to the national and international conventions. In addition to Frances Harper and Sarah J. Early, other influential and noted black women became national organizers and lecturers, including Rosetta Douglass Sprague, daughter of Frederick Douglass, Frances Joseph [Gaudet], Amanda Berry Smith, Mary Cordelia Montgomery Booze, Mary A. Lynch, Frances E. L. Preston, and Lucy Thurman. Membership afforded opportunities for international travel as well. Lucy Thurman was a delegate to the World WCTU in England in 1896, and Frances Joseph served as a delegate to the international WCTU convention in England in 1900. Jessie Carney Smith's note regarding Frances Preston would have applied to other organizers and lecturers as well: "This position [national lecturer for the WCTU] facilitated her speaking engagements and recitations before lecture associations, clubs, churches, lyceums and other groups" (871).

For some African American women committed to improving conditions for their race, the WCTU structure offered a measure of support for achieving those goals. According to Dorothy Salem, "the WCTU offered black women an organized vehicle through which they could improve family life, health and morality" (36). Harper also pointed to the good provided some black communities. She appreciated union efforts at helping African Americans become independent of the curse of alcohol, and she was pleased that the organizational structure aided some black unions in founding orphan asylums for African American children (Boyd 206).

There were other positive aspects to WCTU membership for African Americans as well. Such associations afforded opportunities to influence and change negative attitudes about blacks, especially among those who had the power to model and expedite the change in such attitudes. In 1896, while in England as a delegate to the World WCTU, Lucy Thurman was the house guest of Lady Henry Somerset. In 1900 when Frances Joseph served as representative to the international organization, she too was the house guest of British nobility and met with Queen Victoria in private audience. Joseph also met with President and Mrs. McKinley during the national convention in Washington. According to Jessie Carney Smith, M. A. McCurdy—secretary of the Atlanta city and county WCTU, and later secretary of the state organization and superintendent of presswork for the second Georgia WCTU—"became widely known throughout the state and in major cities" (702) through the WCTU and the *Woman's World*, "a newspaper that focused on the intellectual, moral, and spiritual progress of people" (701). These leaders had a unique opportunity to present a positive image of African Americans to powerful people.

By the end of the century, African American women had organized the many members of black women's clubs into the powerful National Association of Colored Women. Many of the leaders of this and earlier organizations were strong leaders well before they joined the WCTU. But the exposure and experience permitted black women in their relationship with the WCTU might have seemed valuable, even to these women as they formed their own organizations, and would certainly have been helpful to the less experienced. Hazel Carby has noted black women's recognition of the "necessity of systematic organization for their own protection" at the end of the century, but suggests also that "despite the apparent plea for the autonomous organization of black women as black women . . . [many] knew that in order to transform the social and political condition of black women alliances with white women were important, if not crucial" (118). The WCTU was, in many ways, the perfect organization for forming such alliances. Darlene Clark Hine notes similar realizations for Harper:

In this capacity she tried to help those who wished to join the white group to do so and those who preferred to organize themselves separately to do that. For Frances Ellen Watkins Harper it was a matter of coalition building. She recognized and did not apologize for racism among some of the individuals with whom they might need to affiliate but declared this a "relic . . . from the dead past!" (1: 535)

Although racism was practiced by some inside the WCTU, many black women had positive experiences in their association with the organization, and they often used the union for their own benefit, making use of the organizational structure and the reputation of the WCTU to serve their own purposes. The controversy between Wells and Willard, while angering most members, nonetheless heightened racial sensitivity within an organization that had always professed to invite all members equally. The southern states still maintained primarily separate unions, but the national union went on record against lynching. Whether to improve its own image, or out of sincere concern for African Americans (probably some of both), the attention given to black women at the national level increased, and black members were increasingly selected as delegates in favored capacities, such as representatives at international events and the honor guard at Willard's funeral.

5

Red-Nosed Angels and the Corseted Crusade: Newspaper Accounts of Nineteenth-Century Temperance Reformers

We have received with a request for their publication, the proceedings of a Female Temperance organization in Medina. The Proceedings are rather lengthy for our columns. We give the resolution adopted, and the substance of action had.

—"Movement of the Ladies," 1853 Ohio Woman's
Temperance Convention

The Ladies of New York have just held a State Temperance Convintion [*sic*] at Albany. The attendance was very large, the addresses speeches and resolution pithy and posted.

—"Ladies and Temperance," Report of 1853 New York
Woman's Temperance Convention

NEWSPAPER COVERAGE OF nineteenth-century women's temperance activity reflects a general discomfort with women's changing roles, especially as those roles became more public. Temperance women's refusals to be relegated to the private was threatening for many, both within and outside the movement, who feared women would lose their feminine qualities. Therefore, newspaper reporting focused largely on issues of gender rather than on the subject of temperance. Phrases placing added emphasis on gender surfaced repeatedly, such as "male men" and "female women" to connote favorable, conventional behavior; and "male women" and "female men" for derogatory, radical actions. Early critics often noted women's becoming "unsexed" by taking on public personas and concentrated on speakers' masculine or feminine appearance; late in the century, even favorable reports often focused far more on women's physical features and dress, and on their backgrounds and values, than on their words or on temperance reform.

Newspaper coverage of women's temperance activities increased or decreased according to the novelty and excitement surrounding such endeavors. At mid-century, legislation with regards to the liquor problem—such as the Maine Law (1851), which banned the manufacture and sale of alcoholic beverages in the state of Maine—elevated interest and activity in temperance generally. Such legislation spurred hopes for reform, but in other states, judicial action nullifying some legislation for controlling the sale of alcohol and the failure to enforce many laws that remained on the books incited furor and boosted women's efforts on behalf of temperance reform.

Increased involvement on the part of women piqued journalistic interest; at the same time, women's greater involvement met resistance when the novelty wore off or when the women tried to take a more active role in proceedings traditionally controlled by men. Judging from newspaper coverage of women's temperance activity, journalists delighted in reporting such activity because of its novelty, often further sensationalizing events by dwelling on the unusual or by presenting outlandish headers to introduce reports.

Women's temperance activity was especially threatening at mid-century. Women were not vying for men's place and power in equal rights conventions; since such organizations were new, no one was being displaced. But men had traditionally controlled temperance organizations, and women's calls for active involvement questioned men's right to dominate and control such organizations and activities.

Furthermore, since the demands of woman's rights activists appeared to reflect self-interest, antagonists could reject such women as selfish anomalies. But temperance women presented their cause as a selfless concern for the poor, for suffering children, and for wronged women. Such an approach presented a greater problem for opponents, since these women, for the most part, were making use of acceptable cultural codes and, therefore, were less easily dismissed. Newspaper reports reflected a discomfort about how to deal with such women. Some accounts were openly hostile, some supportive, but most subtly undermined the efforts of temperance women.

Understandably, newspaper coverage was greatest when women's actions seemed radical, provoked great controversy, or in some way created widespread public interest. Mid-century activity—controversies over a woman's right to speak in temperance conventions, women marching upon and aggressively attacking liquor establishments, even the novel appearance of women public speakers—led to substantial coverage of women's temperance exercises. Again in the 1870s, the eruption of the Woman's Crusade, wherein women took to the streets and saloons to protest the sale of liquor, attracted great attention. Between these two periods, and especially during the Civil War, women's efforts on behalf of temperance were deemed less newsworthy. Many of the leading temperance women became active participants in the war, working in the U.S. Sanitary Commission or in some way visibly supporting troops in the field. Although they often continued their vigorous support for temperance, press attention generally focused on their war efforts. For example, Eliza Daniel Stewart continued her efforts to protect college students and soldiers from the dangers of alcohol, but public attention focused on her active participation in the U.S. Sanitary Commission and on her other efforts to support the troops.

The first major coverage of temperance women came at mid-century, and the reporting reflects the contemporary cultural notions of woman's place. In the 1850s, some women became active, and sometimes violent, in addressing the abuses of alcohol. Newspaper reporting focused on the excitement created by these women's activities, both the commotion surrounding the exclusion of women from active participation in temperance conventions and the decidedly non-passivist measures some women took in seeking to diminish the effects of saloons. Reports concerning women's aggression against liquor sellers were sometimes humorous but generally sympathetic to women, based on the assumption that women taking such radical action had been victimized and acted out of frustration and desperation. Such empathy reflects accepted notions of gender, portraying women as vulnerable and in need of protection, and thereby justified in their radical action when that protection was greatly undermined.

One such incident in Mount Vernon, Ohio, March 1852, was reported as the act of "five women, rendered desperate by the intemperance of their male relatives." When the women asked the liquor dealer to cease selling alcohol to men in their families, "[h]e treated them roughly and tried to drive them away, but they did not leave till they had smashed the liquor bottles, flasks, jars, and almost everything smashable. The grog-dealer has prosecuted them for damages" ("Temperance Notes" March 1853, 43).

The reporter's sympathy for the "desperate" women is apparent, as is that of a correspondent for the *New York Daily Tribune* reporting on similar action in Baraboo, Wisconsin. The writer there related that "three or four rum-drinking men abused their wives by beating them, turning them out of doors at dead of night, and in various other ways, until their

wives thought that death would be far preferable to their present life."
Finally, "some 50 of our most noble females" destroyed the liquor and ale
in several establishments" ("A Temperance Revolution" 6). Women who
came to the aid of distressed and abused sisters became not only respectable,
but virtuous.

The *Pennsylvania Freeman* picked up a similar incident the following year, one in which a woman tavern owner was implicated:

> *The Cleveland Herald* gives the particulars of a recent move-
> ment on the part of women of Ashland, Ashland County, Ohio,
> to restrain the liquor traffic, which is quite novel. *The Herald*
> says: "Some thirty of them, well backed by gentlemen, pro-
> ceeded to the grocery of Anthony Jacobs, and asked him to
> discontinue the sale of liquor and the use of a 'bagatelle'[1] board
> which had enticed many of the youth and some of the mar-
> ried men from their homes. He refused, and the ladies chopped
> his 'bagatelle' table into kindling-wood and emptied his liquors.
> They then visited another grocery and a tavern, both of which
> capitulated. Mrs. Witz, better known as 'Mother Yonkers,' was
> obstinate; and the spigots were pulled from her whiskey bar-
> rels, and now not a *drop* of the critter can a solitary horse-
> man, which may be seen in the twilight of a springday wending
> his way into that town, obtain to put into his *camphor bottle*."
> ("The Cleveland" 43)

The *Herald*'s favor lies with the women, since their actions were a result
of their desperation and were, therefore, understandable. And even though
the 1853 report ends with humor, the fun is not at the expense of the
women, but of the horseman seeking liquor for his camphor bottle.

Later that year The *Pennsylvania Freeman* approved the exonera-
tion of a woman who took such aggressive action: "Mrs. Gertrude Salisbury,
who was arraigned in Jamestown, New York, a few weeks ago, for smash-
ing whiskey bottles at Laseur's Tavern, a place frequented by her husband,
was tried at Kennedysville, a few days since. A very intelligent jury acquitted her" ("Temperance Notes" September 1853, 139).

Although newspapers nearly always reported action taken on behalf of helpless or abused women favorably, they proved more reluctant
to provide positive coverage of non-victimized temperance women, especially those who assumed the 'masculine' role of lecturer. When Lucretia
A. Wright lectured on temperance in Cleveland, the *Cleveland Daily Plain
Dealer* had no praise to offer:

> Miss Lucretia A. Wright lectured last night. The Hall was full.
> We were disappointed. We expected to hear an eloquent ap-

peal for the temperance cause, but nothing of the sort came
to our ears.—The lady is poorly fitted for public speaking. She
harangues a good deal in the "spread eagle" style. Her voice
is pitched several degrees above *screech-o* and is consequently
unpleasant. Her declamation is parson-like and measured. She
evidently speaks by rote, or memory. She requires to exert her
physical powers too strongly. This produces a labored impression and is unpleasant to the hearer. . . . In our opinion, Miss
Wright is out of her sphere. ("Miss Lucretia" 3)

Such an assault—the uncomplimentary reference to Wright's gesturing
and the disparaging use of negative terms—dwells on characteristics that
would have been acceptable for male speakers but seemed too masculine
for women. Apparently feeling some discomfort at such an ungentle-
manly attack on a woman, the newspaper assured readers that such comments were made in "good faith and all earnestness," and suggested that
"Miss Wright has made herself the object of criticism, and we have felt
at liberty to speak of her plainly, and as if she were a *masculine*. There can
be no distinction of sex on the rostrum,—there is in the nursery" (3).
The reporter made it clear that a woman who went out of her sphere should
not expect the gentle treatment she might be accustomed to when fulfill-
ing her "feminine" role.

Reports of early assaults on liquor establishments focused primarily
on the sensational behavior of the women involved, but for speakers such
as Miss Wright, the attention sometimes shifted, understandably, toward
delivery; but most often accounts of speakers centered on dress and physical characteristics, especially with regards to accepted cultural notions
according to gender. Many mid-century speakers heightened such interest by radically altering their traditional feminine marks. Speakers began wearing the modified dress adopted by Elizabeth Smith Miller,
daughter of Gerrit Smith. Amelia Bloomer defended the use of the dress—
a short skirt (usually knee length or hemmed at mid-calf) over Turkish
trousers—and subsequently had her name forever identified with it. Those
wearing the "Bloomer" costume also usually cut their hair short, a shock-
ing transgression of nineteenth-century feminine markings for women.
Remarks on such an "unfeminine" appearance often superseded remarks
on either the lecturer's purpose or message, and offered an easy means of
attack for newspapers in opposition to a speaker's activity.

For example, commenting on happenings at the Brick Church meeting, The *New York Courier*'s James Watson Webb editorialized,

Anniversary week has the effect of bringing to New York many
strange specimens of humanity, masculine and feminine. Anti-
quated and very homely females made themselves ridiculous

by parading the streets in company with hen-pecked husbands, attenuated vegetarians, intemperate Abolitionists and sucking clergymen, who are afraid to say "no" to a strong-minded woman for fear of infringing upon her rights. Shameless as these females—we suppose they *were* females—looked, we should really have thought they would have blushed as they walked the streets to hear the half-suppressed laughter of their own sex and the remarks of men and boys. The Bloomers figured extensively in the anti-slavery amalgamation convention, and were rather looked up to, but their intemperate ideas would not be tolerated in the temperance meeting at the Brick Chapel. (Ida Harper 91)

The report noted the "perfect warfare of tongues" at the Brick Church meeting during which "the women were compelled to hold their tongues and depart" with "a number of male Betties and subdued husbands," and concluded with the notation that "the Bloomers put their credentials in their breeches pockets and assembled at Dr. Trall's Cold Water Institute, where the men and Bloomers all took a bath and a drink together" (91). The report ignored purpose and message, resorting to negative gender typing for both women and men participants. Such a play on words—here suggesting temperance women who stepped outside their sphere were intemperate—was a tactic the women themselves often used in their speeches.

Other newspapers also focused negatively on appearance and dress, reflecting a fear of change in women's roles. After the women's meeting at Broadway Tabernacle following the Old Brick Church meeting, Moses Beach, editor of the *New York Sun*, reflected such an attitude and relied on biblical authority, as well, to denigrate the women speakers:

Could a Christian man, cherishing a high regard for woman and for the proprieties of life feel that he was promoting woman's interests and the cause of temperance by being introduced to a temperance meeting by Miss Susan B. Anthony, her ungainly form rigged out in bloomer costume and provoking the thoughtless to laughter and ridicule by her very motions upon the platform? Would he feel that he was honoring the women of his country by accepting as their representatives women whom they must and do despise? Will any pretend to say that women, whose tongues have dishonored their God and their Savior, while uttering praise of infidels and infidel theories, are worthy to receive the suffrages of their Christian sisters? (Ida Harper 90)

Even when not focusing on appearance, many newspapers found

ample cause for disparagement. Another report of the meetings held on May 14, 1853, at Broadway Tabernacle, focused nonetheless on gender. Some women and many men had left the Brick Church gathering to call a separate temperance meeting. The account presented the women as aggressive, their voices "unfeminine," and their behavior "unwomanly":

> THE BATTLE OF THE SEXES.—On Saturday evening the Broadway Tabernacle reverberated with the shrill, defiant notes of Miss Lucy Stone and her "sisters," who have thrown down the gauntlet to the male friends of temperance and declared not literally "war to the knife" but conflict with tongues. . . . Henceforth the women's rights ladies—including among them the misses, Lucy herself, Emily Clark, Susan B. Anthony, Antoinette Brown, some Harriets and Angelinas, Melissas and Hannahs, with a Fanny too (and more is the pity for it is a sweet name) and sundry matrons whose names are *household* words in *newspapers*—are to be in open hostility to the regularly constituted temperance agencies, under cover of association with whom they have contrived to augment their notoriety. The delegates at the Brick Church, who took the responsibility of knocking off these parasites, deserve the thanks of the temperance friends the Union through. (*New York Commercial-Advertiser* qtd. in Ida Harper 90)

This interpretation of "The Battle of the Sexes" unequivocally encourages readers to disdain such surly women. The emphasis on "household," a woman's presumed sphere, juxtaposed with "newspapers," unquestionably not of a woman's sphere, is intended to connote inappropriateness; such impropriety is further accented by noting the women's "hostility" to "regularly constituted temperance agencies." Suggesting that these women have defiled otherwise "feminine" and "sweet" names places further negative connotations on their indecorous behavior and suggests that their conduct might astonish anyone with reasonable expectations.

One might expect better treatment from temperance newspapers, but publishers generally participated in the traditionally male-controlled reform organizations and were in league with male temperance leaders who excluded women. Reporting on the same meeting, The *Organ*, the New York temperance newspaper, referred to the women's dress, but angrily blamed woman's rights for creating a bane for the temperance cause:

> The harmony and pleasantness of the meeting were disturbed by an evidently preconcerted irruption of certain women, who have succeeded beyond doubt in acquiring notoriety, however much they may have failed in winning respect. The notorious Abby Kelly, the Miss Stone whose crusade

against the Christian doctrine on the subject of marriage has shocked the better portion of society, and several other women in pantaloons were present insisting upon their right to share in the deliberations of the convention.

We wish our friends abroad to understand that the breeze got up here is nothing but an attempt to ride the woman's rights theory into respectability on the back of Temperance. And what absurd, infidel and licentious follies are not packed up under the general head of woman's rights, it would puzzle any one to say.

The *Organ* correctly made the connection between temperance and woman's rights, but failed to understand that for many women the two issues were inextricably linked.

While highly critical of women who did not fulfill societal expectations according to gender, the newspaper expressed discomfort at the disreputable treatment of women at the Brick Church meeting, reflecting a problem for many reporters given that such attacks on women infringed upon accepted gentlemanly behavior: "While, however, we approve the act excluding the women at the Brick Church, we feel bound to say that we regretted what seemed to us an unnecessary acerbity on the part of some of the gentlemen opposing them" (Ida Harper 91).

Reports that emphasize the Bloomer attire are especially revealing because reporters never commented on or suggested the inappropriateness of other kinds of frivolous and revealing dress worn by some women; the fear obviously arose from the Bloomer's deviation from cultural expectations for women. Bloomers covered women fully, while other "stylish" dress left women's bodies, at least their upper torsos, greatly exposed; such revealing attire was usually worn by wealthy and socially prominent women and was, therefore, generally accepted as proper. Anthony often protested against such dress. In September of 1852, for example, at the New York Woman's Rights Convention immediately following the Whole World Temperance Convention, Anthony protested the nomination of Elizabeth Oakes Smith for president of the organization, a nomination instigated by Smith's friend Paulina Wright Davis.[2] Anthony remembered the dress of the two as follows: "Both attended the meeting and the convention in short-sleeved, low-necked white dresses, one with a pink, the other with a blue embroidered wool delaine sack with wide, flowing sleeves, which left both neck and arms exposed" (Ida Harper 72). According to Ida Harper, "Anthony spoke out boldly and said that nobody who dressed as she [Smith] did could represent the earnest, solid, hardworking women of the country for whom they were making the demand for equal rights (72). Smith was not elected; instead, Lucretia Mott became president.

The press also chose to highlight and question the rights and abilities of women who failed to choose traditional paths for women, especially that of marriage. During the spring of 1853, Susan B. Anthony, Amelia Bloomer, and Antoinette Brown toured "the principal cities" of New York lecturing on temperance. The *Utica Telegraph*, reporting on their stop in Utica, chose to question the femininity of the speakers and, as often happened, focused on Anthony's unmarried status, displaying disdain for single women and revealing common assumptions that such women lived in an unnatural state. Typically, the *Telegraph* attributed her radical position to an anger at men for not having chosen her as a mate and questioned her ability to speak about matters regarding married women. With the heading "Miss Susan B. Anthony and Rev. A. L. Brown on the Stump," the *Telegraph* reported that

> Mechanics' Hall was tolerably well filled last evening by persons wishing to hear the above-named ladies "spout" about temperance. Seven-eighths of the audience was composed of women, and there was noticeable an absence of all rank, fashion and wealth. The *ladies* proper of Utica don't seem desirous of giving countenance to the silly vagaries disseminated by these strong-minded women. We conceived a very unfavorable opinion of this *Miss* Anthony when she performed in this city on a former occasion, but we confess that, after listening attentively to her discourse last evening, we were inexpressibly disgusted with the impudence and impiety evinced in feelings of strong hatred towards male men, the effect, we presume, of jealousy and neglect. . . . With a degree of impiety which was both startling and disgusting, this shrewish *maiden* counseled the numerous wives and mothers present to separate from their husbands whenever they became intemperate, *and particularly not to allow the said husbands to add another child to the family* (probably no *married* advocate of woman's rights would have made this remark). Think of such advice given in public by one who claims to be a *maiden* lady!
>
> . . . if there is one characteristic of the sex which more than another elevates and ennobles it, it is the *persistency* and intensity of woman's love for man. But what does Miss Anthony know of the thousand delights of married life; of the sweet stream of affection, of the golden ray of love which beams ever through life's ills? Bah! Of a like disgusting character was her advice to mothers about not using stimulants, even when prescribed by physicians, for the benefit of the young. What in the name of crying babies does Miss Anthony know about such matters?

In our humble judgment, it is by no means complimentary to wives and mothers to be found present at such discourses, encouraging such untruthful and pernicious advice. If Miss Anthony's ideas were practically applied in the relations of life, women would sink from the social elevation they now hold and become the mere *appendages* of men. Miss Anthony concluded with a flourish of trumpets, that the woman's rights question could not be put down, that women's souls were beginning to expand, etc., after which she gathered her short skirts about her tight pants, sat down and wiped her spectacles. (Ida Harper 83–84)

The *Telegraph*'s account is similar to other reports in a number of ways. The disparaging emphasis placed on "Miss" and "maiden," favorable terms for very young women, denigrates unmarried women past a certain age and questions their propriety and competence in offering counsel in matters of children and marital sexual behavior. Single male doctors and ministers did not meet with such condescension when offering advice on similar matters, even though their time spent with children would have been far less, and they too, presumably, had no personal experience with marital sexual relations. Like early accounts that described women's delivery as shrill and spouting, the lexical choices here—"shrewish," "disgusting," and "pernicious"—further impugn the speaker's credibility. Women's constancy in delivering societal and spousal expectations, here called "persistency," draws accolades from this reporter. Another revealing choice, the double emphasis on sex and gender—"male men"—reflects the fear nineteenth-century reporters had about the changing roles of the sexes. The term "female woman" cropped up in accounts as well.

All reports of the women's activity were not negative, however. Some newspapers reported favorably on the speeches and meetings. In New York, the influential *New York Tribune*, whose editor, Horace Greeley, was active in temperance and women's causes, supported women's public temperance activities. For example, when Bloomer, Brown, and Anthony spoke on temperance in New York City's Metropolitan Hall on February 1853, the *Tribune* declared the meeting "a most brilliant and successful affair," noting that the audience was "almost as large and fully as respectable as the audiences that nightly greeted Jenny Lind and Catherine Hays[3] during their engagement in that hall" ("Great Gathering" 5).

In addition to presumedly "objective" reporting, Greeley responded at great length to derogatory letters to the editor and criticized the conventions that excluded women. For instance, after the World's Temperance Convention (or Half-World's Temperance Convention) in which some men refused to let Antoinette Brown take the platform, Greeley wrote,

The World's Temperance Convention has completed the third of its four business sessions. The results may be summed up as follows:

> *First Day*—Crowding a Woman off the platform;
> *Second Day*—Gagging her.
> *Third Day*—Voting that she shall *stay* gagged.

Having thus disposed of the main question, we presume the incidentals will be finished up this morning. ("The World's" 4)

His biting tone left no doubts as to Greeley's disgust with some temperance men at the Half-World's Convention. But, like other editors, Greeley began to limit the space given to women's causes as the novelty and sensation accompanying their new roles began to subside. By June of 1854, the *Tribune* declared that the newspaper would provide "not as much space as previously" given to women's issues, noting that it could not "provide space to say a truth for the 20th time," but would "publish so much of those proceedings as is essential to a fair history of the times, including such suggestions of Reform as are substantially novel or else particularly adapted to some existing exigency" ("Employment" 4). The newspaper must have become reluctant to spare reporters for coverage of women's conventions. Beginning at this time, reports of women's temperance conventions took the form of letters from the president to the newspapers.[4]

Sometimes positive, "objective" reporting could be clearly undermined by later reports or by accompanying letters or references. On January 14, 1853, the *Cleveland Daily Plain Dealer* reported the Ohio Women's Temperance Convention as "a highly respectable meeting" and praised Medina's Mrs. Bronson for her "most earnest and truthful address, which bore proof of having been prepared with much care" ("Women's State" 2).

But immediately following the convention report, the newspaper printed an obviously bogus letter from "Temperance Valley" under the header "Great Commotion, Motion":

Dear Editor:—All is hurly burly here at Temperance Valley, nothing to be thought of but this great woman's convention. Great commotion among the wives and mothers, all looking out without doubt, for a promotion. But doleful lamentations and mourning are heard among the husbands and little ones. Husbands turned into the kitchen and children wandering about the streets with unwashed faces and uncombed hair, while mothers are making us laws. O! what rich times we shall have, when we women get to voting and being statesmen and stateswomen. Yours, Nina Nial

Even though the letter had no authentic signature, the message regarding neglected husbands and children would have reinforced many of the fears underlying opposition to women speakers.

Many of these trends continued throughout the century, but the WCTU's active efforts to influence press reportage in the last quarter century somewhat altered newspaper accounts. Leaders organized and taught members to provide prepared information for newspapers, and, most significantly, the women appropriated the very emphasis on appearance that had been problematic for earlier speakers in order to reassure readers that women were not becoming masculinized. Early focus on the "manly" or "masculinized" speaker shifted to descriptions of the "womanly" rhetor.

Beginning with the first meeting of the national organization, leaders reserved front seats for reporters and were careful to thank them publicly for "the patience manifested during the sittings, and for the correctness and fidelity with which they reported the proceedings" (*Minutes of the First* 39). Their "Plan of Work" exhibits further evidence of their awareness of the importance of the press.

The lengthiest section of the Plan of Work, "Of Making Public Sentiment," recognizes that "people are informed, convinced, convicted, pledged" (24). This section offers nine points of activity for members, the most important for this discussion being the seventh: "Seeking permission to edit a column in the interests of temperance in every newspaper in the land, and in all possible ways enlisting the press in this reform" (25).

Reporting for the first few years of the organization's existence, if not always positive, was not overtly negative. At Cleveland in 1874, the *Cleveland Daily Plain Dealer* had highlighted disagreements noting that "Most of the afternoon was wasted in a wrangle over a proposition to admit all attending ladies as delegates" and pointed to "innumerable and tedious speeches" before a compromise was reached. On subsequent days the *Plain Dealer* reported the continuation of the "wrangle" ("Another" 3).

The WCTU's minutes offer a different perspective on the incident, or at least a dissimilar rhetorical presentation:

> A motion was made by Mrs. Anna Sabine, of Ohio, that the lady visitors of this convention be admitted to its discussions, as recommended by the Committee on credentials, namely, with the power of discussion—but not by voting.
> The motion elicited warm and protracted debate, in which a large number of ladies participated. It was carried. (*Minutes of the First* 13)

Newspaper reports in Cincinnati and Newark in the ensuing two years were generally favorable. However, when the convention met in

Chicago in 1877, negative reporting angered the women and prompted them to better organize in their efforts to influence the press. For example, bold headers in the *Chicago Times* made the convention seem amusing and insignificant. On October 25, 1877, the headlines ran as follows:

The Product of the Pump

The Members of the Woman's National
Temperance Union Extol It as Far Above Corn-Juice (8)

Rum Routers

Bustline Army of Crusaders Now En-Camped in Farwell Hall
And When They March Forth There Will be Dismay Among John
Barleycorn's Followers (8)

The following day headers were even more outrageous:

There's Whisky in the Jar

And the Ladies at Farwell Hall Have
Discovered That There is More Behind the Bar
Which is Why There is "Much Heap Talk"
and a Vast Amount of Enthusiasm (12)

And the following day:

The Toper's Doom.

It was Sealed by the Temperance Ladies at Farwell Hall on Yesterday
For They Passed a Series of Resolutions Considerably Longer than
the Moral Law. And Adopted a Memorial Petitioning Congress to
Suppress the Liquor Traffic Instanter. They Furthermore Decided on a
Badge and Appointed Several Hundred Special Committees
A Variety of Miscellaneous Business (3)

The *Times* also had fun at the expense of the women speakers:

> Mrs. Pinkham of Fond du Lac, certainly the most enthusiastic and picturesque speaker of all, came on and made a very stirring speech. Prohibition out and out is what she wants, and when she wants anything bad she says so at the top of her voice. The good work will be pushed on in the Badger state she says while she is able to move. She is in robust vigor now. A short-hand reporter died from trying to keep up with her fine flow of language. When her fifteen minutes were up she was

recalled, and, going to the other side of the platform, gave them another stirring up. She had a double round of applause.

Mrs. Mary T. Lathrap of Jackson, Mich., made an able speech, warmly faforing [sic] the cause of prohibition. She took a tilt at tobacco, the twin curse with drink, and the first lesson in intemperance. Mrs. Lathrap occupies a pulpit in Jackson, and is a very excellent and impressive speaker. Her heart is in the work of temperance. ("There's Whiskey" 12)

On the final day of the convention, the *Times* noted that "A long-winded discussion followed and all kinds of drink were fired in," and evaluated the proceedings by explaining that "It was chiefly remarkable for the vast amount of talk indulged in" ("The Toper's" 3).

By the fourth day of the Chicago convention, then Corresponding Secretary Frances Willard, offered the following resolution:

> That in view of the formative influence exerted by the public press, we deprecate the flippant jests and cruel levity with which the degradation and suffering caused by intemperance is often treated by our newspapers, and we beg our journalists to remember that they wield a mighty and subtle power, which may be used either for purification of National character and the permanence of freedom, or for the demoralization and the downfall of a Republic, which can endure only as it rests upon intelligence and morality. (*Minutes of the Fourth* 177)

The organization established a standing committee of six women called "On Influencing the Press," later to become a department, that continued throughout the century. Comprised of some of the WCTU's most influential members, the department labored vigorously to assure more positive reporting of WCTU activities.

One way in which the WCTU redirected traditional reporting to its advantage was in matters of dress and appearance. Members carefully avoided dress that would draw criticism to their persons and away from their cause. Leaders of the WCTU stressed to members that the purpose of dress was to conceal, to protect from the weather, and to suggest rather than to define the shape, especially shaping by means of corsets and other binding paraphernalia. Such meticulous attention to dress served the WCTU well. Newspapers still led with physical descriptions of the women, much of it probably provided by members of the Press Department. At this time, however, the reports usually hinted at an acceptance of the women because of their "proper" attire and their feminine appearance. Accompanying sketches of the conventions depicted appropriately feminine gatherings (plates 23–25). A typical report is that of the *Baltimore*

American and Commercial Advertiser during the 1878 annual convention of the WCTU:

> Persons passing on the leading streets and riding in the street cars yesterday must have met groups of ladies who looked like strangers in the city, and who also bore unmistakable evidences of belonging to some semi-religious body. Some wore simple drab and the small white-frilled Quaker bonnets, others were tall and clad in somber travelling suits looking severely Puritanical, and more again were richly but yet tastefully attired in silk dresses and subdued bonnets, such as suited serious-minded ladies not very juvenile in years. . . . [A]lthough ladies of a middle age predominated among the delegates, yet there were several ladies of twenty years or thereabouts among them, and the Convention was hardly less deficient in representation of beauty than in representation of brains, of which it had a plenty. ("Religious" 4)

The following day, the same newspaper commented approvingly, "One fails to see the short-haired, masculee-looking female, clad in [indistinguishable] and a man's hat, who is associated in the popular mind as the representative delegate in women's conventions" ("Local Events" 4).

Such concern with women's appearance almost always included a categorization according to age. Newspaper accounts generally referred to generational make-up of convention goers; the older age of participants seemed to offer reassurance, probably because of the grandmotherly connotations associated with age, but also because of reassurances that these women were not neglecting motherly and wifely responsibilities at home: "From the platform the auditorium revealed a very serene sea of faces, which on the average have been touched by the passing of 40 years and which were largely motherly-looking and markedly intelligent" ("Notable Women" 2).

Newspapers often included sketches of the most prominent women attending conventions, usually describing each in detail. For example, the *Cincinnati Daily Enquirer* reported on a number of women attending the 1875 convention in Cincinnati. In describing President Annie Wittenmyer, the *Enquirer* noted,

> This lady is a fine specimen of that rarest of beauties, a beautiful old woman. She has experienced the sorrows and troubles of more than sixty summers. Her hair is silvery gray, almost white, and is puffed at the sides and forms a round, full and genial face, which looks like an old style portrait that has escaped from some ancient collection to mingle in the bustle and stir of life. ("Crusaders" 8)

The *Enquirer* also reported that Mrs. S. M. S. Henry "is of medium height, fair complexion . . . a lady of about forty years of age, and some silver threads have crept into the dark hair" (8).

Such obsession with age was standard and seems to be part of an effort to categorize and make sense of this new woman, who could hardly be classified as aggressive but, on the other hand, kindled interest and a certain amount of concern, since she did not fit neatly into traditional categories. Just as a woman's "matronly" appearance provided clues about this "new woman," her age, especially following the Miss or Mrs. always attached to her name, provided a wealth of information that might further define her nature. The *St. Louis Post-Dispatch*, in giving brief summaries of women in attendance at the 1884 WCTU convention, always highlighted their age:

> Miss Anna Gordon . . . is 23, lively and has a trim slight form, which she dresses in colors.

> Miss Jennie Smith . . . 45 years . . . is not cultured, but speaks intelligently. Her features are sharp and clear and her manner is winning.

> Mrs. H. H. Wagoner . . . a retiring lady of 39.

> Mrs. Anna Sneed Carins is exactly 43 years. ("Notable Women" 2)

During the convention, the *Post-Dispatch* also offered a description of Frances Willard both on the day prior to the meetings' convening, October 21, and later on the 24th, along with descriptions of other major speakers. On October 21, the *Post-Dispatch* presented Willard as

> a slight, delicate middle-aged lady, [who] wears her light brown hair brushed smoothly down over her temples. She dresses very plainly but tastefully, in subdued colors. No one can look at her clear, resolute eyes without feeling that the glasses she wears are entirely for use and not at all for ornament. Jewelry is not a weakness of hers, and a pretty little gold watch that peeps out from her waist pocket is the only thing of this kind visible. ("Convention of the WCTU" 2)

Willard's sense of audience aided her in winning reporters to her cause. Her simple hairstyle and natural complexion, along with her modest dress and eschewing of flashy or elaborate decoration, increased her credibility and disarmed would-be cynics, especially since her demeanor suggested that, rather than seeking notoriety for herself, her interest resided in the cause of temperance.

On October 24, the *Post-Dispatch*, in front page coverage, presented

"Sketches of Prominent Members of the WCTU." In introducing the
sketches, the account focuses attention on attire to the point of referring
to the convention as a coming together of "dresses." The front page coverage included pencil drawings and accompanying descriptions of many
of the leaders. Following are excerpts from those descriptions:

> MISS FRANCES E. WILLARD, PRESIDENT, WCTU (plates
> 26, 27) Miss Willard, of all women, is of uncertain age but the
> man that can get any woman of the convention to give the age
> of her associate within ten years of the proper limit was not
> born to die. She is, however, in the neighborhood of forty,
> and were it not for the eye-glasses giving her an older look
> she would pass for thirty. . . . A slender figure and small hands
> and feet show that her life has not been devoted to manual
> toil. Although she dresses well, she is not extravagant in her
> apparel, and when she is to speak on any very important occa-
> sion she is attired in black satin, which is her favorite dress
> material. Her light is [sic] brown hair is brushed smoothly
> down in the good old-fashioned way, and is not crimped or
> frizzed in any modern style. Not a gray hair has yet made its
> appearance visible to the casual observer.
>
> Next to the president, the best-known national officer of
> the Union is Mrs. Mary A. Woodbridge of Ravenna, Ohio,
> the recording secretary. About 45, she has a countenance at
> once austere and sweet. It can draw itself into hard lines, or
> melt into a smile with equal ease. Her voice is penetrating but
> not especially agreeable, as it lacks even the suggestion of tender-
> ness that her face sometimes shows. Her husband is a mer-
> chant of wealth, who fairly idolizes her, and has built a beauti-
> ful residence, filled with everything to please an intellectual
> woman like his wife. She dresses in solemn black and her raven
> hair is gathered in a tight knot in the back. . . . She is a woman
> with great reserve force hidden behind her black eyes and
> beneath the bunch of flowers upon her bosom. ("Notable
> Women" 1–2)

Such "pen pictures" were common reportage in the cities where the
national convention met. Newspaper reports usually highlighted women
leaders' marital associations, as well. For example, when newspapers reported on women who had married prominent men, much of the space
described the honorable activities of the women's husbands. A typical
example is the *Cincinnati Daily Enquirer*'s profile of Zeralda Gray
Wallace: "Among the most prominent ladies of the Convention, Mrs.

Governor Wallace of Indiana, occupies a conspicuous place. She is the widow of the late Governor Wallace of Indiana, a genial, whole-souled politician of the Daniel Webster School" ("Crusaders" 8).

At first reading, today's reader might assume that "a genial, whole-souled politician" refers to Zeralda Wallace, but the description, instead, alludes to her husband. Similarly, when the *Minneapolis Tribune* offered a sketch of Caroline B. Buell, more than half the space was allotted to the military exploits of her husband, brothers, father, and grandfather ("Lively Day" 6).

Women gained credibility and acceptance with reporters according to the approval of their husbands, as does Mary Woodbridge, whose husband idolizes her. The same was true for Mary T. Lathrap:

> She is another lady who has not passed the 40-year line, and she looks about that age. She is doted upon by a husband who has a flourishing mercantile business in Jackson. Although Mrs. Lathrop [*sic*] has not a very well-shaped mouth for public speaking, she manages to make a speech with pretty good effect on account of the interrogative nature of her sentences, which appeal to the audience for an answer. She is a tall, fleshy woman, but is very easy on the platform. Mrs. Lathrop [*sic*], like nearly all the rest, dresses in black and has a penchant for silks. ("Notable Women" 1)

Reporters commented warmly on exceptional examples of traditionally appreciated womanly traits, highlighting especially maternal qualities:

> Mrs. Caroline B. Buell, the corresponding secretary, is one of the quietest, most endearing ladies of the body. Her dark hair, slightly silvered, gives just enough of age to her appearance to make more charming the flush that always mantles her cheek when she rises to speak, or take temporary charge of the meeting. Her eyes are deep brown, and very eloquent of her kind heart. She is about 37, and of reserved, retiring disposition. She has that charm commended by Shakespeare—a "sweet, low voice, an excellent thing in woman." She dresses quietly in dark brown silk, and makes an excellent impression. . . . She is one of the most motherly-looking women of the convention. (1)

Always, reporters looked for signs of femininity or masculinity. Sometimes women seemed to possess both. In reporting about Clara Hoffman, the journalist uses the word "strong" three times and highlights her commanding appearance. At the same time, he lets his reader know explicitly that Hoffman is not masculine, and that she dresses rather elaborately:

> Mrs. Hoffman (Clara Hoffman, State Superintendent of Mis-
> souri) is fully 45, and has an originality entirely her own,
> expressed especially by her strongly-marked nose. Her fea-
> tures are strong throughout and not a suspicion of powder
> glosses her dark skin. Her voice is strong but not masculine,
> her figure commanding. She dresses on public occasions very
> elaborately, and has a decided liking for striped velvet and
> satin. A black bonnet sits firmly upon her gray hairs as though
> put on to stay and is very expressive of the determined woman
> who evidently fears nothing in the shape of criticism. (1)

For those who fit less clearly into quiet, maternal specifications or who
broached traditional standards, descriptions were less favorable and further represented the ambivalence of reporters:

> Mrs. Emily Fitz-Stevens [actually Emily Pitt Stevens (plates
> 28, 29)] enjoys the reputation of being the most richly dressed
> woman in the convention. Of about the conventional age and
> size, she comes upon the stage with her head thrown back and
> fires her speech rapidly at the house like a little cannon bang-
> ing away at the enemy. Her eyes are half closed and not even
> in the most inspiring parts of her talk does she ever open them
> any wider. . . . Her head is covered by a bonnet that is evi-
> dently worn to make her look taller and that matches the rich
> tints of her elaborate costume. . . . She is a large woman of
> striking appearance and is said to be a model wife when at
> home. (2)

A woman who might have seemed "womanly" offstage—a model wife at
home, richly dressed—is less easily categorized as she performs in public.
Here is a woman presented at one and the same time as nondescript—"of
conventional age and size"—and as "a large woman." She is manipulative,
but tasteful—the rich tints match—in her dress, and when she speaks, although inspiring, she resembles a cannon "banging away," hardly a favorable image for any woman. Such ambivalence was common.

   Reporters sometimes commented on presentation. Male orators used
forceful, elaborate gestures, but such obvious flourishes on the part of
women were deemed inappropriate. Reports, then, commented favorably on women who refrained from extravagant gesturing. In reference
to "Mrs. Governor Wallace" of Indiana, the *Cincinnati Enquirer* commented, "She is an eloquent speaker, and her gestures are graceful and

easy. In manner, voice, accent and modulation she could give lessons to some of the eloquent men" ("Crusaders" 8).

At the same convention, the *Cincinnati Daily Gazette* reported that

> Miss Willard's discourse was a sort of porse [sic] setting of the "Psalm of Life," couched in the metaphoric earnest language of woman. Many of its thoughts were poetical, and were delivered in an easy, quiet style, abounding in poetical quotations and womanly rhetoric. ("Silent Forces" 3)

Such stress on "womanly rhetoric" embodies the reporter's highest praise and typifies most of the favorable newspaper accounts about WCTU members. This was especially true of Willard, who was accepted and praised more than any other woman speaker of the century. Even in the South, where women speakers drew the greatest concerns, Willard usually drew accolades because of her womanly appearance and delivery, a style she deliberately and consciously constructed.[5]

Willard was usually exempt from criticism. Rhetorically sophisticated and carefully attuned to the press, she was almost always praised for her womanliness and often contrasted to unwomanly suffragettes, despite her public speaking and support of equal rights and suffrage for women. According to the *Galena Evening Gazette*

> It was really a treat to hear a woman lecture without the constant scold, scold, scold, that one must listen to in hearing Annie Dickinson and Susie Anthony. Miss Willard, by her lady-like and sensible demeanor demonstrated the fact that a woman may not be out of place on the platform: while Misses Dickinson and Anthony have time and again proved that a woman on the stage may be exactly where she should not be. ("Everybody's War")

Even though Willard's preferred nickname was "Frank," newspapers never used a diminutive of her name as they did for other speakers. She was almost always referred to as Miss Willard. Her deliberate attention to the feminine reassured audiences and made them more receptive to her message.

Concern with the femininity of speakers drew interest regarding setting as well. Reporters nearly always gave lengthy, detailed accounts of meeting halls. At Louisville in 1882, the *Courier-Journal* reported that the convention church

> was beautifully decorated for the occasion, the rear of the stage being filled with flags and streamers, while the front was

filled with handsome floral designs. The center piece, a large shield of white balsams, bore the inscription "sobriety," and was particularly noticeable. Around the walls of the church were hung shields bearing the names of the different states and territories represented, there being thirty-eight in all. ("Reason VS. Rum" 4)

Such reporting also reflects the effectiveness of the WCTU's press department. Predictable and similar descriptions of the decor of convention headquarters, and probably the lengthy descriptions of the most prominent participants, suggest that many newspapers used prepared material furnished by the WCTU. Those supportive of the women often described the conventions' "homelike" qualities, intending to alleviate anxiety that women were losing their feminine qualities. When the national WCTU met at Chicago in 1877, the *Chicago Times*, a newspaper highly unfavorable to the women in its reporting, included no such description. But the *Chicago Evening Journal* and the *Inter-Ocean*, both less hostile to the women, described the assembly halls in detail. The *Journal* reported the meetings at Farwell Hall as follows:

> The stand and galleries of the hall have been elaborately decorated with flags and flowers. At the rear of the stage is the beautiful device or "coat of arms" of the National Temperance Union of Women. This was originated by Miss Frances E. Willard and Miss Mary A. Lathburg of New York. An imminence [*sic*] cross of leaves and evergreens forms the center, around which are two large American flags and running vines. Above the cross is a star. Below is a century plant, indicative of the origin of the woman's movement so near the beginning of the new century, and beneath all is a beautiful monogram of the national society. The whole is surmounted with the motto, "For God and home and native land." ("Temperance Women" 4)

The *Inter-Ocean*'s description was similar:

> The rear of the stage, which attracted the attention of everyone, was beautifully decorated with the "coat of arms" of the association. The design was originated by Miss Frances E. Willard of this city, and Miss Mary A. Lathburg, of New York. The cross forms the center, on which lean the American flags. Below is the century plant, indicative of the origin of the woman's movement so near the beginning of the new century, and beneath all is a beautiful monogram of the society. Above, in a graceful circle, is the motto in elegant letters, "For God and Home and Native Land." ("The Cause" 8)

Descriptive words such as "beautiful," and such detail as the significance of the century plant, suggest prepared copy.[6] It is possible, of course, that the *Inter-Ocean* simply drew from the Journal's report of the previous evening, but reports in other cities were often similar. The major newspapers in almost every convention city elaborated on setting and speakers' backgrounds. Like accounts of members' womanly appearance and rhetoric, descriptions of the "feminine" halls in which the women met reassured readers about participants.

After the Chicago 1877 convention, newspapers were generally gracious and presented a reassuring image for readers, although they often subtly questioned parts of the proceedings or highlighted any "unfeminine" behavior. As at the founding meeting in Cleveland, however, reporters delighted in detailing any semblance of infighting. Disagreement, considered unfeminine, offered good copy, and newspapers capitalized on any discord. During the 1878 convention in Baltimore, for example, the *Baltimore American and Commercial Advertiser* reported, over and over, a disagreement among the women about whether or not the official WCTU newspaper should include writing concerning suffrage for women. The dispute was reported, under separate headers, as a fight. The newspaper "recognized" Frances Willard as "one of the leaders of the aggressive minority," and delighted in printing Dwight Moody's reprimand under the header "Mr. Moody's Sharp Lecture":

> The spirit I found here when I entered was such that I felt like putting on my hat and going out again. . . . Instead of talking of Christ and helping the fallen drunkards, you've been passing long resolutions and talking about matters that are entirely outside. Let me beg of you to be of one mind, to see eye to eye, and to let your discussion alone. . . . This *Union* was born in prayer and should stick to its first principles. I would advise a whole month of prayer among the temperance women of the whole United States. . . . You never heard of Christ's apostles meeting and passing resolution, did you? You've got to save the drunkards, and it isn't by resolutions or by talking about resolutions that you're going to do it. ("Mr. Moody's" 4)

The report must have been especially galling to Willard. Willard had assisted Moody in his gospel revivals, an association that helped to establish her reputation, but the relationship was not always a smooth one. Moody initially provided no remuneration for Willard's services. In addition, he opposed her lecturing under any auspices except his own and questioned her association with women he considered radical. Willard finally left the Moody camp meetings to return to Evanston, where she became permanently associated with the WCTU. Behind Moody's request that the women be of one mind and see "eye to eye" rested the implication that they should "become one" with those who opposed taking a stance on suffrage. As we know from her writing, Willard and her closest associates would have chafed at this suggestion that women remain relegated to their limited sphere.

Coverage not only identified any disagreements, but generally highlighted such accounts. In reporting a specific disagreement between Frances Willard and Louise B. Rounds on the suffrage issue, the *Commercial Advertiser* used the headings "A Fight" and "The Fight Renewed," and reported as follows: "Miss Willard (coming forward dramatically, and pointing her finger at Mrs. Rounds)—'And thou, too, Brutus!' Has it come to this? This from Louise Rounds, my friend and room-mate" ("The Fight Renewed" 4).

WCTU references to the disagreement differ greatly from that of the Baltimore newspaper. On the Monday following the Saturday disagreement, and after the *Commercial Advertiser*'s account of the "fight," Mrs. H. W. Smith offered a resolution that was unanimously accepted by members of the convention:

> *Resolved.* That it is the sense of this Convention, that although there have been differences of opinion on some questions of expediency and method incident to all deliberative bodies, we feel profound thankfulness that in the discussions that have occurred, the prevailing sentiment of the Convention has been manifestly one of unusual Christian love and fellowship. (*Minutes of WCTU Annual* 43–44)

Similar emphasis on disputes were common, as in Minneapolis when women disagreed over whether to officially endorse the prohibition party, and in Chicago and for years after, when race became a disruptive issue.

An effort to appear supportive might have motivated positive early coverage. When the national WCTU convention was held at Baltimore in 1878, the *Baltimore and American and Commercial Advertiser* reported after the first day as follows:

> The convention is composed of intelligent, thoughtful women, some young, and others on the downward slope of life. . . . One of the most prominent gentlemen in Baltimore, who had the popular delusion, dropped in to the convention yesterday to see what it looked like, and was agreeably disappointed. "Why," said he, "They are the most distinguished lot of ladies I ever saw together in my life." ("Local Events" 4)

But accounts during and after the convention often undermined the previously positive reporting in order to make light of convention participants. A later *Commercial Advertiser* account of meetings read thus:

> The convention was put in a titter by the first item of business, coming as it did just between prayer and very important proceedings. It consisted in a question of privilege from Mrs. Lathrop [*sic*], of Michigan, who said some one had taken her gum shoes, "lined with red, they were," and she was very anxious about them. ("Temperance: The Suffrage" 4)

At other times, even the semblance of support was abandoned. When the national WCTU convention was held in Washington, D.C., the *Washington Post* portrayed the women as amusing and rather ridiculous. After the first day of the convention, the *Post* reported that

> The sex of the convention crops out in a thousand and one harmless but amusing incidents. Imagine a convention of men requesting the pages to take off their shoes and don slippers so as not to disturb the proceedings! The old adage that likens a woman's tongue to a clapper hung at both ends is momentarily illustrated excepting when one of the "big guns" . . . rises to the floor. . . . And how careless the women are: the announcements of "lost" and "found" read at the close of each session are numberless. Last evening the list included spectacles, handkerchiefs, pocketbooks, memoranda, manuscripts, parasols, and even a blue cotton umbrella. ("Woman's War" 1)

While reporters expected women to behave differently from men and reported favorably their feminine features with regard to dress and delivery, they nonetheless often ridiculed the traits that differentiated the women's conventions from those of men.

Following the convention the *Post*, under the header "The Corseted Crusade," reported on the election of officers: "It was decided that there should be no applause during the election. This was deemed by the profane a precautionary measure to prevent hair-pulling or other manifestations of female wrath" (2).

As they had at mid-century, sometimes newspapers initially reported conventions and participants positively, but later undercut such favorable accounts. A likely explanation is that reporters who attended and met the women were inclined to make affirmative reports. Later, editors, who had no first-hand experience with the women and their proceedings, would editorialize according to their own philosophies. For example, the *Louisville Courier-Journal* provided one of the most favorable coverages the WCTU received throughout its nineteenth-century history, even though editor Henry Watterson often denounced such audacious behavior on the part of women and generally opposed temperance activity. Watterson called the leaders of the temperance movement "red-nosed angels," and insisted that "the woman who assails the soap boxes . . . where such a one is not a lunatic she is a nuisance" (192–93). Watterson charged that women activists were masculinized and suggested a remedy: "To me the younger of them seem as children who need to be spanked and kissed" (199).

The varied and interesting mixture of rhetoric in newspaper accounts of women's temperance activities reflects fear and confusion about, as well as efforts to understand changes in, gender roles in the second half of the nineteenth century. Phrases such as "male men" and "female women" illustrate anxiety about and resistance to change, the redundant wording highlighting the difference between the sexes that many found comforting. Reporters and editors who feared and resisted change between the sexes also focused on women's dress and physical appearance, either to validate their own fears and persuade readers not to take such women seriously, or to reassure themselves and their readers that women's new roles were not undoing the fabric of their society.

By the last quarter of the century, members of the WCTU weakened harsh criticism by employing traditional definitions of femininity to the service of their cause. They successfully turned concern about women's appearance to their own benefit, deflecting criticism by offering detailed, reassuring descriptions of the patriotic and religious decor of meeting facilities, as well as descriptions of women's feminine, modest dress, and their "home-loving" and patriotic backgrounds.

Newspaper accounts reveal a generally more positive coverage for temperance women than for other woman's rights activists, reflecting the conciliatory and complex rhetorical approach taken by temperance women. While temperance women generally supported controversial demands on behalf of women, their strategies proved more disarming than the more confrontational rhetoric of some woman's rights advocates. And although they still received subtly denigrating coverage, their approach and work were less readily dismissed than that of other advocates for woman's rights.

Part Three

Fictional Accounts of Feminine Concerns

6

"The Feelings of the Romantic and Fashionable": Women's Issues in Temperance Fiction

I never saw a bridal but my eyelids hath been wet
It always seemed the saddest sight of all
To see a gay and girlish thing lay aside her maiden gladness,
For a name and for a ring.

WITH THIS TRENCHANT epigraph, Henrietta Rose introduces the chapter "The Bridal Excursion" in her 1858 temperance novel, *Nora Wilmot: A Tale of Temperance and Woman's Rights* (129). Rose questions narrow societal strictures that leave few choices for women, a major concern in much temperance fiction by women. An excerpt from Lydia Sigourney's 1833 sketch, "The Intemperate," illustrates an even more prevalent topic in such fiction: women's often dangerous dependency on men. Sigourney's narrator comments on protagonist Jane Harwood's danger as she moves away from family and friends with her husband John: "He felt she had no friend to protect her from insolence, and was entirely in his own power; and she was compelled to realize that it was a power without generosity, and that there is no tyranny so perfect as that of a capricious and alienated husband" (178).

Such examples typify the issues that nineteenth-century women writers of temperance fiction discussed at mid-century. Authors addressed the very real concerns women had about alcohol, but the temperance topic also allowed them to examine other issues of concern to women, as did women temperance speakers: societal and legal injustices, issues of physical abuse, and the generally unequal treatment of women. Like women speakers at mid-century, they portrayed women as victims of inebriate men, providing both a rallying point and a justification for temperance women's activity; but they were even more likely than speakers to address such sensitive issues as suffrage for women, women's economic dependence on men, marital infidelity, social injustices toward and legal inequities for women, and a woman's right to her own body.

Some writers explicitly connected woman's rights and temperance, as did Henrietta Rose in her 1858 novel. But, like women temperance speakers, fiction writers more often provided a temperance title and frame to their works as they explored other women's issues.

Authors readily addressed temperance and women's issues together, making use of the easy cultural conjunction between intemperance and injustices to women as outlined in previous chapters. Temperance fiction provides specific examples of the rhetorical acumen of women writers as they connect women's issues to the very popular issue of temperance. Women's temperance fiction is important because, while it reflects many of the traits of other women's fiction in the nineteenth century, it differs in its narrative exploration beyond the seemingly happy ending typically offered. It does not end with the wedding, but explores the very real problematic circumstances women must face after the ceremony. Finally, because of its connection with alcohol abuse, women's temperance fiction is more explicitly radical than most women's fiction in the nineteenth century.

Jane Tompkins has outlined the importance of doing such "cultural work," that is, writers' efforts to order their world. While not specifically examining the role of temperance fiction, Tompkins does note the traditional exclusion of temperance texts in the study of a period in our history when temperance preoccupied the country. She argues for the recovery of such texts because of "their cultural work within a specific historical situation," important for "providing society with a means of thinking about itself, defining certain aspects of a social reality which the authors and the readers shared, dramatizing its conflicts, and recommending its solutions" (200).

The unique nature of the temperance issue made it especially amenable to "cultural work" because it permitted an unusually candid discussion of circumstances that left women feeling powerless and in pain. If, as Mary Poovey claims, "literature was the nineteenth-century discourse in which women participated in the greatest numbers and arguably with the least cultural restraint" (38), temperance fiction provided an especially unique and powerful genre for participation, offering even fewer constraints than most fiction. Because temperance became accepted as within the province of women's work, and because it could so readily be associated with many forms of injustices toward women, temperance offered women a popular cultural medium for discussing and exploring women's issues.

Despite their unique and frank discussion of concerns to women, little attention has been addressed to women's temperance writings. Such neglect of women temperance writers is unfortunate, because we have apparently lost much biographical information. Temperance women formed the largest organized movement of women in the nineteenth century, with women writers playing a major and unique role in temperance discussions; yet I have found little information about them, except when scholars have found them interesting and valuable for other reasons. Authors who wrote primarily in other "acceptable" genres—Lydia Sigourney, Sarah Josepha Hale, Caroline Kirkland, Frances E. W. Harper, Ann Stephens, Harriet Beecher Stowe, Catherine Maria Sedgwick, Caroline Hentz, Elizabeth Stuart Phelps, Elizabeth F. Ellet, and Marietta Holley—command attention, but seldom, if ever, is mention made of their temperance stories or novels. Biographical information is available for authors who attained high visibility in major reform causes—Sarah K. Bolton, Frances D. Gage, and Elizabeth Cady Stanton—primarily because the women in those causes wrote their own records. But information regarding other authors seems lost. For example, Mary Dwinell Chellis wrote at least forty-two novels, the majority enjoying several editions, in addition to an indeterminable number of tracts and pamphlets for the American Tract Society and for the National Temperance Publication House. Yet, I have found no information about her except for the cataloguing of her works. For example, no listing is given for these authors in either the National Union Catalogue Manuscript Collection Index or in the indexes that catalogue specifically women's document sources.

Information about these women might broaden our understanding of the connections between women and temperance, but women's temperance fiction itself can shed light on women's thinking in the nineteenth century for a number of reasons. Previous to the nineteenth century, both American women and men consumed alcoholic beverages heavily; but unique divisions during the nineteenth century increasingly led to a dichotomy, whereby most men drank but the majority of women abstained (Blocker, *American Temperance* 10–11, 93), making discussions of alcoholic intake particularly amenable to explorations of men's conduct. In addition, the temperance cause was increasingly taken up by church affiliated groups. Because of support from religious communities, women writers could "go out of their spheres" by writing publicly and still maintain credibility, even among those groups who railed against the dangers of novels. Thus, temperance literature's association with morality assured its availability to thousands upon thousands of women through popular magazines and in tracts and novels, often published by religious presses and distributed in Sunday school libraries. Sunday school distribution was of supreme importance because, for most of the nineteenth century, Sunday school libraries provided the only publicly accessible books for the majority of Americans.

Finally, because male speakers and writers of temperance fiction also depicted violent alcoholic men, often evoking sympathy for women and children victims, women might readily use temperance for discussing issues of injustice. Women quickly appropriated the temperance cause and expanded the examination of intemperance to include women's wrongs.

Much has been written about nineteenth-century women's ability to express the personal dissatisfaction and doubt that lurk beneath the surface of their writing in subversive and sublimated texts,[1] but temperance writers were also able to represent nineteenth-century women's dissatisfaction with their assigned roles more openly than other writers. Fictional presentations of otherwise clandestine subjects permitted a more open challenge to the society women inhabited, and the temperance cause provided a vehicle for an explicit discussion of previously "delicate" subjects.

Since women were dependent on men, both legally and economically, they were, indeed, the victims of intemperance. But problems associated with alcohol might readily be generalized beyond the specific circumstances involving the drunkard. Much of the fiction labelled 'temperance' actually addresses the issue of alcohol only superficially, primarily offering advice to women, presenting role models for them, or indicting unequal legal and social treatment of the sexes. Whether an initial focus on intemperance led to the communal acknowledgment of a woman's unfair position, or whether women recognized the temperance debate as amenable to their complaints, women's temperance fiction is almost always the story of women's lives. Narratives focus on women's precariously subordinated positions, with temperance being addressed primarily in relation to the problems women faced (plate 30).

Temperance fiction provided an ideal vehicle for addressing women's concerns, and early on, women claimed the rights to temperance reform. By 1839, Sarah Josepha Hale openly proclaimed the need for women's perspectives on intemperance in her Preface to *My Cousin Mary: or The Inebriate*:

> It may, at first, seem an unnecessary labor, for a new writer of moral stories to attempt depicting the evils of intemperance, while the popular author of "My Mother's Gold Ring" is still in the field.[2] But a little reflection will show those who have read the interesting and instructive series of "Temperance Tales," put forth by Mr. Sargent, that, notwithstanding all he has done, there is still room for others, in this great work of national reformation. He has, as he naturally would do, addressed his lessons to men, rather than to women, and thus spoken to the heart and mind of the active, bustling world, rather than to the feelings of the romantic and fashionable.
>
> But the evils of intemperance reach all classes, and often involve the helpless and innocent female in deeper sufferings,

than the hardier sex ever endure. Many a fair, delicate girl, reared in the lap of indulgence, and surrounded by all those pleasures and advantages which make youth appear like the opening scene of a sweet romance, which is sure to end in love and happiness, many such have found their dreams of bliss rudely dissipated, while awakening to the reality of wretchedness, which the wife of an intemperate man, in any station in life, must endure.

Hale thus confirms women as the greatest sufferers of intemperance, thereby justifying their right to speak for themselves, and women consistently used temperance fiction to address their concerns and the injustices leveled toward women. That women's temperance fiction focuses on women is evident in the following titles: *Edith Moreton; or, Temperance Versus Intemperance; Alice Waters; or, The Sandown Victory*; and "The Drunkard's Daughter." But, unlike most fiction written by women in the nineteenth century, temperance fiction does not *end* with the marriage of the heroine, but, instead, generally *begins* with the wedding. The bride is usually a well-loved daughter and friend with bright prospects, but her happy dreams for the future fade quickly after marriage, as her promising and loving husband becomes increasingly involved with drinking and the ills that accompany intemperance—gaming, violence, and subsequent economic vulnerability. As the husband moves closer and closer to destruction, so does his family, and the attention focuses on women's difficulties in protecting themselves and their children because of economic, social, and legal roadblocks.

Nearly all women's temperance fiction at mid-century foregrounds the precarious nature of a woman's choosing a life-mate. As a character remarks in Caroline H. Butler's 1850 short story entitled "Emma Alton," "There is always, I believe, a feeling of sadness commingled with the pleasure with which we regard the young and trusting bride. . . . How soon are the bright visions dispelled" (49, 51).

Often women's temperance works open with a discussion among young women with regards to marital prospects. At the beginning of *The Price of a Glass of Brandy* (1841), for example, Laura Somerville and Sidney Barton discuss the young men they might marry. Laura expresses concern at Sidney's choice, Alfred Percey, but Sidney insists Alfred will be a good husband. Sidney incorrectly expects Alfred to change his habits once they are married, but Alfred fails to reform. His drinking increases, and Sidney dies a young woman, a victim of the hardships incurred by a drunkard's wife.

Similarly, in *Nora Wilmot: A Tale of Temperance and Woman's Rights*, Nora reprimands a friend who expects to reform her lover after marriage: "Susie Grey, look at your married acquaintances, and see how many have reformed by a matrimonial alliance. Do they not, nine cases out of ten, indulge far more after marriage than before?" (Rose 11). Such fiction thus accents the precarious and vulnerable position of young women for whom marriage is the expected social avenue, even though their lives may be destroyed by that marriage.

Marriage may prove treacherous for women because they can never be certain that their suitors' kindness will continue; marriage is thus represented as a dangerous gamble. As Sarah Keables Hunt's Alice wryly suggests, "marriage is like a lottery; there are not many who draw prizes after all" (12). This dictum dispels the romantic ideology of the domestic sphere and suggests instead that women carefully evaluate suitors with an eye to their own safety. Authors often suggest that women may improve their odds, however, by carefully considering suitors' past behavior, and they make examples of characters who fail to benefit from such warnings.

In the anonymous *My Cousin Mary*, Mary Dalrymple accentuates just such a concern when she expresses her fear of marriage to Mr. Harvey, a reformed drinker who assures her of his ability to remain alcohol free: "What guarantee have I for this? How can I know, that when the excitement of courtship is over—when a wife ceases to be a novelty—you will not return to the vice which was so lately a habit?" (32). Despite these reservations, Mary weds Mr. Harvey and, like Sidney Barton, suffers the consequences. Mr. Harvey leaves Mary destitute and tainted. An earlier love who had warned Mary to avoid Mr. Harvey, Henry Fullerton, would not now marry her, because "a woman cannot love an unworthy object, without losing, in a degree, that refinement and purity of mind, which I should consider in a wife" (46). Mary becomes a forlorn and miserable woman, a testament to her failure to heed warnings; but the novel also indicts the societal norms that persecute and isolate innocent women because of their association with drunkards.

Writers particularly warned those young women who would marry a drinker in the hopes of reforming him. Agatha Stafford explains to Faith Temple in *John and the Demijohn* (1869), "[T]here is no more miserable delusion than to marry a man to reform him" (Wright 271). This message echoes throughout temperance fiction. For example,

> Mary Lincoln felt it her duty to marry and save John. She did not consider that, if she could not keep him from those vile resorts for drunkards of every type and grade, the low grog-shops and fashionable drinking-saloons, as her affianced lover, she could do nothing for him when the lover had become the legal husband. (Friend 22)

Concerns about women's relationships to men surface throughout temperance fiction by women, primarily addressing the issue of spousal relationships, but also considering dangers in connection with brothers and fathers. Time and again, authors expose women's dangers in a society that excludes women from the legal and social protections afforded men and makes them completely reliant on the men in their lives. In Corra Lynn's *Durham Village* (1854), William Lundley becomes increasingly "enslaved" to alcoholic drink. While the temperance focus revolves around William and his dissipated friends, William's sisters, Edith and Julia, provide the primary interest in the novel. Not only does Lynn encourage the reader to empathize with the sister who "almost felt degraded that she was compelled to close the door on a servant, in order to conceal the condition of her brother" (35), but she points to the very real physical danger created by the brother. Fitzgerald Dunlap, William's deceitful, dishonest cohort, takes advantage of William's intoxicated state to take possession of keys to the Lundley apartment and tries to enter Edith's bedroom. Only quick and clear-headed action on Edith's part saves her from rape. William places Julia in danger, as well, because Dunlap uses incriminating information about William to blackmail her for valuable papers and to "take liberties" with her. But the self-assured young woman rejects Dunlap's improper advances and threatens to expose him if he continues the blackmail attempts (150). Julia's courage and self-sufficiency provide her only protection. The situations of both young women point to the dangers in a society where men provide their primary protection. When the men in their lives fail to meet those responsibilities, the women have no other sources of protection, which serves as a scathing critique of patriarchal culture and of domestic ideology.

Both Edith and Julia exhibit great strength in the face of the danger posed by their brother's problems and ultimately suffer no serious personal harm, but they are remarkable models of positive agency at mid-century. More commonly, women are presented as victims, and although they exhibit remarkable courage and strength, they are often less assertive than Edith and Julia, generally preparing the way for explicit arguments on behalf of women by depicting women as victims. In Metta Fuller Victor's *The Senator's Son* (1853), for example, Alice Madison sacrifices her life's happiness to protect her brother Parke. When the despicable Alfred Clyde threatens to expose Parke's forgery and to demand Parke's imprisonment unless the beautiful Alice marries him, Alice submits to her brother's appeal. Alice lives a miserable and ultimately destitute life, belying the promise of her youth. Although Parke is saved from prison, his drinking increases, bringing about his subsequent ruin and underscoring the futility of Alice's sacrifice.

Alice and her sister-in-law, Lucy, finally join forces at the end of the novel in a show of cooperation, companionship, and self-sufficiency. But both women are now free of husbands, permitting a different form of agency. As do many plots in women's temperance novels, this one suggests that women are a more reliable source of comfort and support than men, and the independence granted single women affords a much more satisfactory degree of protection and companionship than many marriages.

Mid-century writers repeatedly highlight the social pressures for women involved with inebriates. By doing so, these authors expose society's complicity in the degrading and unfair treatment of women. Maria Collins (1853) comments on such inequities that lead women increasingly into danger after one misstep: "[H]ow very partial the conventionalities of society are to the interest and well-being of man. He can be redeemed. She, once fallen, is fallen forever" (149–50). And Maria Buckley (1856) indicts society for similar reasons: "Man seduces, she believes and succumbs— she is banished from society, he is more honored than before" (12–13).

Charlotte S. Hilbourne exposes a parallel danger for women in a patriarchal society—difficulties daughters suffer because of drinking fathers. In Hilbourne's 1867 critique of patriarchal society, *Alice Waters; or, The Sandown Victory*, young Alice beseeches her father to attend a temperance lecture at the town hall, explaining that the children call her a "drunkard's child" and ridicule her because her "father is a toper and because the family lives in a shanty with nothing but bannock and browse[3] for food and wear ragged clothes" (3). While such ridicule might be leveled at both boys and girls, writers most often highlight the specific dangers for young women, especially portraying the compromised marital prospects of daughters of alcoholic fathers.

For example, Caroline Lee Hentz's Kate Franklin in "The Drunkard's Daughter" (1856) becomes the love and marital choice of Harry Blake, but Harry's father forbids his son's union with the daughter of a drunkard. Since Harry depends upon his father for support, opposing his father would bring only poverty and sorrow to Kate, and the two seem hopelessly separated. Harry's father finally agrees to the marriage after witnessing Kate's heroic rescue of her mother and sister from the family home her alcoholic father has ignited, but Kate suffers the loss of an arm during the daring rescue effort, and her redemption in the eyes of society comes at great cost.

Writers also portray economic handicaps for women by presenting the adversity daughters endure in having the burden of support for their families thrust upon them. Such problems are often juxtaposed against already diminished prospects for forming a suitable and happy marriage. Because young women's earning power is so meager, the daughters and the entire family suffer great deprivations. Many times, as for Lydia in Caroline H. Butler's 1854 "Amy" (plate 31), fathers increase hardships by demanding daughters' hard earned pay. Lydia, having no legal rights to her earnings, must relinquish her wages, but finally, desperate to save her mother and young siblings from starvation, Lydia parts with "her only jewel—her innocence" (241).

As it sometimes did in women's platform speeches, especially at mid-century, divorce figures prominently in women's temperance fiction of that period, many authors addressing whether a wife should stay with an inebriate husband. In some cases, women remain simply because they have no alternatives. They may live far from home, or their parents and relatives may no longer survive, and because of the nature of social preju-dices toward victims of the drunkard, few choices are available to them within their communities. More often women make the radical choice to leave. Such concern is evident as early as 1841 in *The Price of a Glass of Brandy*. After her husband becomes a victim of drink, Sidney Percey's "sincere and ardent affection rapidly chang[ed] into feelings of aversion and despondency." The birth of her first child had been "attended with joy and gladness." Her second child was anticipated "with mingled feel-ings of hope, fear, and despondency." When Alfred Percey breaks his vow to reform, Sidney, in desperation, takes the children and moves to a dis-tant city, justifying the abandonment of their marriage in a note:

> My only hopes for you, myself, and all connected with us, are in separation. With you I cannot life [*sic*] and preserve my senses;—near you, we shall always be a source of mutual trouble to each other. I must, therefore, go to some other place where I can earn the means of livelihood in such tranquillity as you have left me. (22)

Sidney thus declares her independence from her husband. She insists that separation provides a superior alternative to remaining with a hus-band who represents danger rather than security and protection.

Another contemporary feminist issue, the notion of a woman's right to her own body, is not addressed explicitly, but nineteenth-century women would have recognized the meaning behind the constant birthing of chil-dren in a situation where the husband has become an alcoholic. Ann Douglas has noted the tendency among American women in the nineteenth century to control the number of their pregnancies, and Linda Gordon notes the two methods that adherents of "voluntary motherhood" pro-moted: a couple's mutual decision to abstain (which Gordon suggests was in actuality the husband's self-imposed celibacy), and "the right of the wife unilaterally to refuse her husband" (103). The wife of a drunkard could hardly have depended on a husband's complicity in either context, and some authors make clear that wives of drunkards retain no "rights" of refusal.[4]

In temperance fiction by men, and in much of women's temperance fiction, the issue of pregnancy is deftly circumvented. But in some novels in which the husband becomes abusive to both wife and children, the author makes a point of noting the yearly addition of children to the family. Writers accentuate the numerous yearly births of women married to intemperate men by creating heroines who themselves are either only children or have only one or two siblings. In addition, friends and neighbors usually have few children, further emphasizing the numerous and closely-spaced additions to the drunkard's household.

For example, in S. A. Southworth's 1854 novel, *The Inebriate's Hut*, Alice Lee, an only child, quickly gives birth to six children. Alice's husband had begun drinking while the couple had only two children, and the last two children are born while Alice and the older children struggle under conditions of poverty and abuse. Feeble from birth, the youngest children die while very young, their weakness another testament to their father's alcoholism and a contrast to today's warnings about alcohol's dangers for the pregnant mother alone. Similarly, in Jane C. Campbell's "Steps to Ruin," James Boynton has begun to drink from the beginning of his marriage, bringing himself and his family quickly to financial disaster. Mrs. Boynton soon has four small children despite the fact that the family must live in a seedy tenement, deprived of basic necessities.

In "Tales of Truth" (1852), Frances D. Gage depicts examples of both infidelity and forced intimacy even more candidly. She also seizes the opportunity to undercut the wisdom of conventional advice that proves detrimental to women's good. Gage tells the story of Mary Cadwallader, who marries Edward Harris. Edward is a young and promising lawyer, but he begins to drink. Mary considers leaving Edward, but "Friends told her the old tale of woman's patient kindness and endearing love." The reader learns that "every feeling of her soul revolted at the idea of living with a drunkard" and that Edward broke his marriage vows: "He did neither *love, cherish* nor protect, nor did he '*leaving all others*, cleave only unto her.'" Furthermore, the author destroys all doubt that Mary might have any sexual attraction to Edward:

> And she did live and suffer on for two years more, and then a pair of twins—two little girls—were added to her heart trials. This was what she had dreaded—that she should, by living with him, add to the number of those whom his hourly self-indulgence was bringing down to wretchedness and woe. Had she yielded to the suggestions of her own heart, there would have been but two to have borne the name of "drunken Harris" children. (3)

This issue surfaces again in Mary Dwinell Chellis's *Out of the Fire* (1869). Elsie Gray marries Clement Foster against the protests of her family and moves away from the community. Clement continues to drink after the marriage and soon becomes abusive to Elsie. "At twenty she was married, and left her father's house a happy bride. At twenty-five she was a drunkard's wife; and the mother of three children" (418). When Elsie's brother Judson hears of her plight and rushes to her rescue, Elsie's youngest child is "but a few weeks old" (411). Elsie pleads with her brother, "Take me and never let me see *him* again" (414). "Eagerly she welcomed her brother and heard the joyful news that her slavery (for by no milder term could her life be called) was at an end" (416). That Elsie's last two children are the products of intemperance is also suggested in their feebleness. Like Alice Lee's children born subsequent to Edward Lee's complete addiction to alcohol, Elsie's two youngest children are weak and die at a young age, an obvious indictment of the genetic harm alcohol visits upon the father. The author explains, however, that the eldest has "more rigor of constitution" and recovers (416).

Elsie, too, continues to be sick for a long time, a possible allusion to illness from sexually transmitted diseases. After wives leave abusive husbands, they are often ill for a lengthy period. Elsie eventually recovers, but Clement Foster dies within two years. "Elsie was then free, and she made no pretence of mourning for one whom she had long ceased to love, and whose very name was a terror" (417).

In the final decades of the century, writers are often more explicit in the issues they address and are less likely to present women as victims, offering strong women role models instead. Having effectively established their right to speak and act on temperance matters, women authors, like women speakers, turn their attention more fully to remedying injustices to women. They unqualifiedly insist upon greater rights for women and concern themselves with creating stronger, more self-sufficient characters for young women to emulate. Some continue to explore the notion of divorce, more explicitly supporting characters' rights to desert drunken husbands by foregrounding justification in the authoritative voices of experienced or respected figures. For instance, while Patsy Quinn, in Mary Dwinell Chellis's *At Lion's Mouth* (1872), stays with her husband, she rejoices at his death:

> Two years longer she dragged out a miserable existence, and then she was free—no one claiming from her aught beyond the common amenities of life . . . not a tear did she shed over her husband's grave; not a sigh did she give to his memory. Henceforth, she was to live as though he had never crossed her path. (226–27)

Not only does Chellis suggest that women need not grieve for the loss of an abusive husband, her male characters validate women's right to leave alcoholic husbands. Tom Magee, son of a reformed inebriate, attests that "if I was a woman, I wouldn't live with a drunken husband and I wouldn't have lived with my father if he had kept on drinking." The father's reply confirms the correctness of such a position: "If I had kept on [drinking] would it have helped my case if a dozen others had gone down with me? Not a bit, and that's why I don't believe in clinging to a drunkard when he's past hope" (279).

In her 1874 novel, *Wealth and Wine,* Chellis enlists the gentle Dr. Saunders to justify divorce and to underscore the lack of legal protection for women. Jane Warland and son, John, have unsuccessfully tried to escape from her abusive husband. Hastings Warland had "made no pretensions to any regard for them; yet he claimed their service, and appropriated the proceeds of their labor. Hoping to rid themselves of his presence, they had removed to a neighboring city. But here he found them" (61). Dr. Saunders ultimately convinces Warland to free the two because Warland has so severely abused his son that the boy is in danger of dying: "If the boy should die, there will be a legal investigation into the matter" (21). Authors thus highlight the lack of legal and community support for women who leave abusive husbands—both Sidney Percey and Jane Warland must seek protection through obscurity in distant communities—and at the same time point to the lack of protection for women who remain. Only in extreme cases, such as abuse resulting in death, do authorities take action.

Dr. Saunders provides transportation money for Warland upon Warland's consent to leave town; he then arranges Mary's return to her father's home. Still, young John Warland does not feel safe. He begs Jane, "You must get the lawyers, or the judge, or somebody else—I don't exactly know who—to give me all to you, so no one else will have any claims upon me." John adds the authority of the abused child to the call for divorce: "[Y]ou must get a divorce from your husband" (65).

Dr. Saunders not only condones the divorce, he places it in a positive light. "You still have much life to live," he tells Jane, and "if you are as sensible as you ought to be, you won't feel it to be your duty to wear sack-cloth and ashes all that time, because you made a mistake when you were twenty" (96). By depicting Jane as an honorable, sympathetic character, Chellis elicits the reader's identification with her. She also undercuts possible criticism of divorce by implying that other women are vulnerable to Jane's predicament. Jane, when young, had seemed an unlikely candidate for divorce and "never before wished to know how divorces are obtained," considering them "dreadful" and "disgraceful." But now she realizes "there are alternatives more dreadful, more disgraceful" (68).

Even when authors praise women who remain with drunken husbands, they seem to undermine that support. Perhaps the most glorified example is that of Mrs. Chester in Julia M. Friend's *The Chester Family* (1869). Friend devotes an entire chapter entitled "Self Sacrifice" to the praise of women who, like Mrs. Chester, remain true to their husbands. Friend calls this "fidelity to her nuptial vow" heroic.

Yet Friend actually undercuts her praise for Mrs. Chester by accusing her of complicity in the trials of her children, insisting that she had no "right to inflict shame and suffering upon her innocent children by becoming the wife of a drunkard" (45). And, although Friend praises Mrs. Chester for remaining "for the sake of her children," readers must have questioned Mrs. Chester's wisdom as Friend highlights the horrors her children endure. Mrs. Chester's third child becomes a cripple, "the result of her father's drunkenness" (40), and Johnny earns enough to purchase crutches for his sister, only to have the father discover and then squander the hidden money on rum.

By the final part of the century, authors begin to explore the psychological implications behind women's continuing to love or stay with an abusive man. Mary Chester stays with her husband out of a sense of duty. But Patsy Quinn, who was unable to leave her drunken husband, "wonders" that all women don't refuse to live with a drunkard, "but women keep hoping for better times" (279). Mrs. Tubbs, in Chellis's *Our Homes* (1881), attempts to explain her attachment. Mrs. Tubbs's husband, Timothy, has deserted her, taken on the pseudonym Renau, and illegally remarried, his new wife ignorant of his previous life. The women discover their situation, and Madame Renau questions Mrs. Tubbs's willingness to rejoin her abusive husband. When Mrs. Renau suggests that Mrs. Tubbs should rejoice at her riddance of such a husband, Mrs. Tubbs suggests that women's accomplishments and self-esteem might provide the necessary impetus for refusing to accept abuse from men:

> Yes, ma'am you'd think so, and I'd think so, but when I heard where he was, the longing in my heart wouldn't let me rest. I can't tell how it is, but women like me, who don't have anything to think of but their work and their families, don't give up a man they've once loved, as easy as women do that study books, or paint pictures, or dress so nice that folks praise them for their good looks. I don't know how it is, and I can't rightly say it, but such as I be, are always going back to the courting times. Timothy pretended to love me then, and seems as though, now he couldn't undo it all. (84)

Like Mrs. Tubbs, Rosie Dunn in Margaret Hosmer's *The Subtle Spell* (1873) also addresses the psychological implications of abuse. She provides money and help for her siblings when able but, understanding the need for distance from violence and abuse, refuses to remain a part of the family household: "[A]buse makes me wild. I've got to keep out of it, or I'll be as bad as any of them" (89).

Madame Renau also addresses a related issue—women's retaking of their identity and name. Learning that she has never been legally married, she despises her name and agonizes about how to proceed: "It seems to me now that I must take my maiden name, and be known as Miss Augusta Blaine. It will be unpleasant, and it will cause many awkward mistakes, but I have no right to the title, 'Madame Renau;' and besides, it is hateful to me" (Chellis 96).

Late-century authors also often hint at husbands' infidelity. Mary Evalin Warren's *Compensation: A Tale of Temperance* (1887) provides a typical example. Readers learn that for Ann Miller, after husband Harry begins to drink, "many and frequent were the long, wary hours of his absence, when he would be compelled to be away, sometimes all night, and often way into the small hours of the night" (18). Apprehension centers explicitly on husbands' late night drinking, as anxious wives wait through the long dark hours for husbands to return. But fears of infidelity would naturally accompany their keeping late hours. After a long period of dissipation, Harry tries to reform, but fails. Finally, he hangs himself, and Mary moves with her son, Alfred, to be near her family. Eventually, she marries Harry's brother, a sober, respectable man.

By the latter part of the century, authors seemed intent on presenting alternatives and strong role models for women. Some offered the single life as a constructive and safe alternative to marriage, introducing the usually denigrated "old maid" favorably. For example, Chellis's *Out of the Fire* presents the story of Rhoda Smith, the daughter of an inebriate, who chooses to remain single rather than to chance marriage. Rhoda becomes a beloved old maid, highly respected, and a paragon of strength.

Throughout the novel, Rhoda demands her rights and serves as a role model for women. After becoming an orphan, she grew up in her cousin's household, where she was treated as a servant. At sixteen she realizes the value of her work and demands that the family pay her wages; if they refuse, she insists, she will leave. The family initially balks at this idea, but realizing Rhoda's worth, they agree to the arrangement. Later, when her cousin's wife, Samantha, needs a new dress, she tells Rhoda, "I'd always rather go without than ask for it." Rhoda responds, "There's no use in being afraid to take your rights in this world. Half the men pay more for rum and tobacco than it would take to clothe their families and then complain that they can't get along, because the women folks are so extravagant" (103). Although several men propose marriage to Rhoda, she "lived to a good old age, unmarried, choosing as she said, with something of the old spirit, to live her own life, in her own way, yet by a large circle of younger friends she was loved and honored scarcely less than a mother" (417).

Similarly, in Chellis's *Wealth and Wine*, Mabel Pease decides not to marry and "sets up housekeeping" for herself. Mr. and Mrs. Archer discuss the implications of Mabel's act, and Chellis places the authority figure on the side of the single woman. Mrs. Archer criticizes Mabel, but Mr. Archer tells his wife, "I suppose it is quite natural that she should want a home of her own." Mrs. Archer worries about Mabel's establishing a precedent, but, again, Mr. Archer takes the opposing view: "If nine out of every ten women could keep house as pleasantly as she will, they would be far better off than they are now" (187–89).

In numerous temperance pieces, women take charge of the family upon the death of an alcoholic husband or father, and maintain a comfortable and now much happier environment. In others, they simply take charge when the husband or father becomes ineffective or destructive. For example, John Carter, the alcoholic father in *Paul Brewster and Son* (1875), brings his family to near destitution. His daughter Mary asks about family finances in an effort to help, and Mr. Carter tells Mary, "For business, such a head as yours wouldn't be worth much" (Chapman 119). But Mary decides to find out about her father's "pecuniary circumstances." She takes charge of the family finances, begins teaching music, and creates a modest but respectable living for the family, dispelling the notion that women's minds are unsuited for such management.

Other spirited role models for women populate women's temperance fiction at the close of the century. Faith Kemp of *The House on the Beach* (1893), provides one such role model. Faith overhears a girl singing on the beach:

> Little Sally Sawyer
> Sittin in a saucer,
> Aweepin' an' awailin' for a young man.
> Rise, Sally! Rise, Sally!
> Wipe the tears from out your eyes, Sally.
> Cease weepin', cease wailin'; here's a young man! (293)

Faith's reaction? "[C]ertainly this Sally she is singing about is a very idiotic young person. What is she 'weepin' an' wailin' for a young man for? Couldn't she find something better to employ her time?" (Wright 294).

Faith makes the young girl consider what she is singing. The child "had evidently never applied any thought to her ditty" (295). Faith tells her, "There are precious few young men worth turning one's self into a fountain for. If I were you, I'd sing about a girl that had some grit. Sally, in my opinion, was simply absurd and disgraceful" (296).

In another incident, Faith registers an unexpected reaction when a young boy she has befriended thinks to frighten her with his collection of insects: "If he expected to be revenged for Faith's tartness by seeing her jump in horror at 'the bugs,' he was disappointed. She examined them coolly, remarking, 'I've found much handsomer plenty of times'" (37).

Such models of composure and self-assuredness surface earlier, as well, in Wright's *John and the Demijohn*. When Ralph Curtis proposes to Agatha Stafford, Agatha refuses him, remarking that she will marry only a thoroughly temperate man. Ralph asks incredulously, "Do you want me to sign a pledge? Give up my liberty?" Agatha responds in the negative: "I do not tell you to sign away your liberty for me, because I am not willing to make a return in kind to you. There is no wisdom for loving just for the sake of making sacrifices" (80).

When Robert Halsey, in Chellis's *The Temperance Doctor* (1868), comes home drunk for the first time, his wife Betsey draws three pails of water, dashes his face with them, and tells him she'll leave him if he shows any further signs of intoxication. He doesn't. In the same novel, John Hosford has become a drunkard, squandering the fortune his wife's wealthy parents have left her. She is forced to support herself and her children, but Hosford demands her earnings as his legal right. Finally, Mrs. Hosford tells John, "I have earned what money I have, and I will keep it for myself and children. You can drink up your own earnings, but you shall never again drink mine" (93). Mrs. Hosford successfully supports her family and regains the respect and esteem of the entire community. Her own strength, along with the support of her neighbors, keeps her husband at bay.

Late in the century, role models represent women's entrance into the work force and professions. For example, Georgenia J. Koppke's Katherine Getsing "had taken a university course and was serving her first term as County Superintendent of Schools." When Katherine shows interest in Doctor Beson's electrical therapy treatment, he seems surprised. Katherine "smiled as she thought how this broad-minded physician had seemed to forget that woman's sphere could be inside the scientific circle" (79). Katherine's brother, Adrein, becomes sexually involved with a young woman, Margarita, who subsequently becomes pregnant. Margarita is taken to a "Home for the Fallen." When Adrein seeks her there, he is greeted by the resident doctor, a woman.

That women's issues are the primary focus in women's temperance fiction is evident, not only because intemperance is often only superficially treated, but also because many times the cases of injustice are not directly related to alcoholic intake at all. Sarah Knowles Bolton's *The Present Problem* (1874) includes vignettes about intemperate men, but protagonist Mary Sharon becomes a victim even though she avoids men who drink alcohol. Mary's husband dies, leaving her a comfortable inheritance. She keeps an adequate amount of money for herself and donates the remainder to charity. Eventually, Mary remarries and when her second husband, also a temperate man, dies, his family claims much of Mary's money, although the entire amount had belonged to her before this marriage. Bolton thus points to legal injustices with regards to property rights for women, and she makes explicit that such injustices exist apart from intemperate husbands.

Marietta Holley devotes several chapters in *Sweet Cicely* (1886) to the injustices of the legal system. When Cicely's husband dies, Cicely has no control over their estate; rather, her son inherits the estate, and a man manages it until the son comes of age. Likewise, Holley's Dorlesky Burpy narrates many instances of "wommin's helpless condition under the law" (145). She tells about the plight of the women in her family, including that of her sister, Susan Clapsaddle, who had five thousand dollars when she married, but whose money and property "has gone down Philemon Clapsaddle's throat"; of her sister Patty, who was happily married to a minister and worked hard to make his small salary stretch to meet the family's needs, but who, upon her husband's death and the loss of his meager salary, had to pay taxes on their previously untaxed property; and of her aunt, Eunice Keeler, who "owns a big property in tenement-houses, and other buildings where she lives. Of course her taxes wus awful high; and she didn't expect to have any voice in tellin' how that money, a part of her own property, that she earned herself in a store, should be used" (148–49).

Holley points to women's being taxed without the privilege of participation in formulating the laws to which they are subjected. She also ridicules the absurd and unjust laws men create. Male lawmakers tax Eunice for the construction of new sidewalks in front of some of her buildings, but when new legislators come to power and tax her again so that they may tear up the existing sidewalks and build new ones, Eunice refuses to comply and is incarcerated. Holley repeatedly highlights the notion of taxation without representation, of women who suffer because of men's intemperance, and of the law's failure to protect women.

Throughout temperance fiction, but especially during the final quarter of the century, women present the need for greater equality between the sexes. When Bolton's Mary Sharon questions her friend Camilla's intentions of marrying Ralph Harmon, a drinker, Camilla responds that all young men must sow their wild oats. Mary insists, "There is no more reason for men to drink than for us, Camilla. It is as respectable for us to go into saloons, as it is for them. A woman who is intemperate, we debar from society; why not do the same by men?" (12).

In the same novel, the narrator regrets that, upon finishing school, Camilla remains idle, waiting for somebody to marry because society disdains her seeking useful employment. She then predicts, "That will all change some day, girls, when all women work. When the rich girl ceases to make herself a burden, work will be an honor and a blessing" (34).

Frances E. W. Harper's Belle Gordon also comments on such inequity in *Sowing and Reaping* (1876–77). When her friend Jeanette questions Belle's breaking her engagement to Charles Romaine because of his drinking, and chides Belle that "young men will sow their wild oats," Belle replies, "A young man has no more right to sow his wild oats than a young woman" (103).

Later in Harper's novel, Mrs. Gladstone's daughter tells her mother,

> I do think it would be a dreadful thing for women to vote . . . being hustled and crowded at the polls by rude men, their breaths reeking with whiskey and tobacco, the very air heavy with their oaths. [I]f we women would use our influence with our fathers, brothers, husbands, and sons, could we not have everything we want? (161)

Mrs. Gladstone refutes the argument that women do not need the vote because their influence on voters is adequate: "No, my dear we could not, with all our influence we never could have the same sense of responsibility which flows from the possession of power. I want women to possess power as well as influence" (161).

Even Julia Friend's narrator, who praises Mary Chester's loyalty to her drunken husband, calls for "*woman's* right to use the ballot." The narrator challenges, "Who will dare come forward, and forbid that wife and mother to use the ballot, to save herself and her helpless little ones from the madness and fury of the drunkard's appetite?" (101).

The largest portion of nineteenth-century women's temperance fiction, like nineteenth-century women's fiction in general, was written during the 1840s and 1850s. It suffered a decline in volume after that period, possibly attesting to the increase in alternative avenues of communication for women and in additional outlets for their talents and energy after the Civil War. Much of the temperance fiction by women in the last quarter of the century does attest to the pervasive influence of the Woman's Christian Temperance Union, founded in 1874.

Koppke's *Bows of White Ribbon* (1899), for example, enumerates the good works of the WCTU, from saving "fallen women" and providing shelter in their maternity homes, to preparing "housewives" (small containers of essential items) for American soldiers in the Spanish-American War. Koppke even includes quotations from Frances Willard.

On the other hand, Mary Dwinell Chellis, the most prolific woman writer of temperance fiction throughout the century, markedly changes her focus in the 1880s when the Woman's Christian Temperance Union had become closely aligned with labor unions. Chellis mentions the creation of local temperance unions in her fiction, even women's temperance unions, but they are never associated with the WCTU. And the primary focus of her temperance fiction during this period is anti-union, as Chellis repeatedly takes up the corporate cause.

In her 1885 *The Workingman's Loaf*, for example, Chellis's Robert Winter explains, "Men earn enough; that isn't the trouble; it is the way they spend their money. Most of it goes for beer, and whisky, and tobacco; and the women and children have to live on the leavings" (31). Later, under pressure from fellow workers, Robert joins mill employees in a strike when their employer cuts wages by 10 percent. But good Mrs. Stearns tells Robert, "If you will give me one-half of what your wages would be, even after ten per cent reduction, I will engage to provide comfortably." And, when Mary and Robert Winter's father does stop drinking and gives Mary "half the workingman's loaf," that is, half his wages, Mary finds she can provide for the previously destitute family comfortably. Her younger brother Luke expresses amazement at how large a share half a loaf is: "a grand, good loaf it is; fresh baked every day, and increased in size, as the appetite of the family demands" (83). Mr. Winter invests the remaining half of his wages, and the family eventually buys property and builds a house. Chellis's message clearly attests to temperance and frugality as remedies for poverty, not higher wages.

Chellis accents her position further by presenting the conversation of two gentlemen who express concern for the animosity that has been created between labor and capital:

> Those who work under the direction of others are inclined to consider their employers as mere task-masters, wrestling from them unrequited labor. For one, I was never so happy as when I worked on a fair, living salary. I knew exactly how much I could spend, and still lay by a little every year. I am richer than I was then; but I work harder and have a thousand times more anxiety. (75)

Late in the century, Chellis wrote numerous novels that the twentieth-century reader would consider anti-labor. *Our Homes* (1881) addresses the issue of "elegant economy," the remedy for "waste which fills our poor houses, and fills, too our streets and alleys with starving women and children" (23). Chellis's works abound with kind employers, such as Ben Jarvis of *Bread and Beer* (1882), who is a "splendid man," always willing to help those who are down. Chellis contrasts good factory and shop owners, such as Ben Jarvis, with their intemperate neighbors who acknowledge, "He [Ben Jarvis] wasn't brought up any better than I was. I am ashamed of myself every time I see him. I might have been well off as he is if, when I started myself, I had started on the right track" (149). Being rich "is easy enough. Spend less than you earn. Stop drinking liquor of every kind and throw away your pipes and tobacco. Keep right on at work and when the year comes 'round you will begin to be rich" (*Old Benches with New Props* 108). Such novels overflow with kind, wealthy men who started at the bottom and achieved success through abstinence, frugality, and hard work. Although Chellis's late-century writing accentuates an anti-labor ideology, much of her work as well as that of other women temperance fiction writers serves as a springboard for women's rights.

The numerous examples of women temperance writers' concern for the unequal status of women suggests that we should reconsider our images of women and temperance throughout the nineteenth century. Cognizant of the sensitive nature of questioning a society that both controlled public communication among women and punished those who broke patriarchal strictures, these women nonetheless appropriated concern about temperance to address delicate matters significant to a very large audience of women. While women addressed the issue of problem drinking, the topic also permitted them to highlight the abusive and unjust treatment of women. Many of these issues, such as spousal abuse and a woman's right to her own body, parallel the concerns of late-twentieth-century women. In addition, authors present strong role models that even today feminists can accept as positive.

An examination of women's nineteenth-century temperance fiction also complements and expands upon recent efforts to recover and understand the works of nineteenth-century women. Knowledge about women temperance reformers is valuable, not only because they participated in the largest mass movement of women in the nineteenth century, but also because they complicate our notion of women's thinking during that period by indicating less passivity and suggesting a greater degree of unhappiness and dissatisfaction among "traditional" women than previously presumed. Temperance historian Jack S. Blocker Jr., correctly, I believe, questions the claim of historians Ruth Bordin and Barbara Epstein that the attitude among women involved in the Woman's Temperance Crusade changed, suggesting instead that assumptions about those women's prior submissiveness seem inconsistent with their actions: "marching upon saloons and coercing saloonkeepers" (*"Give"* 223). Examination of women's temperance fiction suggests that many assumptions about temperance women might be unfounded, since women whom we have regarded as very accepting and conservative wrote and read literature that so openly challenges women's restricted roles and unjust treatment in the nineteenth century.

7

"Wine Drinkers and Heartless Profligates": Water Drops from Popular Novelists

> Among women, excluded as they are from all participation in the conviviality which leads astray so many of the stronger sex, a clearer and more rational view early prevailed. They experienced not the tempting pleasure, but they observed the next day's depression or irritability, and they *counted the cost*!
>
> —Caroline Kirkland, "Agnes: A Story of Revolutionary Times"

TEMPERANCE WAS THE woman's issue of the nineteenth century. Temperance novels and stories proliferated, apparent in titles that announced their subject matter, such as "The Drunkard's Daughter" or "The Intemperate Reclaimed," or because they were published by temperance publication houses. But anxieties about alcohol's use and abuse, and consensus about its detrimental ramifications for women, were so pervasive that scarcely a popular nineteenth-century woman's novel exists that does not make reference to intemperance, attesting to its inherent dangers. Not only did references to problems associated with alcohol surface in the writings of the century's most popular novels, many popular writers wrote explicitly temperance fiction. Such fiction writing was probably comfortable for them. As Mary Kelley suggests, many of these women "could enter the man's world [of writing] because they had not left behind woman's work" (287). By writing temperance fiction, they both contributed to the notion of temperance as rightfully a woman's issue and maintained their own association with woman's work.

While such writing among popular authors was often less "radical" than that written by women who wrote primarily temperance fiction, it nonetheless is significant for two reasons. First, although late-twentieth-century scholars value writings that demand change—writing that encouraged women to remove themselves from abusive situations and to protest against inequalities—works that established the dangerous, helpless situation in which many women found themselves served an important function. A vast number of women in the nineteenth century became united and created change because the temperance issue allowed them to agree upon the need for improved conditions for women. They read and heard about concerns with regards to alcohol's dangers at every turn, and the rising anxiety about alcohol abuse went hand-in-hand with women's rapidly growing involvement in the temperance and other reform movements that brought about change for women.

Second, because alcohol became the focus of women's anger, women with greatly divergent political views united for a common cause—improved legal, social, and economic conditions for women. The temperance problem was one on which nearly all women could agree, whether they personally believed in divorce or eternal fidelity to marriage vows; whether they believed that even a single glass of alcohol was dangerous or simply opposed excessive use of alcoholic beverages; or whether they believed in the possibility of reform for drunkards or believed that, once addicted, the intemperate were lost.

Men who wrote temperance stories often depicted women drunkards; significantly, women authors were much more likely to cast the problem of intoxication in terms of men. Women characters, then, needed to be on guard, seeking means of protection. Alcohol became the primary woman's issue of the century, because it came to symbolize and gave vent to frustrations about women's powerless and precarious situation.

Popular works promoted the notion of temperance as a woman's issue, helping to justify women's active involvement in temperance organizations. By associating use of alcohol with danger for women, they contributed to the notion of temperance as both a woman's concern and responsibility. Although popular women writers were less likely than specifically temperance writers to address controversial issues such as divorce, suffrage, and a woman's right to her own body, many of the issues addressed by temperance speakers and in women's temperance fiction are pervasive in the works of popular women writers as well. And popular writers effectively supported ideals offered by temperance women during the century: heroes and heroines never drank alcohol, signaling their characters' moral integrity.

In order to achieve an accurate reading of the century's most popular novels, one must consider the temperance influence. Placing popular women writers in the context of the temperance movement and its rhetoric allows us to see the dialogue between temperance tracts and fiction that is strongly affected by temperance rhetoric. These works raise questions about female agency and strategies of influence. While contemporary readers of nineteenth-century fiction may ignore the temperance rhetoric in these popular works, the original readership would have been very familiar with it, understanding and accepting alcohol usage as a code that evoked a wide range of cultural ideas and ideals. Such cultural codes permitted authors to comfortably make use of temperance to explore feminist issues and to offer positive role models for young women.

In the century's best-known novel, *Uncle Tom's Cabin* (1852), Harriet Beecher Stowe frequently presents alcohol use as a measure of the worth of her characters. In the opening scene of the novel, even before identifying his occupation, Stowe quickly reveals the nature of the slave trader Haley by the description of his garish dress, physical demeanor, and profane language; but also by the fact that he drinks, in quick succession, wine, two glasses of brandy, and then more wine. Alcohol is also implicated in the horrid activities at Simon Legree's plantation. The wallpaper in Legree's home is "defaced, in spots, by slops of beer and wine"; Legree also plies his henchmen with whiskey (plate 32) and attempts to get Emmeline to drink brandy against her will. While Haley and Legree represent a danger to all, women are uniquely vulnerable. Eliza stands to suffer most from Haley's deal, it seems, because of the danger of being separated from her son. And although the reader may be concerned for Uncle Tom, Stowe portrays Aunt Chloe and the children as also suffering greatly because of the loss of husband and father. Similarly, Simon Legree, both at the slave warehouse and on his plantation, presents special dangers for Emmeline because of the sexual implications attached to his behavior. He passes his hand over her breast before buying her, and his coaxing her to drink alcohol attests even further to his licentious intentions. For Stowe, the heavenly home is the Quaker one, where alcohol is never present. In her pervasive use of cultural codes about alcohol, Stowe convincingly suggests the need for a female influence, one that will effectively counter the problematic influences of inappropriate male behavior.

Similarly, another of the century's most popular novelists, Susan Warner, connotes character by associations with alcohol. Warner's *The Wide, Wide World* (1850) became the nation's first "best seller." As Nina Baym points out, Warner writes of women's "power and lack of it" (144), an issue always underlying nineteenth-century women's writing about intemperance. In *The Wide, Wide World*, Mr. Lindsay's abuse of Warner's protagonist, Ellen Montgomery, is most clearly depicted in his pouring wine for Ellen and insisting that she drink it. The "glass of wine looked to Ellen like an enemy marching up to attack her" (517–18), an important event underscored in many early editions by an illustration depicting the scene (plate 33). Mr. Lindsay even wishes he could "make her drink Lethe!" (551) so that she will forget her American friends and heritage, a culturally despicable intention for nineteenth-century Americans. Ellen underscores the disparity between the Lindsays, her society-conscious and superficial Scottish relatives, and the favored American Humphreys family—who live simple lives devoted to moral, intellectual, and religious concerns—by noting that Alice and John Humphreys never drink wine.

Maria Cummins, to whom Nathaniel Hawthorne referred in his now famous quotation about "a d——d mob of scribbling women," wrote another of the most popular novels of the century, *The Lamplighter* (1854). According to James D. Hart in *The Popular Book*, the novel represented "the thoughts and feelings of the majority" (Freibert and White 243). Indeed, the disdain for alcohol and the hardships it causes for women appear to represent the feelings of the majority of women, if not of men. In *The Lamplighter*, Willie Sullivan is saved from taking a glass of wine when his mother's touch causes the glass to fall from his hand and break into a thousand pieces (171), attesting to women's important involvement in temperance. Later, while in Paris, Willie becomes intrigued by "polished gentlemen" and the "ornaments of the sphere" in which members of a favored class move, and he fails to keep up his guard; he almost allows himself to be enticed into drinking wine, but his mother's influence continues to assert itself when his "recollection" of her "warning counsels . . . springing up and arming themselves with a solemn meaning" save Willie from danger (355–56). Without the guidance of a woman on temperance matters, Willie would have been lost. His mother is instrumental in Willie's salvation, but his resistance to the dissipating effects of drink also help to demonstrate that he is morally worthy of Gerty, the novel's protagonist. The author thus enacts through plot what temperance reformers attempted to do politically.

E. D. E. N. Southworth, another of the century's most popular women authors, also claimed that she "tried to please the multitude and satisfy the cultured" (Dobson, Introduction, xi). In doing so, she was aware of and sensitive to cultural implications connected with alcohol. Southworth was so popular with the public that Robert Bonner, editor of the *New York Ledger*, paid her handsomely for the exclusive rights to her stories for more than thirty years. Bonner also capitalized on the extreme popularity of Southworth's *The Hidden Hand* (1859) by serializing it three times before permitting its publication in book form. *The Hidden Hand*'s protagonist, Capitola Black, was one of the best-known heroines of the nineteenth century. She became an icon—so popular that articles of clothing and other paraphernalia sported her name. In *The Hidden Hand*, Capitola, a daring and unconventional character who has lived on the streets, comments wryly on the dangers of alcohol. When her guardian,

Major Warfield, encourages her to drink wine, the feisty Capitola replies, "Ah, sir, my life has shown me too much misery that has come of drinking wine" (52). Old Hurricane (Major Warfield) does drink intoxicating beverages and his behavior is often questionable. For example, described as a "self-indulgent old Sybarite, who dearly loved his own ease" (9), Old Hurricane sips his gin punch and would gladly neglect his responsibilities except for the continued insistence of Reverend Goodwin that the Major perform his duties of office.

Alcoholic intake marks other characters negatively as well. The only other characters to imbibe alcoholic drinks are outlaws. Capitola and other model characters never drink, and Herbert Greyson, Capitola's betrothed, notes that "I never use intoxicating liquors . . . because I gave a promise to that effect to my dying mother!" (55), attesting both to his worthiness and to the importance of women in saving youth from dissipation. Even Old Hurricane acquiesces: "Drink water if you like. *It won't hurt you*" (55).

One of the most famous nineteenth-century male protagonists was St. Elmo Murray in Augusta Evans's popular novel, *St. Elmo* (1866). Like Capitola, the novel and its reformed hero were so popular that St. Elmo's name surfaced on representative commodities, such as cigars. St. Elmo is the only character in the novel explicitly represented in terms of alcoholic beverages. He refills his champagne glass at dinner (150) and drinks, gambles and carouses during his days of dissipation in Paris (271). After his reformation and installation as minister (and especially after his marriage to Edna Earle), the reader would have been shocked by any further alcoholic consumption. Although Edna refuses to "save" St. Elmo, her example is essential to his reform.

Louisa May Alcott's Meg in *Little Women* (1868) takes a stand against intoxicating beverages as well. An early chapter entitled "Meg Goes to Vanity Fair" depicts Meg's dangerous flirtation with the trappings and excitement of a pleasure-loving society. Meg attends the ball with "frizzled head, bare shoulders, and fantastically trimmed dress," wears jewelry and powder, and is generally "made to look a fashion plate" (106). She also drinks champagne with boys who behave "like a pair of fools" (108). Meg suffers a "splitting headache" and remains ill the entire day following the ball. The boys' foolish behavior reflects their consumption of alcohol, and Meg's eventual rejection of the showy excesses of the alcohol-imbibing social group attests to her progress toward maturity and virtue.

Later in the novel, when Meg marries, her alcohol-free wedding evinces her good character and implies that her married life will be happy. Meg determines to make her wedding one of her own choice, not a conventional one. At the reception following the wedding, in communion with her father's wishes, she sets a good example by banning alcoholic beverages. Even though Mr. Laurence has offered vintage wines for the celebration, and Aunt March has actually brought along wine for the occasion, only water, lemonade, and coffee are served along with the cake and fruit. Mr. March retains a small amount of the gift wine for medicinal purposes and sends the remainder along to the old soldiers' home, presumably to be used as health remedies as well. Alcott's Meg exemplifies both the cultural rejection of alcohol appropriate for admirable characters and the ability of women to influence others by example.

Because the temperance focus accommodated a variety of philosophies about the proper means of rectifying disturbing conditions for victims of alcoholic men, nearly all women could feel comfortable with temperance fiction. Popular authors' interest in writing temperance fiction served to increase both their own visibility and that of the temperance problem as a woman's issue. For authors, the acceptable temperance topic permitted widespread publication of temperance works, which were often published over and over. For example, Harriet Beecher Stowe's "The Coral Ring" was featured in an 1843 gift book, *The Christian Souvenir*. In 1848, the same story was published in *Godey's Lady's Book*, and in 1853, the Scottish Temperance League published *The Coral Ring* under its own cover. In addition, Stowe included the story in her collection, *May Flowers and Miscellaneous Writings*, as well as in a later collection, *Stories, Sketches and Studies*. Similarly, "Let Every Man Mind His Own Business," in *The Mayflower and Miscellaneous Writings* (1855), was originally published in 1839 in the *New-York Evangelist* as "The Drunkard Reclaimed," in *The Christian Keepsake and Missionary Annual* in 1839, and again in *The Christian Keepsake* in 1848. Other authors also made ample use of the popularity and acceptability of temperance fiction.

In addition, publication of temperance works by such loved and established writers as Stowe, Lydia H. Sigourney, and Alcott gave further credibility to the idea that alcohol abuse was, indeed, a serious problem, one with major implications for women. Popular writers were less likely than those who wrote primarily temperance fiction to explore underlying implications for women or to suggest remedies, such as separation, divorce, and suffrage, but their works do sometimes address such issues and unquestionably highlight the many injustices and marked dangers for nineteenth-century women.

Such popular works helped both to promote temperance ideals and to confirm women's importance in advancing those ideals. Popular writers did not relegate temperance messages only to these major best sellers, however. Other renowned works by these authors and others address the issue as well. Unlike explicitly labeled temperance fiction, these popular works nearly always allow for the heroine's happy ending; but as in women's temperance fiction, alcohol is nearly always associated with either physical or emotional danger to women. Alcohol jeopardizes the bright hopes of young women who trust their futures to intemperate men; it also often endangers children physically, economically, and socially, especially daughters, who must live with alcoholic fathers; and mothers, daughters, and sisters face heartbreak because of the devastating effect drink has on sons and loved ones.

As did women temperance speakers and writers, popular women novelists at mid-century often portrayed women as the victims of intemperance. For example, emotional and psychological abuse figure prominently in the temperance works of Ann Stephens. Stephens first gained renown as a contributor to such periodicals as the *Ladies Companion*, *Graham's*, and *Peterson's*. She later successfully wrote novels and contributed to Beadle's dime novels. Stephens's 1847 contribution to a temperance gift book, "The Tempter and the Tempted," demonstrates how alcohol can be used by an antagonist to punish women. When Ellen Fleming rejects a young suitor named Brownson, partially because of his drinking habits, Brownson threatens Ellen: "Look on me Ellen Fleming, you will yet sleep in the bosom of a drunkard" (16). Brownson purposefully befriends Ellen's betrothed, a young lawyer named Franklin, in order to punish Ellen. He arranges to accompany Franklin on a trip south and maliciously convinces Franklin to drink wine, gradually encouraging him to take ever greater quantities. Ellen and Franklin are married immediately upon Franklin's return, but Franklin's addiction to wine increases. Recognizing the financial and emotional ruin he is bringing upon Ellen and their infant, Franklin decides to commit suicide. As Brownson grabs Franklin's arm to prevent the deed, the gun misfires, striking Ellen. The wound does not prove to be fatal, but horror at his deed and initial belief that he had killed his wife lead Franklin to promise never again to touch alcohol. Stephens thus accents unique ways in which alcohol can present dangers for women. In addition, such stories might suggest the need for legal and social reform. After all, Franklin, like many characters in women's temperance fiction, was not dissipated when Ellen fell in love with him. Problems that ensue after a marriage, or about which wives learn too late, cannot readily be avoided or remedied without some legal or societal support. The story thus points to the need for the legal autonomy for women.

In another of Stephens's short stories, "The Wife" (1847), Lucy Sprague, an orphan and wealthy heiress, marries Thomas Burke against the wishes of her uncle and guardian, Mr. Stewart. Stewart warns Lucy that Thomas is "a wine drinker, a heartless profligate in every thing" (45). Lucy acknowledges Thomas's problem, but insists that he is not heartless. After their marriage, Thomas drinks increasing amounts of liquor, eventually coming home drunk every evening and squandering Lucy's fortune.

Finally, his drunken acts lead to his imprisonment. Lucy's guardian has had the forethought to ask Thomas to sign a prenuptial agreement keeping a small portion of Lucy's estate in her name. Thomas had gladly signed, and after his ruin, he begs Lucy to take the money and forget him. Instead, she uses the money to effect his release and to leave the country with him to begin a new life; however, the many hardships she has endured lead to her early death shortly after the emigration. Stephens does not explicitly address notions of separation or divorce, but Lucy's early death might be seen as a form of murder, especially when read in conjunction with "The Tempter and the Tempted." If not a direct appeal for leaving intemperate husbands, the stories certainly foreground both the dangers of engaging in a relationship with men who drink and of remaining with drunken husbands. Stephens presents a complex problem here for women, that of appreciating and loving good men who become victims to alcohol. Thomas is, after all, profligate but not heartless; the use of alcohol diminishes men's goodness, leaving women in a difficult and dangerous situation.

Caroline Lee Hentz's women characters do not suffer direct physical abuse at the hands of the inebriates in their lives, but the consequences associated with intoxicated relatives do endanger them. Hentz, a New Englander by birth, moved to the South and became a noted writer about that region. She, too, was a major contributor to periodicals, especially to *Godey's Lady's Book*. Her popular *The Planter's Northern Bride* (1851) offered a Southerner's response to Harriet Beecher Stowe's *Uncle Tom's Cabin*. Hentz's temperance stories were originally serialized, primarily in the *Philadelphia Saturday Courier*, but also in popular periodicals. She later included the stories in her collected works. For example, "The Drunkard's Daughter," which also appeared in *Godey's*, was later collected in both *The Mob Cap and Other Tales* (1850) and in *Courtship and Marriage* (1856).

Mr. Franklin, the inebriate in Hentz's "The Drunkard's Daughter," attests to the mortal dangers for women associated with alcoholic men. Mr. Franklin relates details of his mother's slow death, providing confirmation of the problem from a voice of experience. He saw her "cheek grow paler and paler, and knew that my father's curses and threats and brutal treatment were the cause—when I saw her at length die of a broken heart and heard the neighbors say that my father had killed her, and that he would have to answer for her death at the great bar of Heaven!" (357). Watching the consequences of his father's drinking does not save Mr. Franklin from repeating the pattern, however. His own wife becomes an invalid because of hardships consequent to her husband's drinking, and the presentation of women's suffering is a clarion call for change.

A further example of women's endangerment can be found in Hentz's

"The Tempest" (1856). Rose Somers refuses to go boating with Augustus Norwood because he has been drinking, but Augustus's younger sister, Mary, accompanies him. Augustus tries to protect Mary but, in his intoxicated state, fails to prevent her from falling into the water. Inebriated and confused, his efforts to rescue her come too late, and Mary is pronounced dead. Mary later revives unexpectedly, but Augustus has already wandered off in a drunken and shocked state, and family and friends believe he has drowned himself in the river. Augustus returns years later, a reformed man, but his previous behavior endangered the life of his sister and caused much grief and sorrow among the other women who love him. As do Hentz's other temperance stories, this one suggests the need for women to have greater power and influence over the dangerous habits and habit-forming vices in society.

Some popular women authors did address the divorce issue, always in relation to physical abuse, but seldom offered definitive advice. Physical abuse figures prominently in the temperance short story of Elizabeth F. Ellet. Ellet, a popular contributor to periodicals, apparently wrote only one temperance story. In "A Country Recollection; or the Reformed Inebriate" (1859), Ellet equivocates about how women should address such issues as divorce and separation. Jane B.'s husband, Walter, becomes physically abusive to both wife and children, even building a fence around their cottage to keep the knowledge of his abusive treatment from neighbors. Jane finally leaves Walter in order to protect her children, but she does not desert her husband. When Walter is unjustly accused of murder and incarcerated, Jane takes his Bible and tracts to him, seeking to reform him. Walter is eventually acquitted of the murder charge but is wasted and sick, and Jane works "day and night" to "procure him comforts." Thus, Ellet protects both wife and children from abuse without the final desertion of the spouse. The imprisoned husband and father is also a safe husband and father, and by the time of his release from prison, Walter is an invalid and no longer an alcoholic. Further, the thankful, but sick and wasted man is unlikely to represent further physical danger for the family. So, while Jane is rewarded for her faithfulness to her husband, the text also suggests that women are endangered by men; and Walter's imprisonment intimates a possible avenue for protecting women and children. Only after his incarceration is Walter no longer a threat to his wife and children, suggesting that positive results might be gleaned from making abusive men accountable for their actions.

The best-known woman poet of the century, Lydia Sigourney, also wrote prose prolifically. A testament to her popularity is the fact that John S. Hart devoted eight pages to her biography in his 1852 *Female Prose Writers of America*. No other writer claimed that much space, and most writers' biographies are allowed only one-half to three pages. At the time of Hart's writing, Sigourney had produced thirty-five volumes of writing, several pamphlets, and had contributed vastly to contemporary periodicals and gift books.

Sigourney's temperance writings include *Water-Drops* (1850), a volume of poetry and prose. In addition, she contributed temperance short stories to gift books and to newspapers. Her short story, "The Intemperate," highlights a young wife's danger, as well as that of her children, at the hands of an intemperate husband. James Harwood becomes abusive to his wife Jane and causes permanent injury to their son. Sigourney links a woman's happiness to her husband and children, suggesting, thereby, the impossibility of happiness for the wife of an intemperate man: "But, to a woman, a wife, a mother, how small is the portion of independent happiness! She has woven the tendrils of her soul around many props. Each revolving year renders their support more necessary. They cannot waver, or warp, or break, but she must tremble and bleed" (186–87).

Like many writers, Sigourney holds that a woman's greatest duty is to her children: "There was one modification of her husband's persecutions which the fullest measure of her piety could not enable her to bear unmoved. This was unkindness to her feeble and suffering boy" (187). James abuses the son to punish his wife. Still, Jane remains with James, and his alcohol-induced behavior leads to the death of her son when he administers the wrong medication to the ailing child. Sigourney praises a wife's fidelity to her spouse, but the emotional and physical abuse, and the eventual death of her child, highlights a woman's powerlessness in such a marital situation and calls into question the wisdom of such loyalty.

Stowe's early "Let Every Man Mind His Own Business" demonstrates an ambivalence to, and eventual compromise on, the issue of abandoning alcoholic husbands in a way similar to that of Ellet. After Augusta Melton marries Edward Howard, the couple spends a pleasant, loving winter at home enjoying one another's company. But both Augusta and Edward are accustomed to "habitual excitement," and in the spring they rejoin society. When "the cares and duties of a mother beg[i]n to confine her at home" (163), Augusta recognizes her husband's physical and mental deterioration caused by a dependence on alcohol. As problems escalate, and Edward loses the fortune Augusta has brought to the marriage, Augusta struggles to earn sufficient money to save her family from starvation. Finally, when Augusta's brother Henry locates the family, Augusta must decide whether to leave Edward or to remain by his side. Caught between duty toward her children and duty toward her husband, Augusta compromises, sending her children with her brother so that she may make a final effort to save Edward from "*everlasting* despair." With the help of temperance reformers, Augusta is able to save Edward, and the family is reunited in love and harmony. Stowe is thus able to finesse both the divorce issue and concern about the damage inflicted upon children when women stay in a bad relationship. While she does not address such issues directly, her contention that women, by their influence, can save men from the dangers of alcohol nonetheless helps to establish temperance as a woman's issue, since only women, it seems, have the power to effect change.

Thus, although women are often depicted as victims, especially at mid-century, they are also presented as agents of change, primarily through their ability to influence. For example, Harriet Beecher Stowe's temperance stories demonstrate her faith in women's ability to influence. Although Stowe was not actively involved with temperance organizations, she did write at least one public letter praising women for their effectiveness in temperance work,[1] and she wrote numerous temperance short stories. In Stowe's "The Coral Ring," Edward Ashton asks Florence Elmore to use her influence to save Colonel George Elliot, one of her admirers. Edward and others have considered Elliot a lost man because men of Elliot's acquaintance have not been able to convince Elliot to stop his reckless bouts of drinking. In soliciting Florence's help, Edward asks her

> What are you women made with so much tact and power of charming for, if it is not to do these very things we cannot do? It is a delicate matter—true; and has not Heaven given to you a fine touch and a fine eye for just such delicate matters? Have you not seen a thousand times, that what might be resented or an impertinent interference on the part of a man, comes to us as a flattering expression of interest from the lips of a woman? (381)

Florence agrees to accept Edward's charge and successfully convinces George to sign the temperance pledge, attesting to the power of her influence beyond that of the young men.

In Stowe's "Betty's Bright Idea" (1875), the protagonist, again named Florence, uses her Christmas allowance to buy presents for the poor family of John Morley, a former employee of her father who has been discharged because of his drinking. Florence convinces John to sign the temperance pledge and then persuades her father to renew John's employment, attesting to her ability to influence these men. In providing such "influential" models, however, Stowe is careful that those women using their influence are squarely outside a romantic involvement with the men they seek to help. Thus, she implicitly acknowledges the danger and difficulty other writers point out—that of trying to reform a love interest.

Louisa May Alcott also suggests that women can readily address the problem of intemperance through their ability to influence. Coming from a tradition of reform, Alcott must have been comfortable with the temperance movement. She participated actively in reform organizations, serving as President of the Concord, Massachusetts WCTU in 1883. She makes reference to temperance in nearly all of her novels. She titles a chapter in *Jack and Jill* (1880) "Good Templars," devoting the entire chapter to Frank and Jack's participation in the temperance cause. Like many of the works of other temperance workers, the chapter could readily serve as an outline for how to ask others to take the pledge, how to construct a temperance newsletter, and how to become involved in other temperance activities. There are similar references to temperance in most of Alcott's works. In *Jo's Boys* (1886), for example, the danger associated with alcohol threatens each of Jo's boys at one time or another; Rose, in *Rose in Bloom* (1876), exacts a promise from Charlie that he will not drink, but Charlie takes a final fling with champagne and is subsequently thrown from his horse and killed; and *Little Men*'s (1871) Mr. Bhaer openly opposes drinking, gambling, and swearing.

Alcott published explicit temperance works as well. In 1876, she published two stories in the book *Silver Pitchers, and Independence: A Centennial Love Story*. "Silver Pitchers" is a specifically temperance story and outlines ways for young women to do their part for the cause. In "Pitchers," Alcott presents three young women who determine to take action after someone spikes the cider at a community function and puts brandy in the coffee, the drink used by young women who avoid even cider. As the story unfolds, we learn how each of the "Sweet P's"—Portia, Priscilla, and Polly—takes action in favor of temperance according to her own individual nature and in a way tailored to her circumstances. Written shortly after the Woman's Crusade, "Silver Pitchers" suggests a way for these young women to use their "influence" and to do their "duty," even though they are too young to "preach and pray in streets and bar-rooms" (6). Despite suggestions that the young women must carefully work within acceptable parameters for women, Alcott's characters, like Stowe's, exhibit a remarkable power to remedy societal ills. Portia conspires with her mother to dissuade her father from his overuse of alcohol; she also sets a standard for parties among young people by creating the most interesting of parties in the community, even though she serves only cake and tea. Priscilla begins a temperance group, "The Water Babies," among her pupils, who subsequently influence their parents to give up wine. Polly creates a humorous newspaper, *The Pollyantha*, to entertain and persuade her sick brother of the dangers of alcohol, and the witty newspaper circulates widely among the young people of the community. Although the newspaper becomes widespread and influential, Polly's original (and humble) intent was merely to impress a member of her home circle. Like actual women writers for temperance in the nineteenth century, Polly's writing exerts a widespread and powerful influence despite, or perhaps because of, her womanly and appropriate presentation. All three young women remain well within the accepted traditions of feminine influence, making effective change from within their own spheres.

By contrast, the absence of good influence presents grave problems. As the primary positive influence for children, a mother's failure or inability to inspire her young toward good motives presents another common theme for popular women novelists. For example, Sigourney's "Louisa Wilson" (1850) depicts an alcoholic wife, a presentation relatively rare in women's temperance fiction. Louisa, a good and kind orphan, revels in social entertainments. She has no mother or siblings to guide her or to offer companionship, so Louisa eagerly attends numerous social engagements where wine is usually prominent. Louisa marries and is happy for a time, but her increasing addiction to alcohol threatens to destroy her marriage. She makes great efforts at reform, but when her doctor prescribes alcoholic tonics for her, she again succumbs to the disease and eventually, in an intoxicated stupor, drops her child into the fire, charring its hand and arm so badly they must be amputated. The baby's father is unable to forgive Louisa, and she languishes and dies. Louisa's dissipation, Sigourney suggests, would have been prevented with the guidance of a good mother during her childhood.

Caroline Kirkland, a successful and respected teacher and author, was best known for *A New Home—Who'll Follow? or, Glimpses of Western Life* (1839). She wrote novels as well as shorter sketches and reviews, sometimes including her work in the gift books she edited. Kirkland often published in popular periodicals as well, and served as editor of the *Union Magazine of Literature and Art*. Two pieces of Kirkland's temperance writing appear in Alice Cary's *The Adopted Daughter* as well. Kirkland focuses largely on proper parenting. "Comfort" tells the story of a son who has become dissipated and alcoholic, largely as a result of his mother's overindulgence and failure to discipline him as a child. The mother invites her pretty niece to visit in the hopes that an attraction to her will bring her son to reform. Kirkland points out her willingness to sacrifice this young woman in order to rectify her own mistakes, not surprising given her history of influence with her son.

Kirkland's "John Hinchley" (1850) draws attention to the other extreme of improper parenting. John's too strict father refuses to let John attend huskings, quiltings, and raisings. John, then, eventually seeks solace in alcohol rather than in the more positive and innocent entertainments from which his father has kept him. Kirkland pleads for a middle ground for parenting that is neither too strict nor overindulgent. She asks that parents require obedience in the spirit of love.

In line with her beliefs about women's ability to create change through influence, Kirkland's "Agnes: A Story of Revolutionary Times" (1846) tells the story of Agnes Manning, who disregards convention and refuses to serve alcoholic beverages to young men who visit her father's home.

Agnes's intoxicated brother-in-law, Philip Lebrand, places Agnes in danger by suggesting to his British cronies that Agnes's father would pay extravagantly for her freedom should they take her hostage. Like many authors, Kirkland associates alcohol with negative character: Philip, un-American by his Tory allegiance, drinks even more than most of his contemporaries. Eventually, Agnes's heroic and composed behavior influences Philip, as well as other young Americans in Washington's army, to denounce the use of intoxicating drinks. Philip not only gives up drink, but he becomes a patriotic American as well, a testimony to the power of Agnes's influence.

One way in which popular women writers chose to use their own influence was in pointing out the unfairness of societal prejudices against those associated with the inebriate. Throughout the century, authors suggest that women must become self-sufficient in order to overcome and change unjust prejudicial treatment. In doing so, they often present remarkably strong role models. For example, in the early 1800s, Catharine Maria Sedgwick was already writing about many of the concerns regarding the consequences of alcohol abuse that would surface throughout the century. Sedgwick, from a well-to-do Massachusetts family, was accepted as a major American author during her lifetime and hosted one of the most important literary salons of the nineteenth century. Her best-known works are *Hope Leslie* (1827) and *The Linwoods* (1835). In her fiction about intemperance, Sedgwick highlights problems encountered by women who marry drinking men, and she presents strong women models who heroically overcome hardships created by those men. In her 1822 *Mary Hollis: An Original Tale*, Mary Lowe, an orphaned girl from a respectable family, is reduced from "comfortable circumstances to penury when her husband resigns himself to the habits of intemperance" (4). Similarly, after six months of marriage to a young New England lawyer, Mrs. Lee, in *Live and Let Live; or, Domestic Service Illustrated* (1837), "discovered that her husband was in the habit of intemperate drinking" (11). In each work, the wife and mother takes control after an alcoholic husband depletes the family's economic resources and brings social embarrassment to his wife and children; despite very difficult circumstances, the women in both tales find the means of creating livable, even happy, situations. Divorce never becomes an issue in Sedgwick's works as drunken husbands conveniently die while still young. Their deaths may attest to the mortal dangers associated with intemperance, but they also allow for women protagonists to remedy the doleful consequences of their marriages without divorcing or separating from their husbands. Still, Sedgwick does present the physical harm caused by intemperance. Jemmie, Mrs. Lee's son, becomes an invalid because his intoxicated father, despite Mrs. Lee's desperate entreaties, puts the three year old on a horse, and the child "suffered a debilitating fall" (35).

Sedgwick also focuses on the issue of the prejudicial treatment of in-nocent victims of the alcoholic father and husband. Neighbors taunt both wives and children of the inebriates, but the women protagonists in both novels show disdain for such attitudes and work consciously to build their children's self-image and future happiness. Wives of alcoholic husbands show great wisdom and strength in addressing very difficult situations, and through the guidance of their mothers, children of intem-perate fathers become happy, successful adults. Sedgwick addresses so-cial issues that few other writers address until much later in the century, but like many other authors who follow her, she implies that poverty is the direct result of intemperance.

Hentz also foregrounds strong women and the social embarrass-ments they face. Kate in "The Drunkard's Daughter" leaves her home in a raging storm at midnight in search of her alcoholic father, fearful that he cannot survive the storm in his drunken state: "How strong must have been the impulse, how intense the anxiety, which could have induced a timid young girl to come out at that lone, silent hour, on such a night, without a protector or guide!" (349).

Despite her courage, Kate must contend with the shame and embar-rassment wives and daughters must suffer because of drunken men. Harry Blake happens upon Kate as she tries to revive her father: "She was over-whelmed with shame; for she knew, as Harry inhaled the burning exha-lation of his breath, his disgraceful secret would be revealed—that secret which her mother and herself had so long in anguish concealed" (350).

Like Sedgwick and Hentz, Elizabeth Stuart Phelps presents strong women protagonists. Also like Sedgwick and Hentz, Phelps tries to make readers aware of the prejudicial treatment toward victims of the alco-holic. Unlike Sedgwick, however, Phelps makes social environment the heart of her works, and she implicates hierarchical societal structures in the evils of the disease. Phelps was active in temperance causes, and she contributed to the formation and continuation of a temperance organi-zation in Gloucester, while living among members of an alcoholic com-munity. In Phelps's novels, perils associated with alcohol are even greater than those in Sedgwick's works, because the dangers include murder and suicide—the murder, in Phelps's works as well as in that of other writers, often connoting a form of martyrdom.

Phelps's temperance concern shows up in a number of her shorter works, but she wrote two explicitly temperance novels. *A Singular Life* (1894) narrates the struggles of a minister to the people of a seaport fish-ing community. Because he refuses to accept some orthodox doctrines, Emanual Bayard is refused ordination into the ministry for which he has spent his life preparing. He becomes, instead, the spiritual leader of The Church of the Love of Christ on Angel Alley, a street lined with grog shops. The novel indicts orthodox religion, especially for its refusal and inability to offer assistance to society's neediest people. Bayard's efforts to help his people overcome the addictive effects of alcohol, as well as his work for the closure of saloons, places him at odds with church members and ministers from wealthier congregations and in danger from liquor interests. Phelps's presentation of the struggle to survive and to overcome hardship by the people of Angel Alley is a complex examination of the societal implications in alcohol and dissipation. She offers no happy resolution; Bayard dies, murdered by a representative of the saloon owners, and the reader realizes that false witnesses will testify for and assure the freedom of Bayard's killer. But Phelps implicates an oppressive class system in creating the problem and dismisses the pervasive notion that the poor create and are responsible for their own poverty through their idle and dissipated ways.

Phelps's *A Singular Life* extends beyond personal dangers to encompass dangers to the society at large. The situation on Angel Alley exposes dangers from alcohol interests for the legal system, for churches, and for economic and social institutions. But Phelps also highlights perils to women personally. The primary love interest in the novel occurs between Bayard and Helen Carruth, who eventually becomes Bayard's bride. Helen also labors with the people of Angel Alley, and the reader empathizes with the suffering she endures when she loses the love of her life. In addition, Bayard has worked to support the women victims of alcohol—prostitutes and wives and children of drunkards. With his death, they have lost their primary source of care and support.

Phelps's temperance novella, *Jack the Fisherman* (1887), also presents the difficulties of overcoming the poverty and violence into which one is born. Even though Jack and his wife, Teen, struggle to create a better life, they are products of a society whose attitudes and behaviors entrap the couple. Jack eventually murders Teen in a drunken, jealous rage. When he realizes what he has done, he commits suicide by drowning himself in the ocean. Their child does present some measure of hope for future generations. Mother Mary, who has tried to provide assistance to Jack and Teen, adopts the child, suggesting a possibility for breaking ongoing generational behavior. Significantly, the woman representing that hope, Mother Mary, is a temperance worker.

Popular women authors generally avoided controversial subjects, such as suffrage and equal rights for women, but some did address such concerns. While rarely remembered as a popular writer today, Sarah Knowles Bolton wrote a number of popular nineteenth-century works. Her best-known and greatest sellers were her series of biographies for children and her series on women. Bolton served as secretary of the first WCTU meeting in Cleveland and later as assistant corresponding secretary of the National WCTU. She wrote a history of the Temperance Crusade for the WCTU centennial volume and published poetry and short stories for magazines, later collecting them into volumes. Bolton's single temperance novel, *The Present Problem* (1874), illustrates the frequent commingling of temperance and woman's rights issues by women reform leaders in the nineteenth century. A vast number of women were involved in both movements or believed that working for one equated working for the other. Frances D. Gage, in an 1854 letter to *The Lily*, espoused this idea: "I gave twenty-five lectures on the two great subjects of reform, Temperance and Woman's Rights (which indeed seem but one, so closely are all the interests united)" (104).

In the Preface explaining the need for her novel, Bolton tells her reader, "Intemperance and immorality are on every side. We have tacitly countenanced them in one sex, while we have condemned them in the other. The women of America are beginning to feel the magnitude of the evils they are called upon to meet, and the greatness of the work God has laid upon them."

Bolton discusses issues of intemperance, but addresses numerous other issues with regards to women as well. She questions the moral and social double standard for men and women; she also offers explicit support for "strong-minded women," for women who break traditional gender roles, and for "working" women. In addition, she emphasizes women's need and right to support themselves, to become self-reliant, and to be something other than "mere playthings" for men.

Some authors may have written temperance fiction to capitalize on the subject's broad appeal, but there can be little question of the interest in temperance reform for many authors. Louisa May Alcott, Sarah K. Bolton, and Elizabeth Stuart Phelps took active parts in temperance organizations. Others, such as Harriet Beecher Stowe, Sarah Josepha Hale, and Caroline Kirkland had a history of interest in reform issues and in issues of concern to women. But, I have been able to find no obvious interest in temperance among some of the popular novelists who occasionally wrote temperance fiction, except in the one or two works written for gift books explicitly earmarked for a temperance audience. Their celebrity status was likely important in some of them being invited or persuaded to contribute to such publications, and the broad acceptance of the temperance cause, especially among women, would have made it convenient for them to write for such a specific purpose.

Elizabeth F. Ellet may have been one such author, Metta Fuller Victor another, although Victor wrote very popular temperance novels. The prolific Victor was a frequent contributor to periodicals and gift books, often writing under a variety of names and doing editorial work during part of her career. Her *The Senator's Son* (1853) and *Fashionable Dissipations* (1854) are not atypical temperance novels, but Freibert and White suggest that Victor capitalized on opportunities, having "changed her subject matter and style to accord with public taste" (306). In the first part of her career, she wrote reform novels. Later, after marrying Orville Victor, she took advantage of his position as general editor of Beadle and Adams's dime novels and wrote for that series (or may have been persuaded to do so, since she was already a popular writer). Later, in the 1870s, Victor turned to the lighter, humorous sketches of childhood that were becoming popular.

Like much of women's temperance fiction, *The Senator's Son* relates the story of men's drunkenness and the subsequent devastating effects on the women in their lives. Victor does, however, address women's legal inequities. Both Alice Madison, who marries Alfred Clyde in order to save her brother Parke, and Lucy, Parke's beautiful wife, become destitute and have difficulty providing for their children, even though the Madison estate should have provided well for both. Parke even demands what little money Lucy earns from her painting.

Like Lucy Sprague in Stephens's "The Wife" and Augusta Melton in Stowe's "Let Every Man Mind His Own Business," Alice Madison had come to her marriage to Alfred Clyde with a vast fortune, a common theme in women's temperance fiction. That women are comfortably provided for but become destitute at the hands of their husbands serves to point out the dangers of marrying an intemperate man, but also emphasizes the great injustice toward and powerlessness of women in a country where married women must relinquish all legal rights to their own money. Parke's right to demand Lucy's hard earned money also points to the failure of the legal system to protect women. Anger and frustration about just such situations led to efforts to change these unjust laws, and the difficulties women encountered in making changes fueled demands for more rights for women, including the right to participate in elections.

Victor's *Fashionable Dissipation* does less to draw attention to injustices and inequities for women. Blanche Guyarre does anguish over her brother Pierre's problem with drinking, but he has reformed before the novel begins. Her fear revolves around temptations that might cause her brother's second fall. Both Charles Lennard and Evelyn Hubbard succumb to the temptations of alcohol. But Evelyn is an "insincere woman" with whom the reader is unlikely to identify, and Charles has deserted the novel's chief protagonist, Rose Lee, when a train derailment injures her and he believes that she will be an invalid for life. Perhaps by the time she wrote *Fashionable Dissipation*, Victor was already losing interest in the temperance issue.

Other well-known writers contributed at least one temperance story to gift books or collections. Grace Greenwood (pseudonym for Sara Jane Lippincott), for example, wrote a temperance short story, "James Blair; or, Love in the Valley of Juniata," for *The Fountain*, a temperance gift

book. James Blair is actually a minor character except that he is the inebriate. The story focuses on the relationships between Henry Elbridge,
minister son of a rich and aristocratic Virginia family; Katherine Denny,
the beautiful belle in the region where Henry goes to preach; and Elizabeth Blair, daughter of the inebriate James Blair. Like many temperance
stories that highlight society's injustices to victims of the inebriate, the
story ends with the happy marriage of Henry Elbridge and Elizabeth
Blair, the wise Henry having chosen the good and kind drunkard's daughter over the beautiful, fashionable, but manipulative Katherine.

Numerous popular authors also wrote temperance poetry, but most
notable was Lydia Sigourney, who includes poetry in her *Water-Drops*
and who contributed temperance poetry to periodicals and gift books.
Others, such as Alice and Phoebe Cary, wrote temperance poetry for gift
books, and Caroline Hentz contributed temperance poetry to periodicals.

Ironically, at least some of the women writers who wrote about temperance made use of addictive substances themselves. Both Harriet Beecher
Stowe and Louisa May Alcott grew up in households where addictive substances were banned, and both acknowledged dangers from such substances in their writing. But, Stowe drank wine throughout her life, and
Alcott made use of opium.[2]

Nineteenth-century women did comprise the majority of users of patent
medicines, many of which contained alcohol, sometimes nearly 50 percent
(Green 140). And both paregoric and laudanum, commonly used for
medicinal purposes, were opium derivatives. But manufacturers often reported the alcoholic content on labels, and some temperance women,
such as Julia Colman, encouraged women to test for the presence of alcohol in questionable medicines and foods, while others wrote about the
dangers of such substances as laudanum. Although doctors did prescribe,
and women used, such patent medicines, the use of such products by
women does not provide proof, as Alcott's biographer Charles Strickland
suggests, of these women's "moral hypocrisy" (143). Rather, this may
demonstrate that their fear of alcohol and its use was associated primarily with men and subsequently to women's precarious situation in relation to men. Even Frances Willard, President of the WCTU, drank wine
regularly while abroad before her presidency but after her claim to believe in the temperance cause. Significantly, when offered wine by a
woman in whose home she was staying while president of the WCTU,
Willard's response had nothing to do with the dangers of alcohol for her:

No sooner had I reached my beautiful and quiet room, than
the hostess, who had greeted me at the door, came in, saying
earnestly, "Will you not allow me to send you up a glass of wine?
You must be very tired after your journey." The blood flushed
in cheek and brow as I said to her, "Madam, 200,000 women

> would lose somewhat of their faith in humanity if I should
> drink a drop of wine." . . . Evidently this lady lived in a world so
> different from my own that it did not occur to her that a temper-
> ance woman was a total abstainer! (Willard, *Glimpses* 492)

Willard's concern here is for her image with union members, not the fear
of her own addiction.

Alcohol abuse permitted women to focus their fears and anger, and
to unite in a common cause: improving conditions for women. Nina Baym
suggests that

> In striking contrast to woman's fiction, which frequently uses
> the motif of the drunkard, the temperance novel stresses, as
> it must, the failure or inadequacy of feminine moral influ-
> ence to solve this problem. Many women sacrifice themselves
> and exert influence to no avail. A temperance novel must show
> woman's power as insufficient because its purpose is to get
> temperance legislation passed. (267)

Temperance fiction does often differ from woman's fiction, primarily because fewer stories end happily for women protagonists in temperance fiction, and because the happy bride appears at the beginning of
the story rather than at the end. Nonetheless, in a great deal of temperance fiction by popular writers, influence does solve the problem. Numerous writers present woman's influence as a powerful and often
successful deterrent or remedy for problems associated with intemperance. And, although the fiction often shows women's powerlessness
amidst unjust legal laws and societal conventions, often the narrative
explores options and suggests ways in which women might increase their
power. Sometimes those suggestions include legal changes, but often they
present other ways in which women may protect themselves and maintain a certain measure of power—by remaining single, by very carefully
assessing a suitor before agreeing to marriage, and by leaving a marital
relationship when the husband and father endangers the physical and
economic well-being of his family. The compelling stories written by
women about temperance permitted nineteenth-century women to focus their fears and angers, and to unite in efforts to improve their conditions. That, once organized, they were forced to recognize how very powerless
they were led them to explore new and more effective means of addressing inequities.

Conclusion:
Women of the Century

The nineteenth century is woman's century [a] marvelous promise of the twentieth century.

—Frances Willard and Mary A. Livermore
Preface, *American Women*

THE NINETEENTH-CENTURY temperance movement provides lessons for us at the end of the twentieth century. A major contribution to the temperance movement's success was the ability of its leaders to appeal to women across socio-economic, racial, religious, and national identities. Everyday women came to accept the tenets offered by temperance leaders, including the necessity for suffrage and other equal rights for women. Leaders from mid-century through the end of the 1800s understood the need to approach women rhetorically on their own terms, accepting their level of consciousness and practical needs. Frances Willard expressed such awareness best:

> [I]f we are going to win, there is one individual we have got to win—she is the key to our position—the average woman. For the abstract principle of justice on which the woman question is really based, the average woman does not care a farthing; though for the sake of justice in the concrete she often plays the part of a heroine. If she thinks she ought to want the ballot she will seek it with persevering zeal; but she honestly believes that it is more womanly to cry out against than for it. She has been told this from press and pulpit since her earliest recollection, and she has learned the same doctrine from her husband at home. ("The Average Woman" 623)

163

Willard understood both that change for women would come only when large numbers of women demanded change and that those women would demand change only if convinced to do so by leaders whom they could safely and proudly emulate. Most nineteenth-century women were at least as fearful of being identified as "suffragettes" as many women today are of being labeled "feminists." Willard sometimes protested that the term "strong-minded" should be a designation of pride, but she carefully limited such remarks to such audiences as the National Council of Women and avoided the term at mass gatherings.

Willard also understood the fragile and precarious relationship she held with most women, noting that the "average woman" was not "too well pleased with platform women." She held great respect for the average woman, acknowledging that she might not be versed in current theories, "but this same average woman has a hard sense in the snug round box on top of her head, and whoever counts her out, let not the progressive women do so if they expect to win" ("The Average Woman" 623–4). Nineteenth-century temperance women leaders never "counted out" average women. Rather, they relied on these women to bring about change. In the last quarter of the nineteenth century, leadership came from educated and professional women who understood, accepted, and made room for "the average woman."

Today, however, the average woman may be more difficult to define. Many of the changes brought about by nineteenth-century women have provided diverse opportunities and widened the image and identity of twentieth-century women. Women occupy a greater variety of educational levels, employment positions, and familial roles. Nonetheless, with modern techniques for polling women for their beliefs and for gauging their participation in various activities, both inside and outside the home, feminist leaders should be able to understand and appeal effectively to women of different consciousness levels. But to appeal to a broad spectrum of women, academic feminists must abandon complex, theoretical jargon when speaking outside the academy. If they take a lesson from the successful temperance movement, they will learn to speak a language non-threatening to most women. An understanding of parallels and differences with the largest movement of women in the nineteenth century provides helpful models for feminists today.

Women's political situation at the end of this century in many ways parallels their situation at the end of the last. Important correlations apply to leaders' general theoretical approaches. Both groups have recognized the power of language and popular appeal, for example, in reconstructing attitudes and in reproducing culture. In 1892, Frances Willard told her national membership,

> Because language is one of life's greatest educators, let us now attack the phrase, "man and wife" (still standing in the odor of sanctity upon the pages of Catholic and Episcopal ritual), because it incarnates all the serfdom of woman's past, exaggerates sex out of its due subordination to personality, and is false to the facts of the case. (*Minutes of Nineteenth* 117)

Willard recognized the enculturating effect of words, hoping to change their customary use in order to alter modes of thinking. Because of their awareness of such potential, women of both centuries have tried to change societal attitudes by including moral suasion in reform efforts. Nineteenth-century temperance leaders understood the necessity of persuasion, refusing to discard it totally in favor of legislation: "The old battle cry of moral suasion has been a constant weapon . . . [b]ut moral suasion or any other conciliatory means will not accomplish the end we seek. . . . [L]aw and gospel must go hand in hand" (Woodruff 27). Twentieth-century feminists, ostensibly, have focused more on legal redress, but their participation in the late-eighties and early-nineties political correctness movement to change acceptable attitudes differs little from late-nineteenth-century efforts at moral suasion, with both groups understanding the importance of subconscious viewpoints.

Both groups also reflect the importance of the popular press and media in communicating their messages. In the nineteenth century, women made use of both popular fiction and newspaper reporting to change opinions and to garner support. Today's women use television and music to present stirring messages about abuse of women. They also court the news media and capitalize on current events to emphasize their points. Recent made-for-television movies, such as *The Burning Bed*, in which a battered wife strikes back by setting her husband's bed on fire and killing him, as well as attention to real-life happenings, such as the Lorena Bobbitt case and the Clarence Thomas hearings, have served to highlight pervasive sexual harassment and abusive treatment of women; such efforts have helped feminist messages to reach a wide circle of women outside academic venues.

Parallels are also reflected in the specific battles women fight, with late-nineteenth-century rhetoric resonating strongly with issues of the 1990s, such as a woman's right to her own body, equal pay for equal work, and the imperative for women to focus on their own needs. These issues are still unresolved today, and women continue to fight comparable battles. For example, in Iowa at the end of the century, Marion H. Dunham was calling for the right for married women to control their own bodies similar to current efforts to provide legal protection from rape within marriage: "[T]he wife must be conceded the right to retain as full control over her body after marriage as before, a right now denied both by law and custom, and because of which the foulest outrages have been perpetrated through the ages" (37).

And in 1896, Susanna M. D. Fry from Minnesota highlighted the need for better pay for women:

> There is a sentiment abroad in the land that the Utopian condition expressed in the above caption [Equal Pay for Equal Work] has been attained, at least to a good degree. . . . Women have climbed up to high places to-day, but few of them, even in the schools, receive what men do in similar positions. (33)

Such sentiments reverberate today in women's concerns about efforts to remove affirmative action, and their concern about the inequality of compensation between the genders remains a major issue.

Women continue to care for family at the expense of their own needs. Increased employment and career responsibilities among women have not lessened their family obligations proportionally. Women repeatedly remind one another to make time for themselves. In 1887, Lide Meriwether from Tennessee encouraged women to focus realistically upon their own needs:

> I rejoice in the knowledge that in the ranks of our own, and many other progressive and beneficent organizations, so many thousands of American women are finding themselves, and taking their true and rightful place in the world. . . . The special need of the nineteenth-century-woman is to find herself, and that in a very practical sense! ("President's Address" 26)

The need for women to counter opponents' arguments for limiting women's options are similar as well. Much of the rhetoric associating the "decline of the family" with a woman's changing role reverberates over the centuries. Mary T. Lathrap railed against efforts to contain women's progress based on the sanctity of the family: "If self-respecting women make protest against these things, they are met with the cry that the political and ecclesiastical progress of women will destroy the family" (*Poems* 399).

And much like late twentieth-century leaders, Mary E. Griffith, president of the District of Columbia WCTU, reminded listeners that many women were leaving their "sphere" out of necessity, rebutting the argument that women had less need for just compensation for labor than men: "Men claim higher wages than women for equal work because they have wives and children to support, but *some* women have *husbands* and children to support also" (16).

Nonetheless, temperance women, like many of today's women, believed they had made considerable, permanent progress. Today we hear about the "year of the woman," for example, signifying unusually large numbers of women political candidates. Repeatedly, nineteenth-century women referred to the "age of woman" and the "century of the woman" to extol the place they had created for women in nineteenth-century culture. Typical is this passage from Pamela L. Otis's address before the eleventh annual meeting of the Arizona state WCTU: "This has been called a woman's age. It is indeed the epoch of the awakened woman, and to convince one that it is high time that we recognize the need of this period does not require keen observation or logical deductions" (7).

Such rhetoric is associated with women's charting a new course. Today's women celebrate their pioneering entry into areas previously denied them: Sally Ride—first woman astronaut; Geraldine Fararro—first woman vice-presidential candidate from a major political party. They point to numerous other reasons for pride as women have broken restrictive barriers to career paths: women combat pilots, women professionals, women in public offices. Likewise, nineteenth-century women extolled their own originality and advancement despite a lack of models to emulate:

> In 1874 women, seperated [sic] by denominational differences, political preferences and sectional strife; as far apart as nationality, tradition, inheritance, temperment [sic] and education could place them, without experience in business or public affairs, with the old landmarks and ideas of woman's sphere left behind and with no precedent to guide them, but feeling the impulse of a divine call, had to be welded into a homogeneous whole, had to be united in a common purpose, had to learn step by step and costly experience what the purpose should be, had to discover, invent and test their methods, and all this to be done in a voluntary society. (Dunham 32)

Women had forged ahead, making progress. Women's claims to unity today are more likely to be along international lines (as for example, the International Conference on Women), and they are unlikely to claim divine guidance. Nonetheless, they continue to believe they are pioneers, testing new waters, creating change for future generations of women, and measuring progress.

Over and over, at state and national conventions, temperance women measured improvement. Because temperance readily accommodated a variety of women's grievances, the movement was both popular and effective. For example, Mary T. Lathrap enumerated to Michigan union members some of the accomplishments of the WCTU: "Ask," she prompted them,

why Lucy Hayes's portrait is in the White House? Why the
girls' Industrial School is at Adrian? Why intoxicating wine
is banished from the communion table? Go read the record
on Constitutional Prohibition in Kansas, Iowa, Maine, and
Rhode Island; and of Local Option in Atlanta and through
the Sunny South land. Search the state books of fourteen States
and one territory for laws compelling the study of temperance physiology; stand by the presses pouring out books to
meet the demand of these laws. Then go to Washington and
ask why Congress has just passed the first temperance measure since we had a country, and you will find that Mary H.
Hunt and the WCTU are a very clearly defined power to the
men who voted for the national Temperance Education bill.
(*Poems* 336)

In fact, the 1886 Temperance Education Bill passed unanimously in
the Senate and with a 209 to 8 vote in the House: "When the President
had signed the Bill, he handed the pen, with which he had signed it, to
our National Superintendent of Scientific Temperance Instruction, Mrs.
M. H. Hunt of Massachusetts—saying that the Bill owed its passage to
her" (Meriwether, "President's Address" 31). Hunt had written the bill,
and it passed, unamended, as she had written it.

Lathrap and Meriwether mention activities directly related to temperance, but the WCTU was instrumental in achieving legislation in numerous areas of importance to women, some related to temperance only
tangentially, if at all. For example, they also effectively worked to raise
the age of consent in nearly every state, to guarantee the presence of police
matrons for jailed female prisoners, to improve property rights for women,
and to amend laws against prostitution in order to equalize punishment
for men and women. In addition, they created homes for "fallen women"
in many states.

Cornelia B. Forbes, state president of the Connecticut WCTU, extolled this "awakened woman" as follows:

To her the gates of the future have swung outward. She has a
glimpse of wonderous possibilities of achievement, glorious
opportunities lie before her. . . . Because of her there is today
in place of the timid and retiring, or frivolous, vain, helpless spe-
cies of woman kind, a vast army of energetic, educated, self-
reliant and self-supporting women. (37)

Forbes continued, noting women's newly gained skills in "parliamentary
tactics" and in "addressing vast audiences with marvellous power," and
provided statistics to show women's entry into education, medicine, religion, dentistry, law, architecture, and more.

Today, women still measure their success by statistical records of women in the professions, as well as by legislation, although the concerns sometimes differ in focus, such as with laws affecting abortion and the continued efforts for an Equal Rights Amendment. For many, such efforts do not focus on substance control, and they are unlikely to draw up legislation or to be credited with it if they have. Efforts to influence education, while still a concern for many women, are unlikely to proceed from a national level.

And much as the initial energy from the late-sixties and seventies women's movement diminished, altered, or diverged into new paths, so did enthusiasm for the broad causes espoused by temperance women. Membership that had grown so quickly in the first decade of the union showed substantially less growth by the 1890s. The reasons are complex and probably entailed the union's changing public image, increasing dissension within the union, and failure to attract young women.

Leaders broadened the union's agenda, but although leaders boasted of the union's forty departments and two-hundred-thousand-plus members, and although such breadth permitted a wide variety of women to become active as public leaders, such diverse interests also changed the identity of the union and eventually promoted dissension from within and criticism from without. The broader focus diminished the easily identifiable and respectfully safe image of the union.

Early criticism of the WCTU was readily absorbed. That women were the primary sufferers from drink had been firmly established, both in speeches and in temperance fiction, and most reproaches centered on women's taking a public role. Such criticism served to further unify members as these attacks were seen as assaults upon women in the union as a whole. However, as leaders included an increasingly varied number of causes and a more diverse membership, the dignified and respectable facade of unity began to crumble, and critics, especially in newspaper accounts, seized upon the opportunity to portray members as petty, squawking shrews.

Perhaps the greatest strength of the Woman's Christian Temperance Union in amassing such a large number of women was that of establishing an effective network of local, county, district, and state unions—a system nonexistent for women today. Unity among women from a variety of ideological, economic, and regional backgrounds, despite many unpopular and "radical" stands by national leaders, was sustained in large measure by the ability of state and local leaders to mediate differences. The national organization's position on states' rights was intended early on to deflect the discomfort of local and regional groups with more progressive national stands. State and local leaders nonetheless found it necessary to remind members of their right to differ with the position of the national union, and often found it necessary to explain national policy as well. The issue of race, as noted in chapter 4, created severe discomfort for many union members. But efforts at appeasing some members had become necessary much earlier with regards to such controversial national stands as support for suffrage for women, official affiliation with political parties, and the use of local dues to support state and national efforts. Such efforts on the part of Maryland's corresponding secretary to direct members' attention to basic premises is typical:

> I ask those who sometimes fear we are straying from the original purposes of the organization to note particularly the foundation on which we have built, the purpose to use all possible means toward the suppression of the liquor traffic, and to enter into any Christian work connected with this as the Lord may direct. ("Corresponding" 23)

Local and state leaders continually pointed members to the original purpose and strength of the union in an effort to assuage discomfort with more progressive national policy. And as major controversial issues arose, they strove to palliate those matters with their own membership, especially regarding concerns such as suffrage, political affiliation, and the parting with precious money.

Frances Willard's early support for woman's suffrage dismayed and alarmed some local women. In 1878, when Willard called for a resolution supporting suffrage for women, some national leaders expressed concern about how to mediate such a volatile issue with their local members. Mrs. E. B. Hoyt explained that "the public would not understand." Hoyt insisted that she had been asked time and again if she were in favor of women's voting and believed that if she had answered yes, she would have been ineffective. She pleaded that the convention not take an official stand on suffrage for women lest she "feel I cannot go back to the State to which I belong, to do work I hope to do" (*Minutes of WCTU Annual* 32).

After the national organization adopted a suffrage resolution the following year, however, state leaders displayed sophisticated rhetorical acumen in mollifying uneasy members. In an effort to appease her Maryland membership, for example, Mrs. Summerfield Baldwin reminded members of their justifiable pride in the extensive membership of their organization. She also relied upon the diversity within the large numbers to justify the national position:

> Let us always remember that our National Society is composed of women from every State and Territory, women who have voted, women who have acted successfully on School Boards, women who have come from States where there are success-

ful women doctors, lawyers and preachers. They may not
think about women's work as many in Maryland do. We all
meet together annually to plan for better methods of work,
but we can't all be expected to think alike. (21)

Baldwin continued by carefully offering rationales based on temperance
and the Bible. Like many leaders, Baldwin made the liability an asset by
placing arguments in favor of suffrage before her membership in a manner
that might serve to alter their thinking, while attributing the reasoning
to others. She thus offered support for the national position while maintaining her affinity with local members:

> The majority think we will never get national prohibition until
> the women are allowed to vote; again others believe it is a
> fact that God made man in his own image; male and female
> created He them, and gave them dominion over every living
> thing, and think because it was God's plan for woman to be
> man's helpmeet everywhere, it is the best plan, and the nearer
> we keep to God's plan for this the better it will be for all
> humanity. (21)

State and local leaders also served to mediate differences when the
national organization moved toward official support of the Prohibition
Party. The issue was especially problematic in Iowa, where J. Ellen Foster strongly opposed such action.[1] Mary J. Aldrich, president of the Iowa
WCTU, acknowledged members' feelings of bitterness at the stands
taken by the national leadership and, at the same time, recognized their
many sacrifices for the cause. After empathizing with members, she asked
for unity and reminded members of the right of states to take a different
stand in such matters: "Miss Willard and the National officers have ever
kindly recognized the right of our State Union to maintain a non-parti-
san attitude." Aldrich continued to seek unity by invoking the "god terms"
of Christianity for a spirit of acceptance and unity in support of an image of solidarity:

> [D]ifferent minds will so read events as honestly and consci-
> entiously to reach different conclusions, and I have come to
> feel that greater, even than the interests of prohibition, so
> dear to us all, is the importance of each one deciding these ques-
> tions in such a manner and with such a spirit that we ourselves
> and the world outside may see that our *christianity* is able to
> triumph over our *party spirit* in differences of opinion con-
> cerning political methods of prohibition work. (6)

Despite efforts at amelioration, however, J. Ellen Foster and the official Iowa delegation finally walked out of the national convention in 1889 and began a separate Nonpartisan Woman's Christian Temperance Union. Although no other states made such a strong show of opposition, many others found it necessary to pacify local and state members on this issue. In Illinois, Mary Allen West dealt with the problem by taking the middle ground:

> Early in the year, we, as Illinois women, were called to take a stand antagonistic to the wishes of our national president, for whom we would gladly have laid down our lives, but for whom we could not yield what seemed to us principle. In our own ranks have come wide divergence of convictions concerning duty. Many of us feel with all the intensity of our nature that the accepted time is *now*. . . . [T]onight I stand between them, with a hand clasping each, thanking God for both and the work he has enabled them to do. ("President's Annual" *Eleventh* 23)

Thus, West pointed to divergent parties within Illinois, acknowledging the validity of each, but, as mediator, exhibiting a desire to somehow join the two oppositions.

Resistance to sending local dues outside of the area of collection also created dissension. Many local unions severed relationships with state and national unions because auxiliary status meant sharing a portion of dues, and many believed that dues "could accomplish more good by being retained at home" than by being sent to a "foreign field" (Hobart 37). However, leaders usually mediated opposition to dues collection. West's effort to mollify members' opposition to a dues increase is typical. She first prepared members by evoking the strength of the WCTU, based on its network of unions:

> The centre of our organization, around which stand State, district, county and local unions grouped in concentric circles, is the National Union, the mother of us all. She has no constituency except in the hearts of her children, who are always loyal to her. (37)

West continued by further emphasizing loyalty and by offering a compromise, one that might not please members altogether, but one that would not increase the personal burden of individual members. West suggested that, rather than increase membership dues, Illinois supplement the national portion of current dues from the state treasury. She concluded her appeal by alluding to the pride of Illinois state members at being special among national groups and pointing to the attendant responsibility of such a position: "Numerically we are the strongest State union in America, paying more dues into the National treasury last year than did any other State. We that are strong should esteem it a privilege to assist in carrying the burdens of the weak" (37). West both invoked members' pride and duty to ameliorate difference and offered compromises in her effort to please both local and national constituents.

Organization alone, however, was inadequate to sustain previous membership growth because, while local and state leaders might have appeased veterans, they failed to attract younger members. In spite of efforts at conciliation, national membership did not continue its rapid growth after 1885. In its first ten years, the WCTU had rapidly increased in membership, official dues-paying participation reaching 135,253. In the subsequent fifteen years, membership grew by just over 20,000 members, reaching 158,477. Concern over slowing growth surfaces throughout WCTU minutes. Often leaders expressed concern that local unions were being "swallowed up by the Reform Clubs" that were part of the "great tidal wave that has swept over" their areas; such leaders stressed the unique character of the WCTU, noting that all temperance and all reform groups did not work for the same end (Moore, "President's Report" *Proceedings* 12).

But most often leaders lamented their inability to attract young women to the organization. Active participation in the WCTU does appear to be strongly generational. Crusade leaders had been described as "matronly," middle-aged mothers or older women, women who had become comfortable with themselves and secure enough in their position to lead public demonstrations. Annie Wittenmyer was forty-seven when she became the union's first president; Frances E. Willard was forty, but her style and primary acquaintances remained relatively fixed over her two-decade reign. Other women who had helped to establish both the national and state unions continued in positions of leadership until their deaths. And, upon Willard's death, Lillian Stevens and Anna Gordon followed as union presidents, both closely aligned with Willard and representative of the established leadership.

From the beginning there were few young members. Young mothers were probably too busy caring for small children and were less likely to have the funds to participate in state and local conventions. Newspaper reports nearly always attested to the white and graying heads that filled the audiences of national conventions, and they acknowledged explicitly that the young women in attendance were unusual. Members also recognized the aging image of union members. In 1887, Mrs. C. S. Abbot reminisced before the Connecticut WCTU convention:

> It was my delight once to be present at a national convention; as
> I looked over the vast assembly coming from every State in the

Union I was surprised to see so many beautiful white-haired women. On almost every head it seemed as if there were silver threads. These, I thought are the women in the middle of life. (10)

Very shortly after the union's beginning, WCTU leaders had become concerned that young women were not being enrolled in sufficient numbers. Bands of Hope and other youth organizations flourished, but parents usually determined young children's participation in these groups. Young women were less inclined to join, and union leaders across the country expressed concern.

As early as 1881, Iowa's president, Mrs. V. W. Moore, was expressing concern that "One department of work suffers—that of interesting the young ladies of the State in the work of temperance" ("President's Report" *Eighth* 12). The following year, President Mrs. L. D. Carhart conveyed the national president's concern and recommendation: "[I]f a young lady superintendent of young people's work were secured in each local Union and left free to enlist her friends in her own way, we should soon see the present apathy changed to interest and enthusiasm" (25). In suggesting that young women should be permitted to recruit members according to their own methods, Willard seemed to recognize the need for a different kind of excitement to attract a younger generation. Carhart added her own recommendation that efforts be directed through local unions located in towns with seminaries and colleges to interest young women in membership.

Such problems were not confined to Iowa. Unions across the country were expressing such concern. In Oregon, President Anna R. Riggs "mourn[ed] the lack of advance" in recruiting young women and suggested, as remedy, "more earnest effort along the line of L.T.L. [Loyal Temperance League] work, for this Department is to cover our future recruits for the Y's" (46). But members of the Loyal Temperance League failed to join the Young Woman's Christian Temperance Union in substantial numbers. In Connecticut, Ida M. T. Pegrum explained part of the problem: "Since October last, one Y. auxiliary has been organized and one disorganized. New London Y. was organized in the William Memorial Institute, and quite naturally died as an organization when the members graduated and scattered" ("Young" *Report Twenty-Second* 59). The following year, Pegrum noted that the previous year's report had been inaccurate, suggesting more Y. auxiliaries than actually existed—"two of those auxiliaries were deceased"—and further acknowledged that since that time "four more have ceased to be" ("Young" *Report Twenty-Third* 75). State and local unions repeatedly noted the merging of Y's because of insufficient numbers to sustain separate ones.

The temperance cause, especially with its roots in the Woman's Crusade, was an exciting place for women of the generation of its early leaders. But younger generations, like today's generations who reap the rewards of the late-sixties and seventies feminist wave, were accustomed to many of the successes of the union and apparently found the organization of their mothers less exciting. They were busy making their own inroads, made possible by earlier reforms, and when joining organizations, they had a much wider variety of choices. Despite efforts on the part of leaders to interest younger women in becoming members of the WCTU, the new generation simply did not enroll in large numbers.

The failure of young women to enroll was disconcerting, too, because union members began dying in large numbers. National meetings began incorporating memorial services in the early 1880s, and in 1887 the national union designed a specific service to be used at members' funerals because so many were dying. Minutes of state conventions also attest to lost state members, each year publishing memorials to those who had died during the previous year. In 1890, for example, Minnesota's memorial list included twenty-one members, and in Connecticut the list grew from two in 1880 to forty in 1890 (plate 34).

Even today, members of the WCTU lament this problem. The average age of its membership is now fifty-five. According to Frances Thompson, a seventy-year-old WCTU member from Ohio, one hundred members in Ohio alone died last year. And even though the organization targets church youth groups and makes particular efforts to recruit young members, she says, "Many younger women are too busy with their jobs and families to get involved" (Hannah).

Because the WCTU had been so successful in creating change for women, perhaps young women saw less urgency in its causes. Women speakers and workers, if not quite commonplace, were no longer an oddity. Newspaper accounts of temperance activities changed dramatically over the years. Early reports openly ridiculed and indicted women for their unwomanly ways, and even though some derogatory reports continued, by the end of the century most accounts were either favorable or very subtle in their criticism, attesting to changing attitudes toward women's public role. Other venues reflected changing attitudes as well. By 1880, J. Ellen Foster was noting the change in the reaction of legislators when women sought hearings: "We were granted every possible courtesy in hearing before the committees, and in personal interviews with senators and representatives." Foster noted that "many kind things were said of our fidelity and truth to principle and 'a'that' . . . but very little of the old epithets or abuse of women who worked in temperance reform, as being out of their sphere, etc.,—very little of that" (34).

Young women who had been active in Loyal Temperance Leagues or other temperance youth organizations would have been prepared, not only for leadership in the WCTU, but for other independent choices as well. Temperance women both modeled a more public and independent woman and helped to make professional and public employment, as well as higher education, more acceptable for women; in doing so, they may have undermined membership among young women in their own organization. Temperance reform had served to show unity among women who had become conscious of and disgusted with abuses toward, and unequal treatment of, women. It had also served as a means of escape and for broadening experience for many. But younger women, by and large, may have seen the temperance movement as their mothers' cause.

The union may not have inspired a younger generation, but as they matured, they returned to the reform of their mothers. As a new enthusiasm for reform caught hold in the early-twentieth century, membership in the WCTU again grew rapidly, helping to accomplish the drives for the Eighteenth and Nineteenth Amendments to the Constitution. WCTU membership remained far greater than that of the suffrage association. By the turn of the century, membership in the National American Woman's Suffrage Association (NAWSA) was still less than 6 percent of the total membership of the WCTU. After the turn of the century, NAWSA, with its younger leaders and a rhetoric more attuned to a new generation, attracted increasingly larger numbers of young members; however, despite this growth, by the time of the passage of the two amendments, NAWSA membership had grown to only 20 percent of that of the WCTU.[2]

No such network as that established by the WCTU exists today. The National Organization of Women (NOW), while a national organization, more closely resembles NAWSA than the WCTU, and it lacks the grassroots membership that so strengthened the WCTU. Other efforts to strengthen the rights for women endure. Unity among women exists within specific, special interest categories, such as battered women's shelters and rape crisis centers. But such organizations remain primarily local. Even RAIN (Rape and Incest Network), funded by Lilith concerts of women musicians in an effort to organize a national network for dealing with abuse, seems unable to link with established local programs for greater effectiveness. On the political front, in addition to efforts by NOW, women members of Congress call attention to issues of sexual harassment, abuse, and the special needs of women and children. Still, no major organization has been able to unite women of diverse economic and educational backgrounds in order to provide the political force such numbers would entail. Building such a network requires leaders who can bridge the chasm between intellectual feminists, historically the leaders in such efforts, and other women, such as homemakers and women outside the academic arena.

Perhaps the rhetoric of the WCTU can provide a model of how feminists can more successfully appeal to the "average" woman. As Willard noted more than one hundred years ago, the average woman is not always "clear concerning the relations of cause and effect in politics and law, but she must be" ("The Average Woman" 623). Women who make such a connection must be willing to help other women reach that vision, in a language meaningful for those women. Studying the use of temperance rhetoric in both speech and fiction should, at the very least, provide hope and inspiration that women can help one another reach a meaningful understanding of their situatedness, and that they will prevail if they work together.

Notes

———•–•–•———

Works Cited

———•–•–•———

Index

Notes

Introduction: Silenced Voices

1. Be present at our Table Lord
   Be here and everywhere ador'd
   These creatures bless & grant that we
   May feast in paradise with thee.

2. Unfortunately, thousands of actively vocal temperance women are not represented here. Women who did not publish or take part in highly visible proceedings are, by and large, absent, and records for many of those who did participate more fully have been lost.

3. There does seem to be an increasing awareness of and appreciation for the impact temperance women had on changes for women. Jack S. Blocker's *"Give to the Winds Thy Fear": The Women's Temperance Crusade, 1873–1874* examines the Woman's Crusade, and Janet Giele has recently revised her already valuable 1961 dissertation, acknowledging her failure to appreciate temperance women fully in its earlier form, now recognizing the major influence these women exerted. Still, remarkably little has been published in appreciation of this large, active group of women.

1. Woman's Rights in Woman's Wrongs: Temperance Women at Mid-Century

1. Elizabeth Bowles Warbasse provides the most complete account of changes in women's legal rights and coverture through mid-century. Additional helpful sources include Giele (51–54), Flexner (62–70), Salmon (14, 193), and contributors to Cott, *History of Women in the United States.*

2. Cott calls marriage "a building block of public policy" and explains that "presumptions about the provisions for the obligations and benefits of marriage have always been built into many legal and governmental structures in the United States, from property-holding to citizenship and from immigration to military service and tax policy. Marriage operates as a systematic public sanction, enforcing privileges along with obligations" (107).

3. The Maine Law, passed in the state of Maine in 1851, outlawed the manufacture and sale of alcoholic beverages.

4. The Daughters of Temperance, an auxiliary of the powerful Sons of Temperance, had previously been confined to sequestered, "secret" meetings that provided no public visibility.

5. While Anthony never again officially joined a temperance organization, she did attend temperance conventions, becoming a regular at meetings of the Woman's Christian Temperance Union.

6. For a more complete discussion of the public debate surrounding divorce at mid-century, see Riley 62–84. For further examination of various state laws governing divorce at mid-century, see Chused, Halem 9–26, Riley 34–60, Hareven, and contributors to Cott, *History of Women in the United States*.

2. Patriotic Reformers: "Called by the Spirit of the Lord to Lead the Women of the World"

1. Blocker, *"Give to the Winds Thy Fear,"* and Tyrell estimate women's membership during the 1820s and 1830s at one-third to one-half of total membership. According to Rorabaugh, women dominated temperance societies as early as the 1830s (257).

2. Semiramis, mythical queen of Assyria, founded the ancient city of Babylon and conquered Persia and Egypt; Dido was the legendary founder and queen of Carthage; Zenobia led the armies of Palmyra and Odoenathus to conquer Egypt and Asia Minor, A.D. 269–70; Boadicca (also Boudicca or Boadicea), queen of the Iceni, led the Iceni and other British tribes in a revolt against their Roman rulers. Miriam and Deborah are biblical figures: Miriam, sister to Moses and Aaron, and along with them a leader of the Exodus; Deborah, prophetess, judge, and leader of armies against the Canaanite army.

3. The most complete study of the Woman's Crusade is Jack S. Blocker, Jr.'s *"Give to the Winds Thy Fears: The Women's Temperance Crusade, 1873–1874.* Numbers that I use are based substantially on Blocker's work.

4. Many of the women they celebrated had been actively involved in temperance reform, often in unique and astounding ways, since mid-century. For example, one of the most celebrated women of the Crusade, Eliza Daniel Stewart, who led the Crusade in Springfield, Ohio, had given her

first temperance lecture in 1858. She had been active in numerous other temperance activities, as well. She had disguised herself, entered a saloon, and bought a glass of wine on Sunday, then had the owner prosecuted for violating the Sunday closing law; after passage of the Adair Law in Ohio, Stewart travelled from court to court, pleading (and almost always winning) the cases of impoverished women and children and organizing supportive demonstrations among the women of the community. Mattie McClellan Brown, honored by the WCTU for her leadership in the Crusade, was also Grand Chief Templar of the Ohio Grand Lodge of the Independent Order of Good Templars.

5. A typical example appears in the minutes of the 1879 meeting in Indianapolis: "By motion, and by invitation of the chair, the following ladies were invited to the platform, introduced to the Convention and received with applause: Mrs. E.J. Thompson, Mother Hill, Mother Stewart and Miss Maria Stanton" (*Minutes of National Sixteenth* 18).

6. Instruction to put on Christian armor is based upon numerous biblical references to warfare, but especially on Paul's description of Christian armor in Ephesians 6:

> Therefore take up, the whole armor of God, so that you may be able to withstand on that evil day, and having done everything to stand firm. Stand therefore, and fasten the belt of truth around your waist, and put on the breastplate of righteousness. As shoes for your feet put on whatever will make you ready to proclaim the gospel of peace. With all of these, take the shield of faith, with which you will be able to quench all the flaming arrows of the evil one. Take the helmet of salvation, and the sword of the Spirit, which is the word of God. (6.13–17)

7. Such naming is one of the chief characteristics of temperance women's speeches at national meetings. The minutes of the various meetings include hundreds of women's names, cited publicly at the national forum, and printed in minutes of the national organization for the benefit of members and future generations. The 1881 minutes, for example, cite women 1026 times.

8. Paul declares that since there is one Lord, one faith, and one baptism, Christians should patiently "bear with one another in love, making every effort to maintain the unity of the Spirit and the bond of peace" (Eph. 4.3). According to Paul, this is not a creation of unity since Christians are already one in Christ; the necessity is to maintain the unity.

9. "For there is one God; there is also one mediator between God and humankind, Christ Jesus, himself human, who gave himself a ransom for all" (I Tim. 2–5).

10. Mary T. Lathrap was herself a leader in the Woman's Crusade

and helped to found the WCTU. A licensed preacher, Lathrap was also a prolific writer. She published from the age of fourteen, writing both poetry and prose. According to Willard and Livermore, Lathrap was "Equally at home on the temperance platform, on the lecture platform, in the pulpit or at the author's desk" (2: 450). She was often recognized as the "Daniel Webster of Temperance."

11. Willard and other WCTU leaders often made overtures to members of the Catholic religion to join forces with women of the WCTU. Leaders such as Mary Allen West praised the Catholic Church for its Catholic Total Abstinence Union and noted cooperation between "white ribbon women" and Catholic women who "took communion together" early September of 1886 in Brooklyn's St. Agnes Roman Catholic Church ("President's Annual" *Thirteenth* 104). Willard insisted that the WCTU was open to women of all nationalities and creeds, but Catholic and Protestant women generally joined forces in occasional public displays opposing alcohol while maintaining their separate organizations. Few Catholic women and even fewer Jewish women joined the WCTU. Although theoretically the "Christian" in the organization's name would have included Catholics, the heavy evangelical fervor and reliance on quotations from scripture would not have fit comfortably for women outside mainstream Protestant religions.

12. Lathrop's speech here continues as follows:

> Then, on the other hand, blessed by the fevered lips of the drunkard ready to perish; sought by the wandering feet of the boy or girl who went astray; hallowed by loving thought at thousands of firesides; baptized with holy tears by the mothers whose battle it wages; perfumed by the stainless prayers of the little children; endorsed by the expressed principles of organized Christianity; sustained by the highest and freshest authorities in the scientific world; praised by lips grown careful through statesmanlike speech; believed in by the best, trusted by the most needy, it has been granted them also to find the "love of love." (*National WCTU* 141)

3. Woman-Tempered Rhetoric: Public Presentation and the WCTU

1. See Weidner 119–25 for similar circumstances at Butler University. Women's colleges, in an effort to offer women an education equal to that of men's colleges, adopted textbooks used at men's schools, and trained women "to be teachers, to transmit [rhetorical] knowledge . . . rather

than to act upon it themselves (Lawrence 17). At both coeducational and women's schools, young women created room for freer expression and practice in delivery by forming their own extra-curricular literary societies. (See Lawrence and Weidner for role of women's literary societies.)

2. Instructions were often printed in more than one publication. Where more than one source is available, I cite both.

3. The original Chautauqua Institute was founded in 1874; a Sunday school assembly located on Lake Chautauqua in southwestern New York State, its primary purpose was to train Sunday school teachers. From its beginning, the Institute combined intellectual, spiritual, and recreational activities, incorporating lectures (by John B. Gough in 1874 and President Ulysses S. Grant in 1875) as well as concerts, courses, and recreational activities. The idea became so popular that clone chautauquas surfaced across the country, numbering nearly two hundred by 1890.

4. Annie Wittenmyer, first president of the WCTU and also active in the Woman's Foreign Missionary Society, had traveled the country speaking about her battlefield experiences as one of the best-known members of the U. S. Sanitary Commission during the Civil War. And Frances E. Willard, second president of the WCTU from 1879 until her death in 1898, had taught rhetoric, composition, and elocution over a period of sixteen years, primarily in academies and colleges for women; had been the first woman president of a woman's college, Evanston Ladies' College; and had served as dean of women at Northwestern University, where she taught rhetoric and composition to both men and women. Willard had spoken to large gatherings, such as the National Education Association and Women's Foreign Missionary Society, and to local groups about her travels abroad; in addition, she had spoken daily to large gatherings as Dwight Moody's assistant at his revival meetings in Boston.

5. Willard also uses such an approach in her chapter "Women's Bright Words" in *Woman and Temperance*. Here she narrates a meeting between two local WCTU members "behind the scenes," the obvious intent, again, to present a model for local members (461–66).

6. Willard also sometimes suggested that members use demonstrational aids. In *How to Organize a WCTU*, for example, she suggests that speakers "draw a fifty-cent coin on the blackboard—or make a drawing of the same—and have it hung up" for demonstrating how members' dues are apportioned (9; *Woman and Temperance* 620).

7. Susannah Wesley (1669–1742) was mother of John Wesley, founder of the Methodist Church. She herself was a preacher and the mother of nineteen children. Catherine Booth (1829–1890), preacher, worker on behalf of women and children, and co-founder of the Salvation Army, was the mother of nine children. Willing's point is that these women were active, committed preachers, but nonetheless good mothers.

4. Dissension and Division: Racial Tension and the WCTU

1. For example, Harper notes that a West Virginia "Union has invited the colored sisters to join them," and that "The colored President of an Alabama Union represented a Union composed of white and colored people" ("The Woman's Christian Temperance Union and the Colored Woman" in Boyd 206). Accounts of both mixed unions and separate unions in the North and West are reported in state minutes.

2. I have tried to incorporate the major points of argument between Wells and Willard, but the ongoing controversy entailed numerous, detailed features. For a fuller exposition of the controversy, see Douglass's address, Thompson, and Townes.

3. African American state presidents included in the 1899 Minutes are as follows: Alabama No. 2, Mrs. Booker T. Washington, Tuskegee; Arkansas (Harper), Mrs. F. C. Potter, Cotton Plant; Georgia No. 2, Mrs. A. S. Bowen, South Atlanta; Louisiana (Willard), Frances Joseph, New Orleans; North Carolina (Thurman), Mary A. Lynch, Livingston College, Salisbury; Tennessee No. 2, Mrs. L. Tappan Phillips, Jackson; Texas (Thurman), Mrs. E. E. Peterson, Texarkana. Previous presidents had included Mrs. C. L. Bullock of Greensboro, NC; Ida M. Lane, Jackson, TN; M. Wicker, New Orleans, LA; and Mrs. W. E. Miller of Houston, TX.

5. Red-Nosed Angels and the Corseted Crusade: Newspaper Accounts of Nineteenth-Century Temperance Reformers

1. Bagatelles were similar to games of pool, using a cue and balls on an oblong table, and cups for receiving balls.

2. Elizabeth Oakes Prince Smith (1806–1893), author and editor, edited *The Mayflower*, a Boston annual, and assisted journalist husband Seba Smith in other editorial efforts; Smith was a regular contributor to popular magazines. Paulina Kellogg Wright Davis, wealthy and socially prominent publisher of *The Una*, a woman's rights newspaper, was active in the abolitionist, temperance, and woman's rights causes.

3. Jenny Lind (1820–1887), the very popular "Swedish Nightingale," was opera's most admired and feted star. She toured America between 1850 and 1852. Catherine Hayes, the "Swan of Erin," also toured the United States giving concerts during 1852–53.

4. See Vaughan's letter to the *Tribune* dated June 10, 1854, for example.

5. For an extensive account of Willard's "womanly style" and further newspaper accounts specific to Willard, see Amy Slagell's dissertation on Willard, especially pages 20–70.

6. Both newspapers also omitted the customary period following the initial in Lathburg's name.

6. "The Feelings of the Romantic and Fashionable": Women's Issues in Temperance Fiction

1. See for example Papashvily, Douglas, Dobson, Harris, Sanchez Eppler.

2. Lucius Marcellus Sargent was probably the most popular writer of temperance fiction in the nineteenth century. He was best known for his *Temperance Tales*, a collection which, according to Mark Edward Lender, saw 130 editions and was translated into a number of foreign languages. "My Mother's Gold Ring," the best loved of his short works, was anthologized in *Tales*, under its own cover, and in other compilations as well.

3. Bannock is unleavened griddlecakes made from grain—usually oats, barley, or wheat. Browse refers to young shoots of plants or shrubs, food usually reserved for animal feed.

4. For such a discussion about Mary Todd Lincoln, Elizabeth Cady Stanton, and Harriet Beecher Stowe, see Sklar.

7. "Wine Drinkers and Heartless Profligates": Water Drops from Popular Novelists

1. Stowe's letter was written to the National Era but reprinted in *The Lily*, October 1850.

2. We know, for example, that Stowe drank wine regularly with meals while travelling in Europe and while completing *Dred* (Hedrick 290). In a letter to her brother Henry late in her life, Stowe wrote, "I have some pretty fair sherry which Hatty serves out to me a small wine glass full at dinnertime at tea time and again at bed time, and if I fell on my knees to her I could not get it at any other time" (quoted in Hedrick 396). Some biographers have taken this to mean that only her daughter's vigilance kept Stowe from being completely dependent upon wine.

And at least one of Alcott's biographers, Charles Strickland, suggests that Alcott was addicted to opium. According to Strickland, her literary crusade against alcohol seems less than consistent, given her private addiction to opium. Her use of the drug was evidently habitual, for, as she confided to her diary in 1870, "I slept without any opium or anything— a feat I have not performed for some time" (143).

But a reader of the entire passage might find proof of Alcott's addiction inconclusive. The wording actually comes from a letter addressed to "Dearest People" from the Hotel D'Universe, Tours, June 17, 1870— not from a private journal entry as Strickland implies—suggesting that Alcott felt no shame at her admission. She hints, instead, at the medicinal purposes behind her use of opium:

> We had a pleasant trip in the cool of the day, and found
> Tours a great city, like Paris on a small scale. Our hotel is on

the boulevard, and the trees, fountains, and fine carriages make our windows very tempting. We popped into bed early; and my bones are so much better that I slept without any opium or anything,—a feat I have not performed for some time. (Cheney 230)

Conclusion: Women of the Century

1. J. Ellen Foster had been a staunch supporter and friend of Willard and one of the best-known leaders in the WCTU. For several years, she protested efforts to align the WCTU with the Prohibition Party. In 1889, she finally led the Iowa delegation out of the national convention and began a separate union, which was never very effective.

2. Official membership numbers are probably low, since they reflect only those participants who paid annual dues. Frances Willard consistently claimed that the union represented more than two hundred thousand members in the late-eighties and early-nineties. Some of the discrepancy may reflect the fact that many rural and "colored" unions did not pay dues, and others refused to send the required portion of local and state dues to the national organization. Some official membership numbers according to minutes of the two organizations follow:

WCTU		NAWSA	
1901	158,477	1900	8,981
1911	245,299	1910	19,404
1919	346,638	1914	70,240

I have included membership numbers for the early-twentieth century because NAWSA has so often been credited with passage of the Nineteenth Amendment; however, the WCTU's larger numbers were probably more instrumental in bringing about passage of the amendment.

Works Cited

Abbott, C. S. "Response." Minutes of the *Fourteenth Annual Convention of the Connecticut Woman's Christian Temperance Union*. Brooklyn: Martin, 1887. 9–12.

"About Southern Lynchings." *Baltimore Morning Herald* 20 Oct. 1895. Folder 70, WCTU Headquarters.

"Address of the Woman's Temperance Convention. Held at Doe Run Meeting House on Fifthday, the 21st of Eleventh Month. To the People of Chester County." *The Pennsylvania Freeman* 9 Jan. 1951: 1–2.

Alcott, Louisa May. *Jack and Jill: A Village Story*. Boston: Roberts Brothers, 1880.

———. *Jo's Boys, and How They Turned Out*. Boston: Roberts Brothers, 1886.

———. *Little Men: Life at Plumfield with Jo's Boys*. Boston: Roberts Brothers, 1871.

———. *Little Women: or, Meg, Jo, Beth and Amy*. 1868. Boston: Little, 1920.

———. *Rose in Bloom: A Sequel to "Eight Cousins."* Boston: Roberts Brothers, 1876.

———. "Silver Pitchers." *Silver Pitchers, and Independence: A Centennial Love Story*. Boston: Little, 1908. 1–55.

Aldrich, Mary J. "President's Annual Address." *Twelfth Annual Meeting of the Woman's Christian Temperance Union of Iowa*. Cedar Rapids: Daily Republican Steam Printing and Binding House, 1885. 1–14.

"Another Wrangle." *Cleveland Daily Plain Dealer* 21 Nov. 1874: 3.

Baldwin, Summerfield. "The President's Address." *Minutes of the Sixteenth Annual Convention of the Woman's Christian Temperance Union of Maryland*. Baltimore, 1890. 16–22.

Barker, H. M. "President's Address." *Minutes of the Dakota Woman's*

Christian Temperance Union at the Eighth Annual Meeting, 1889. Madison: Sentinel, 1889. 25–30.

Baym, Nina. *Woman's Fiction: A Guide to Novels by and about Women in America 1820–70*. Urbana: U of Illinois P, 1993.

Blocker, Jack S., Jr. *American Temperance Movements: Cycles of Reform*. Boston: Twayne, 1989.

———. *"Give to the Winds Thy Fears": The Women's Temperance Crusade, 1873–1874*. Westport: Greenwood, 1985.

Bloomer, D.C. *Life and Writings of Amelia Bloomer*. 1895. New York: Schocken, 1975.

Bolton, Sarah Knowles. *The Present Problem*. New York: Putnam, 1874.

Bordin, Ruth. *Woman and Temperance: The Quest for Power and Liberty, 1873–1900*. Philadelphia: Temple UP, 1981.

Boyd, Melba Joyce. *Discarded Legacy: Politics and Poetics in the Life of Frances E. W. Harper 1825–1911*. Detroit: Wayne State UP, 1994.

Brody, Miriam. *Manly Writing: Gender, Rhetoric, and the Rise of Composition*. Carbondale: Southern Illinois UP, 1993.

Buckley, A. B. "President's Address." *Minutes of the Eleventh Annual Convention of the Arizona Woman's Christian Temperance Union*. Prescott: Journal-Miner Print, 1900. 7–11.

Buckley, Maria L. *Amanda Wilson; or, The Vicissitudes of Life*. New York, 1856. 5–30.

———. *Edith Moreton; or Temperance Versus Intemperance*. Philadelphia, 1852.

Buell, Caroline B. *The Helping Hand; or the A-B-C of Organizing A WCTU*. Chicago: Woman's Temperance Publication Association, 1887.

Butler, Caroline H. "Amy." *Household Narratives for the Family Circle*. Philadelphia: Peck & Bliss, 1854.

———. "Emma Alton." *The Fountain and the Bottle*. Hartford: Case, 1850. 48–60.

Campbell, Jane C. "Steps to Ruin." *The Fountain and the Bottle*. Hartford: Case, 1850. 333–40.

Campbell, Karlyn Kohrs. *Man Cannot Speak for Her*. New York: Greenwood, 1989.

———, ed. *Women Public Speakers in the United States, 1800–1925*. Westport: Greenwood, 1993.

Caraway, Nancie. *Segregated Sisterhood: Racism and the Politics of American Feminism*. Knoxville: U of Tennessee P, 1991.

Carby, Hazel V. *Reconstructing Womanhood: The Emergence of the Afro-American Woman Novelist*. New York: Oxford UP, 1987.

Carhart, L. D. "President's Report." *Ninth Annual Session of the Woman's Christian Temperance Union of Iowa*. Des Moines: Capital, 1882. 18–30.

"The Cause of the Crusade." *Inter-Ocean* [Chicago] 25 Oct. 1877: 8.

Chapman, Helen K. *Paul Brewster and Son; or, The Story of Mary Carter*. New York: National Temperance Society and Publication House, 1875.

Chellis, Mary Dwinell. *At Lion's Mouth*. New York: National Temperance Society and Publication House, 1872.

——. *Bread and Beer*. New York: National Temperance Society and Publication House, 1882.

——. *Old Benches with New Props*. New York: National Temperance Society and Publication House, 1891.

——. *Our Homes*. New York: National Temperance Society and Publication House, 1881.

——. *Out of the Fire*. New York: National Temperance Society and Publication House, 1869.

——. *The Temperance Doctor*. New York: National Temperance Society and Publication House, 1868.

——. *Wealth and Wine*. New York: National Temperance Society and Publication House, 1874.

——. *The Workingman's Loaf*. New York: National Temperance Society and Publication House (Fife and Drum Series), 1885.

Cheney, Ednah D., ed. *Louisa May Alcott: Her Life, Letters, and Journals*. Boston: Roberts Brothers, 1889.

"The Chivalry of the Nineteenth Century." *The Lily* Feb. 1851: 14.

Chused, Richard H. *Private Acts in Public Places: A Social History of Divorce in the Formative Era of American Family Law*. Philadelphia: U of Pennsylvania P, 1994.

Clark, Gregory, and S. Michael Halloran. *Oratorical Culture: Transformations in the Theory and Practice of Rhetoric*. Carbondale: Southern Illinois UP, 1993.

"The Cleveland Herald." *The Pennsylvania Freeman* 17 Mar. 1853: 43.

"Close of Session." *Courier Journal* [Louisville] 29 Oct. 1882: 1, 8.

Collins, Maria. *Mrs. Ben Darby; or, the Weal and Woe of Social Life*. Cincinnati: Moore, Anderson, Wilstack and Keys, 1853.

Colman, Julia. *The Temperance Handbook for Speakers and Workers*. New York: National Temperance Society and Publication House, 1889.

"Convention of the WCTU." *St. Louis Dispatch* 21 Oct. 1884: 2.

Coon, Anne C. *Hear Me Patiently: The Reform Speeches of Amelia Jenks Bloomer*. Westport: Greenwood, 1994.

"Corresponding Secretary's Report." *Minutes of the Sixteenth Annual Convention of the Woman's Christian Temperance Union of Maryland*. Baltimore, 1890. 23–28.

"The Corseted Crusade." *The Washington Post* 30 Oct. 1881: 2.

Cott, Nancy F. "Giving Character to Our Whole Civil Polity: Marriage and the Public Order in the Late-Nineteenth Century." *U.S. History as Women's History: New Feminist Essays*. Eds. Linda K. Kerber et al. Chapel Hill: U of North Carolina P, 1995. 107–21.

———, ed. *Domestic Relations and Law. Vol. 3 of History of Women in the United States*. Munich: K. G. Saur, 1992.

"Crusaders in Council." *The Cincinnati Daily Enquirer* 19 Nov. 1875: 8.

Cummins, Maria S. *The Lamplighter*. 1851. Ed. Nina Baym. New Brunswick: Rutgers UP, 1988.

Davis, Angela. *Women, Race and Class*. New York: Random, 1983.

Dobson, Joanne. "The Hidden Hand: Subversion of Cultural Ideology in Three Mid-Nineteenth-Century American Women's Novels." *American Quarterly* 38 (Summer 1986): 223–42.

———. Introduction. *The Hidden Hand*. By E. D. E. N. Southworth. New Brunswick: Rutgers UP, 1988.

Douglas, Ann. *The Feminization of American Culture*. New York: Knopf, 1977.

Douglass, Frederick. "Lessons of the Hour: An Address Delivered in Washington, D.C., on 9 January 1894." *The Frederick Douglass Papers.* Vol. 5 of *Series One: Speeches, Debates, and Interviews*. Eds. John W. Blassingame and John R. McKivigan. New Haven: Yale UP, 1992. 575–607.

Dunham, Marion H. "President's Address." *Tenth Annual Meeting of the Woman's Christian Temperance Union of the State of Iowa held at Des Moines, Iowa, 1899*. Lyons: W. B. Farver, 1899. 30–41.

Earhart, Mary. *Frances Willard: From Prayers to Politics*. Chicago: U of Chicago P, 1944.

Editorial. [Philadelphia newspaper] 12 June 1876. Scrapbook 4, WCTU Headquarters.

Ellet, E. F. "A Country Recollection; or, the Reformed Inebriate." *An Adopted Daughter and Other Tales*. Ed. Alice Carey. Philadelphia: J. B. Smith, 1859. 133–44.

"Employment for Women." *New York Daily Tribune* 18 June 1853: 4.

Epstein, Barbara Leslie. *The Politics of Domesticity: Women, Evangelism, and Temperance in Nineteenth-Century America*. Middletown: Wesleyan UP, 1981.

Evans, Augusta. *St. Elmo*. Chicago: M. A. Donahue, n.d.

"Everybody's War." *Galena Evening Gazette*. 1875. Scrapbook 3, WCTU Headquarters.

"A Fight." *Baltimore American and Commercial Advertiser* 10 Nov. 1878: 4.

"The Fight Renewed." *Baltimore American and Commercial Advertiser* 11 Nov. 1878: 4.

Flexner, Eleanor. *Century of Struggle: The Woman's Rights Movement in the United States*. Cambridge: Harvard UP, 1975.

Forbes, Cornelia B. "Annual Address of the President." *Report of the*

Twenty-Second Convention of the Connecticut Woman's Christian Temperance Union. Portland: Middlesex County Printery, 1895. 35–42.

Foster, Frances Smith. "Frances Ellen Watkins Harper." Hine 1: 532–37.

Foster, J. Ellen. "Report of Committee on Legislation." *Seventh Annual Session of the Woman's Christian Temperance Union of Iowa, 1880*. Des Moines: Prohibitionist Letter Print, 1881. 31–38.

"Frances, A Temporizer." *The Cleveland Gazette* 24 Nov. 1894: 2.

Freibert, Lucy M., and Barbara A. White, eds. *Hidden Hands: An Anthology of American Women Writers, 1790–1870*. New Brunswick: Rutgers UP, 1985.

Friend, Julia M. *The Chester Family; or, The Curse of the Drunkard's Appetite*. Boston: William White, 1869.

"from the *Madison Argus*." *Daily Free Democrat* [Milwaukee] 24 Oct. 1853: 3.

Fry, Susanna M. D. "Annual Address." *Minutes of the Twentieth Annual Meeting of the Woman's Christian Temperance Union of the State of Minnesota*. Austen: Register, 1896. 28–36.

Gage, Frances D. Letter. *The Lily* 15 July 1854: 104.

———. "Tales of Truth." *The Lily* Jan. 1852: 2–3.

Giddings, Paula. *When and Where I Enter: The Impact of Black Women on Race and Sex in America*. New York: William Morrow, 1984.

Giele, Janet Zollinger. "Social Change in the Feminine Role: A Comparison of Woman's Suffrage and Woman's Temperance 1870–1920." Diss. Radcliffe College, 1961.

———. *Two Paths of Women's Equality: Temperance, Suffrage, and the Origins of Modern Feminism*. New York: Twayne, 1995.

Gifford, Carolyn DeSwarte, ed. *"Writing Out My Heart": The Journal of Frances E. Willard, 1855–1896, A Selected Edition*. Champaign: U of Illinois P, 1995.

Ginzberg, Lori D. *Women and the Work of Benevolence: Morality, Politics, and Class in the Nineteenth-Century United States*. New Haven: Yale UP, 1990.

Gordon, Elizabeth Putnam. *Women Torch-Bearers: The Story of the Woman's Christian Temperance Union*. Evanston: National Woman's Christian Temperance Union Publishing House, 1924.

Gordon, Linda. *Woman's Body, Woman's Right: Birth Control in America*. New York: Penguin, 1990.

"Great Gathering of Women of New York." *New York Daily Tribune* 8 Feb. 1853: 5.

Green, Harvey. *The Light of the Home: An Intimate View of the Lives of Women in Victorian America*. New York: Pantheon, 1983.

Greene, E. G., ed. *Pathfinder for the Organization and Work of the Woman's Christian Temperance Union.* Rev. ed. New York: National Temperance Society and Publication House, 1886.

Greenwood, Grace [Sara Jane Lippincott]. "James Blair; or, Love in the Valley of Juniata." *The Fountain and the Bottle.* Hartford: Case, 1850. 258–82.

Griffith, Mary E. "President's Address." *Minutes of the Twenty-First Annual Meeting of the Woman's Christian Temperance Union of the District of Columbia, Held at Foundry M. E. Church, September 26 and 27, 1895.* N.p., n.d.

Hale, Sarah Josepha. "The Only Sister to Her Only Brother." *The Sons of Temperance Offering: for 1850.* Ed. T. S. Arthur. New York: Nafis & Cornish, 1850.

———. Preface. *My Cousin Mary: or The Inebriate.* By Anonymous Author. Boston: Whipple and Damrell, 1839.

Halem, Lynn Carol. *Divorce Reform: Changing Legal and Social Perspectives.* New York: Free P, 1980.

Hannah, James. "Membership Dwindling in Temperance Group." *The Advocate* [Baton Rouge] 10 June 1995: 2E.

Hareven, Tamara, ed. *Themes in the History of the Family.* Worcester: American Antiquarian Society, 1978.

Harper, Frances E. W. *Sowing and Reaping. Minnie's Sacrifice, Sowing and Reaping, Trial and Triumph: Three Rediscovered Novels by Frances E. W. Harper.* Ed. Frances Smith Foster. Boston: Beacon, 1994.

Harper, Ida Husted. *The Life and Work of Susan B. Anthony.* Vol. 1. Indianapolis: Hollenbeck, 1898.

Harris, Susan K. *19th-Century American Women's Novels: Interpretive Strategies.* Cambridge: Cambridge UP, 1990.

Hart, James S. *The Female Prose Writers of America.* Philadelphia: E. H. Butler, 1852.

Haslup, Mary Rider. "The President's Address." *Minutes of the Sixteenth Annual Convention of the Woman's Christian Temperance Union of Maryland, 1890.* N.p., n.d.

Hedrick, Joan D. *Harriet Beecher Stowe: A Life.* New York: Oxford UP, 1994.

Hentz, Caroline Lee. "The Drunkard's Daughter." *Courtship and Marriage; or the Joys and Sorrows of American Life.* Philadelphia: T. B. Peterson, 1856. 348–77.

———. *The Mob Cap & Other Tales.* Philadelphia: T. B. Peterson, 1850.

———. *The Planter's Northern Bride.* Philadelphia: T. B. Peterson, 1851.

———. "The Tempest." Hentz, *Courtship* 413–47.

———. "The Victim of Excitement." *The Victim of Excitement, The Bosom Serpent, Etc., Etc., Etc.* Philadelphia: A. Hart, 1853. 17–39.

Hilbourne, Charlotte S. *Alice Waters; or, The Sandown Victory. A Temperance Story, for Old and Young*. Portland: F. G. Rich, 1867.

Hine, Darlene Clark, ed. *Black Women in America: An Historical Encyclopedia*. 2 vols. Brooklyn: Carlson, 1993.

Hobart, H. A. "Annual Address of State President." *Report of the Tenth Annual Convention of the Woman's Christian Temperance Union of the State of Minnesota, Held at Faribault, September 14, 15 and 16, 1886*. Red Wing: Red Wing, 1886. 34–38.

Holley, Marietta. *Sweet Cicely; or Josiah Allen as a Politician*. New York: Funk & Wagnalls, 1886.

hooks, bell. *Ain't I a Woman? Black Women and Feminism*. Boston: South End, 1981.

Hosmer, Margaret Kerr. *The Subtle Spell: A Temperance Story*. Philadelphia: Alfred Martien, 1873.

Hunt, Sarah Keables. *The Brook, and The Tide Turning*. New York: National Temperance Society and Publication House, 1875.

Kelley, Mary. *Private World/Public Stage: Literary Domesticity in Nineteenth-Century America*. New York: Oxford UP, 1984.

Kirkland, Caroline. "Agnes: A Story of Revolutionary Times." *The Fountain. A Gift: "To Stir Up the Pure Mind by Way of Remembrance."* Ed. H. Hastings Weld. Philadelphia: Wm. Sloanmaker, 1846.

———. "Comfort." *The Adopted Daughter and Other Tales*. Ed. Alice Carey. Philadelphia: J. B. Smith, 1859. 180–96.

———. "John Hinchley." *The Fountain and the Bottle*. Hartford: Case, 1850. 48–60.

———. *A New Home—Who'll Follow? or, Glimpses of Western Life*. New York: C. S. Francis, 1839.

Koppke, Georgenia J. *Bows of White Ribbon: A Romance of the Spanish American War*. Chicago: Woman's Temperance Publishing Association, 1899.

"Ladies and Temperance." *Summit Beacon* [Akron] 2 Feb. 1853: 2.

La Fetra, S. D. "President's Address." *Minutes of the Nineteenth Annual Meeting of the Woman's Christian Temperance Union of the District of Columbia, 1893*. N.p.: Mitchell, n.d. 12–16.

Lathrap, Mary Torrans. "The National Woman's Christian Temperance Union." *Transactions of the National Council of Women of the United States Assembled in Washington, D.C., 1891*. Ed. Rachel Foster Avery. Philadelphia: Lippincott, 1891. 141–52.

———. *The Poems and Written Addresses of Mary T. Lathrap*. Ed. Julia R. Parish. N.p.: WCTU of Michigan, 1893.

———. "President's Address." *Minutes of the Michigan State Woman's Christian Temperance Union, Coldwater, Michigan, May 22, 1888*. N.p., n.d. 36.

Lawrence, Leeanna Michelle. *The Teaching of Rhetoric and Composi-*

tion in the Nineteenth-Century Women's Colleges. Diss. Duke U, 1990. Ann Arbor: UMI. 1991DA9100120.

Lender, Mark Edward. *Dictionary of American Temperance Biography: From Temperance Reform to Alcohol Research, the 1600s to the 1980s*. Westport: Greenwood, 1984.

Lender, Mark Edward, and James Kirby Martin. *Drinking in America*. New York: Free P, 1982.

Levine, Robert S. "Fiction and Reform." Sec. 1. *The Columbia History of the American Novel*. Emory Elliott, gen. ed. New York: Columbia UP, 1991.

"A Lively Day." *The Minneapolis Tribune* 26 Oct. 1886: 6.

"Local Events." *Baltimore and American Commercial Advertiser* 8 Nov. 1878: 4.

Logan, Shirley Wilson. *With Pen and Voice: A Critical Anthology of Nineteenth-Century African American Women*. Carbondale: Southern Illinois UP, 1995.

Lynn, Corra. *Durham Village: A Temperance Tale*. Cleveland: Jewett, Proctor and Worthington, 1854.

McKeever, Jane L. "The Woman's Temperance Publishing Association." *Library Quarterly* 55.4 (1985): 365–97.

Meriwether, Lide. "President's Address." *Minutes of the Fifth Annual Meeting of the Woman's Christian Temperance Union of Tennessee, 1886*. Brattleboro: P of Frank E. Housh, 1886. 22–45.

———. "President's Annual Address." *Minutes of the Sixth Annual Meeting of the Woman's Christian Temperance Union of Tennessee, Held in Chattanooga, Sept. 14, 15, & 16, 1887*. Memphis: P of S. C. Toof, 1887. 26–39.

Minutes of the First Convention of the National Woman's Christian Temperance Union, 1874. Chicago: Woman's Temperance Publication Association, 1889.

Minutes of the Fourth Convention of the National Woman's Christian Temperance Union, 1877. Chicago: Woman's Temperance Publication Association, 1889.

Minutes of the National Woman's Christian Temperance Union at the Eleventh Annual Meeting in St. Louis, Missouri, 1884. Chicago: Woman's Temperance Publication Association, 1884.

Minutes of the National Woman's Christian Temperance Union at the Fourteenth Annual Meeting in Nashville, Tenn., 1887. Chicago: Woman's Temperance Publication Association, 1888.

Minutes of the National Woman's Christian Temperance Union at the Ninth Annual Meeting, 1882. Brooklyn: Martin, Carpenter, 1882.

Minutes of the National Woman's Christian Temperance Union at the Sixteenth Annual Meeting, Chicago, 1889. Chicago: Woman's Temperance Publication Association, 1889.

Minutes of the National Woman's Christian Temperance Union at the Sixth Annual Meeting, in Indianapolis, 1879. Cleveland: Fairbanks, 1879.

Minutes of the National Woman's Christian Temperance Union at the Tenth Annual Meeting, in Detroit, Michigan, October 31st to November 3d, 1883. Cleveland: Home Publishing, 1883.

Minutes of the National Woman's Christian Temperance Union at the Thirteenth Annual Meeting, 1886. Chicago: Woman's Temperance Publication Association, 1886.

Minutes of the National Woman's Christian Temperance Union at the Twelfth Annual Meeting in Philadelphia, Pennsylvania, October 30th, 31st, and November 2nd and 3d. Brooklyn: Martin & Niper, 1885.

Minutes of the National Woman's Christian Temperance Union at the Twentieth Annual Meeting Held in Memorial Art Palace, Chicago, Illinois, October 18–21, 1893. Chicago: Woman's Temperance Publication Association, 1893.

Minutes of the Nineteenth Annual Meeting of the National Woman's Christian Temperance Union, 1892. Chicago: Woman's Temperance Publication Association, 1892.

Minutes of the Second Convention of the National Woman's Christian Temperance Union. 1875. Chicago: Woman's Temperance Publication Association, 1889.

Minutes of the Third Convention of the National Woman's Christian Temperance Union. Held in Newark, N.J., 1876. Chicago: Woman's Temperance Publication Association, 1889.

Minutes of the Twenty-First Annual Convention of the Woman's Christian Temperance Union, 1894. Chicago: Woman's Temperance Publishing Association, 1894.

Minutes of the Woman's Christian Temperance Union at the Annual Meeting Held in Baltimore, 1878. Cincinnati: A. H. Pugh, 1879.

Minutes of the Woman's Christian Temperance Union at the Eighteenth Annual Meeting, 1891. Chicago: Woman's Temperance Publishing Association, 1891.

Minutes of the Woman's Christian Temperance Union at the Eighth Annual Meeting in Washington, D. C., October 26th to 29th, 1881. Brooklyn: Union-Argus Steam Printing, 1881.

"Miss Lucretia A. Wright." *Cleveland Daily Plain Dealer* 12 Apr. 1853: 3.

"Miss Wells Lectures." *The Cleveland Gazette* 24 Nov. 1894: 1.

Mitchner, Lillian. *The WCTU at Chautauquas.* Chicago: Woman's Temperance Publication Association, n.d.

Moore, V. W. "President's Report." *Eighth Annual Session of the Woman's Christian Temperance Union of Iowa.* Des Moines: State Journal Printing and Publishing House, 1881. 9–14.

———. "President's Report." *Proceedings of the Woman's Christian*

Temperance Union of Iowa, 1879. Iowa City: Brant, Katzenmeyer
& Armentrout, 1879. 9–19.

———. "Report of the President." *Proceedings of the Woman's Christian Temperance Union of Iowa, 1878.* Iowa City: Brant, Katzenmeyer & Armentrout, 1878. 11–14.

"The Morning News and Woman's Rights." *Daily Free Democrat* [Mil-
waukee] 19 Oct. 1853: 3.

"Movement of the Ladies on Temperance." *Summit Beacon* [Akron] 2
Dec. 1852: 1.

"Mr. Moody's Sharp Lecture." *Baltimore American and Commercial
Advertiser* 7 Nov. 1878: 4.

"Mrs. Bloomer." *Daily Free Democrat* [Milwaukee] 19 Oct. 1853: 3.

"Mrs. Harper's Report." *New Haven Register* 21 Nov. 1894. Folder 70,
WCTU Headquarters.

"Mrs. Ostrander's Address." *Daily Free Democrat* [Milwaukee] 30 Sept.
1853: 1–2.

The National Woman's Christian Temperance Union. Evanston: Signal, n.d.

"Notable Women." *St. Louis Post-Dispatch* 24 Oct. 1884: 1–2.

Otis, Pamela L. "The President's Annual Address." *Minutes of the Eleventh Annual Convention of the Arizona Woman's Christian Temperance Union, held at Phoenix, Arizona, 1899.* Prescott: Journal-
Miner Print, 1900. 7–11.

*Our Leaflets: Catalogue of the Woman's Temperance Publishing Asso-
ciation.* Chicago: Woman's Temperance Publishing Association, 1901.

Papashvily, Helen Waite. *All the Happy Endings: A Study of the Domestic Novel in America, the Women Who Wrote It, the Women Who
Read It, in the Nineteenth Century.* New York: Harper, 1956.

Pegrum, Ida M. T. "Young Woman's Work." *Report of the Twenty-Second Convention of the Connecticut Woman's Christian Temperance
Union, 1895.* Portland: Middlesex County Printery, 1895. 59–60.

———. "Young Woman's Work." *Report of the Twenty-Third Annual
Convention of the Connecticut Woman's Christian Temperance
Union, 1896.* Norwich: P of the Bulletin Company, 1896. 74–76

Penny, L., ed. *The Juvenile Temperance Reciter No. 5: A Collection of
Choice Recitations and Declamations, in Prose and Verse, For Use
in Sabbath-Schools, Day-Schools, Bands of Hope, Juvenile Temples,
Loyal Temperance Legions, Junior Societies of Christian Endeavor,
and All Juvenile Organizations.* New York: National Temperance
Society and Publication House, n.d.

Phelps, Elizabeth Stuart. *Jack the Fisherman.* Boston: Houghton, 1887.

———. *A Singular Life.* New York: Regent P, 1894.

Poovey, Mary. "Speaking of the Body: Mid-Victorian Constructions of
Female Desire." *Body/Politics.* Eds. Mary Jacobus et al. New York:
Routledge, 1990. 29–46.

The Price of a Glass of Brandy. Baltimore: Robert Neilson, 1841.

"The Product of the Pump." *Chicago Times* 25 Oct. 1877: 8.

"Reason vs. Rum." *Louisville Courier-Journal* 26 Oct. 1882: 4.

"Religious." *Baltimore and American Commercial Advertiser* 7 Nov. 1878: 4.

Report of the National Woman's Christian Temperance Union Twenty-Second Annual Meeting Held in Music Hall, Baltimore, Maryland, October 18–23, 1895. Chicago: Woman's Temperance Publishing Association, 1895.

Report of the National Woman's Christian Temperance Union Twenty-Sixth Annual Meeting Held in The First Presbyterian Church, Seattle, Washington, October 20–25, 1899. Chicago: Woman's Temperance Publishing Association, 1899.

Report of the National Woman's Christian Temperance Union Twenty-Third Annual Meeting. Chicago: Woman's Temperance Publishing Association, 1896.

Report of the Twenty-Fourth Annual Convention of the Massachusetts Woman's Christian Temperance Union. Boston: J. A. Cummings, 1897.

Riggs, Anna R. "Annual Address." *Minutes of the Tenth Annual Convention of the Woman's Christian Temperance Union of Oregon, 1892.* McMinnville: Yamhill County Reporter Job Printing Office, n.d. 39–47.

Riley, Glenda. *Divorce: An American Tradition.* New York: Oxford UP, 1991.

Rorabaugh, W. J. *The Alcoholic Republic, an American Tradition.* New York: Oxford UP, 1979.

Rose, Henrietta. *Nora Wilmot: A Tale of Temperance and Woman's Rights.* Columbus: Osgood & Pearce, 1858.

"Rum Routers." *Chicago Times* 26 Oct. 1877: 8.

Ryan, Mary. *Womanhood in America From Colonial Times to the Present.* New York: New Viewpoints, 1975.

Salem, Dorothy. *To Better Our World: Black Women in Organized Reform, 1890–1920.* Brooklyn: Carlson, 1990.

Salmon, Marylynn. *Women and the Law of Property in Early America.* Chapel Hill: U of North Carolina P, 1986.

Sanchez-Eppler, Karen. *Touching Liberty: Abolition, Feminism, and the Politics of the Body.* Berkeley: U of California P, 1993.

Sedgwick, Catharine Maria. *Hope Leslie; or, Early Times in the Massachusetts.* New York: White, Gallaher, and White, 1827.

———. *The Linwoods; or, "Sixty Years Since" in America.* New York: Harper, 1835.

———. *Live and Let Live; or, Domestic Service Illustrated.* New York: Harper, 1837.

———. *Mary Hollis: An Original Tale.* New York: New York Unitarian Book Society, 1822.

Seventeenth Annual Meeting of the Woman's Christian Temperance Union of Iowa. Cedar Rapids: Daily Republican Printing and Binding House, 1890.

Sigourney, Lydia. "The Apples of Sodom." *The Lily* Feb. 1850: 10.

———. "The Intemperate." *The Intemperate, and the Reformed: Shewing the Awful Consequences of Intemperance, and the Blessed Effects of the Temperance Reformation.* Boston: S. Bliss, 1833.

———. "Louisa Wilson." Sigourney, *Water-Drops.*

———. *Water-Drops.* New York: Robert Carter, 1848.

"Silent Forces." *Cincinnati Daily Gazette* 15 Nov. 1875: 2–3.

Sklar, Kathryn Kish. "Victorian Women and Domestic Life: Mary Todd Lincoln, Elizabeth Cady Stanton, and Harriet Beecher Stowe." *Women and Power in American History: A Reader Vol. I to 1880.* Eds. Kathryn Kish Sklar and Thomas Dublin. Englewood Cliffs: Prentice Hall, 1991.

Slagell, Amy R. *A Good Woman Speaking Well: The Oratory of Frances E. Willard.* 2 vols. Diss. U of Wisconsin-Madison, 1992. Ann Arbor: UMI, 1992. DA9231225.

Smith, Jessie Carney, ed. *Notable Black American Women.* Detroit: Gale, 1992.

Smith-Rosenberg, Carroll. *Disorderly Conduct: Visions of Gender in Victorian America.* New York: Knopf, 1985.

Southworth, E. D. E. N. *The Hidden Hand.* Ed. Joanne Dobson. 1859. New Brunswick: Rutgers UP, 1988.

Southworth, S. A. *The Inebriate's Hut; or, The First Fruits of the Maine Law.* Boston: Phillips, Sampson, 1854.

Stanton, Elizabeth Cady. "Henry Neil and His Mother." *The Lily* 1 Nov. 1849: 86; 1 Dec. 1949: 86–87; Jan. 1850: 4; Feb. 1850: 14; Mar. 1850: 20; July 1850: 54; Aug. 1850: 60.

Stanton, Elizabeth Cady, Susan B. Anthony, and Matilda Joslyn Gage, eds. *History of Woman Suffrage.* Vol. 1. 1881. Rochester: Charles Mann, 1889.

Stephens, Ann. "The Tempter and the Tempted." *The Fountain: A Gift.* Ed. E. H. Hastings Weld. Philadelphia: William Sloanaker, 1847.

———. "The Wife." *A Drop from the Bucket.* Ed. Maria Woodruff. Auburn: Alden & Markham, 1847. 33–63.

Stewart, Eliza Daniel. *Memories of the Crusade.* 1889. New York: Arno P, 1972.

Stowe, Harriet Beecher. "Betty's Bright Idea." Stowe, *Stories* 234–53.

———. *Betty's Bright Idea and Other Stories.* New York: National Temperance Society and Publication House, 1875.

———. "The Coral Ring." *The May Flower and Miscellaneous Writings.* 1855. 24th ed. Boston: Houghton, 1884. 375–87.

———. *The Coral Ring.* Glasgow: Scottish Temperance League, 1853.

———. "Let Every Man Mind His Own Business." *The Christian Keep-*

sake and Missionary Annual. Ed. John A. Clark. Philadelphia: W. Marshall, 1839.

———. *The May Flower and Miscellaneous Writings.* Boston: Phillips Sampson, 1855.

———. *Stories, Sketches and Studies.* Boston: Houghton, 1896.

———. *Temperance Tales.* London: J. Cassell, 1853.

———. *Uncle Tom's Cabin; or, Life Among the Lowly.* Boston: John P. Jewett, 1852.

Strickland, Charles. *Victorian Domesticity: Families in the Life and Art of Louisa May Alcott.* University: U of Alabama P, 1985.

"Temperance Meeting." The *Pennsylvania Freeman* 15 Feb. 1849: 1.

"Temperance Notes." The *Pennsylvania Freeman* 11 Mar. 1852: 43; 17 Mar. 1853: 43; 1 Sept. 1853: 139.

"A Temperance Revolution." *New York Daily Tribune* 4 July 1854: 6.

"Temperance: The Suffrage Question Again." *Baltimore and American Commercial Advertiser* 11 Nov. 1878: 4.

"Temperance Talkers." *St. Louis Post-Dispatch* 22 Oct. 1854: 2.

"Temperance Women." *Chicago Evening Journal* 24 Oct. 1879: 4.

"There's Whisky in the Jar." *Chicago Times* 27 Oct. 1877: 12.

Thirteenth Annual Report of the Woman's Christian Temperance Union of the State of Illinois, 1886. Chicago: Woman's Temperance Publication Association, 1886.

Thompson, Mildred I. *Ida B. Wells-Barnett: An Exploratory Study of an American Black Woman, 1893–1930.* Brooklyn: Carlson, 1990.

Tompkins, Jane. *Sensational Designs: The Cultural Work of American Fiction 1790–1860.* New York: Oxford UP, 1985.

"The Toper's Doom." *Chicago Times* 28 Oct. 1877: 3.

"To the Women of Chester County." The *Pennsylvania Freeman* 1 Feb. 1849: 1–2.

Townes, Emilie M. *Womanist Justice, Womanist Hope.* Atlanta: Scholars P, 1993.

Tyrell, Ian R. *Sobering Up: From Temperance to Prohibition in Antebellum America Eighteen Hundred to Eighteen Sixty.* Westport: Greenwood, 1979.

"The Union and Lynching." The *Baltimore Sun* 19 Oct. 1895: 8.

Vaughan, Mary C. Letter. *New York Daily Tribune* 10 June 1854: 5.

Victor, Metta Fuller. *Fashionable Dissipation.* Philadelphia: Peters, 1854.

———. *The Senator's Son; or, The Maine Law; A Story Dedicated to the Law Makers.* Cleveland: Tooker & Gatchel, 1853.

Warbasse, Elizabeth Bowles. *The Changing Legal Rights of Married Women, 1800–1861.* New York: Garland, 1987.

Warner, Susan. *The Wide, Wide World.* 1850. New York: Feminist, 1987.

Warren, Mary Evalin. *Compensation: A Tale of Temperance.* New York: National Temperance Society and Publication House, 1887.

Watterson, Henry. *"Marse Henry": An Autobiography.* New York: George H. Doran, 1919.

"WCTU Election." *The Cleveland P* 20 Nov. 1894: 1.

Weidner, Heidemarie Z. *Coeducation and Jesuit Ratio Studiorum in Indiana: Rhetoric and Composition Instruction at 19th Century Butler and Notre Dame.* Diss. U of Louisville, 1991. Ann Arbor: UMI, 1992. DA9219356.

Wells, Ida B. *Crusade for Justice.* Ed. Alfreda M. Duster. Chicago: U of Chicago P, 1970.

West, Mary Allen. *Leaflet 1. Organization: Local Unions.* Chicago: Woman's Temperance Publication Association, n.d.

———. "President's Annual Address." E*leventh Annual Report of the Woman's Christian Temperance Union of the State of Illinois.* Chicago: Jameson & Morse, 1884. 22–40.

———. "President's Annual Address." *Thirteenth Annual Report of the Woman's Christian Temperance Union of the State of Illinois.* Chicago: Woman's Temperance Publication Association, 1886. 97–115.

"Whole World's Temperance Convention." *The Pennsylvania Freeman* 8 Sept. 1853: 142.

Willard, Frances E. "The Average Woman." Slagell 2: 622–24.

———. "Decoration Day Speech Before the Army of the Blue & Gray." Willard, *Glimpses* 447–52.

———. *Do Everything: A Handbook for the World's White Ribboners.* Chicago: Miss Ruby I. Gilbert, n.d.

———. *Glimpses of Fifty Years: The Autobiography of an American Woman.* Chicago: Woman's Temperance Publication Association, 1889.

———. *Hints and Helps in Our Temperance Work.* New York: National Temperance Society and Publication House, 1875.

———. *How to Conduct a Public Meeting.* N.p.: Ruby I. Gilbert, n.d.

———. *How to Organize a Woman's Christian Temperance Union.* Chicago: Woman's Temperance Publication Association, n.d.

———. "A New Departure in Normal Higher Education." Slagell 1: 147–59.

———. *A New Profession for Women.* N.p., n.d.

———. *Woman and Temperance; or, The Work and Workers of the Woman's Christian Temperance Union.* Hartford: Park Publishing, 1888.

———. "Woman's Work in Education." *Report of the Proceedings of the National Education Association* (1884): 161–68.

———. "Women and Organization (President's Address)." *Transactions of the National Council of Women of the U.S.* Ed. Rachel Foster Avery. Philadelphia: Lippincott, 1891. 23–57.

Willard, Frances E., and Mary A. Livermore, eds. *American Women [A*

Revised Edition of Woman of the Century]: A Comprehensive Encyclopedia of the Lives and Achievements of American Women During the Nineteenth Century. 2 vols. 1893; 1897. Detroit: Gale, 1973.

Willing, J. F. *The Potential Woman. A Book for Young Ladies.* Boston: MacDonald and Gill, 1886.

Wittenmyer, Annie. "President's Address." *Minutes of the First* 17–22.

"Woman's Rights and Woman's Wrongs." *Daily Free Democrat* [Milwaukee] 22 Oct. 1853: 3.

"Woman's Temperance Convention." *New York Daily Tribune* 22 Apr. 1852: 4.

"Woman's War on Rum." *The Washington Post* 27 Oct. 1881: 1.

"Women in the Pulpits of Chicago." *Chicago Evening Journal* 29 Oct. 1877: 2.

"Women's State Temperance Convention." *Cleveland Daily Plain Dealer* 14 Jan. 1853: 2.

"Women's Temperance Convention." *New York Daily Tribune* 21 Apr. 1852: 5.

"Women Workers." *St. Louis Post-Dispatch* 21 Oct. 1884: 2.

Woodruff, O. D. "Report on Reformatory Work." *Minutes of the Woman's Christian Temperance Union of Connecticut. Eighth Annual Meeting, 1882.* N.p., n.d. 26–27.

"The World's Temperance Convention." *New York Daily Tribune* 9 Sept. 1853: 4.

Wright, Julia McNair. *The House on the Beach.* Boston: Congregational Sunday-School and Publishing Society, 1893.

———. *John and the Demijohn; A Temperance Tale.* Boston: Henry Hoyt, 1869.

Index

abuse: as theme in popular fiction, 149–51; as theme in women's temperance fiction, 123, 134–36

Adair Law, 39

age: and newspaper coverage of temperance activities, 110, 111–12

alcohol, 97, 98; and danger to women, 144; and history of intemperance, 13; and universal suffrage, 79

Alcott, Louisa May: influence of temperance rhetoric in fiction of, 147–48, 153–55

Aldrich, Mary J.: on prohibition, 171–72

Alice Waters; or, The Sandown Victory (Hilbourne), 130

Allen, Mary Marriage, 90

American Woman's Suffrage Association, 25, 49

"Amy" (Butler), 130–31

Anthony, Susan B., 4, 9, 16, 29, 53, 182n. 5; on divorce, 27; and education of women in rhetorical skills, 71; newspaper coverage of, 103, 104; role of, in temperance organizations, 22–25

At Lion's Mouth (Chellis), 133

Baldwin, Mrs. Summerfield: on WCTU and suffrage, 170–71

Baltimore American and Commercial Advertiser, 109–10, 117–19

Beach, Moses: on Broadway Tabernacle meeting, 101–2

Benjamin, Anna Smeed, 63, 77

Blocker, Jack, 7, 42, 125, 181n. 5

Bloomer, Amelia, 15, 32, 106, 107; on divorce, 27–29; role of, in temperance organizations, 23, 25, 26; use of temperance rhetoric by, 18

Bloomer, D. C., 24

"Bloomer" costume (see also dress), 100, 101–2, 103

Bolton, Sarah Knowles: influence of temperance rhetoric in fiction of, 158–59

Bonner, Robert, 146

Bordin, Ruth: on racial tension within WCTU, 76

Bows of White Ribbon (Koppke), 140

Boyd, William: on racial tension within WCTU, 77

205

Carol Mattingly is an associate professor of English at Louisiana State University and the director of the National Writing Project at LSU.